THEY SAY OUR DAYS ARE NUMBERED

THEY SAY OUR DAYS ARE NUMBERED

LIVERPOOL'S SEASON OF CHANGE

IAN SALMON

First published by Pitch Publishing, 2016

Pitch Publishing
A2 Yeoman Gate
Yeoman Way
Worthing
Sussex
BN13 3QZ
www.pitchpublishing.co.uk
info@pitchpublishing.co.uk

ISBN 978-1-78531-193-2

Typesetting and origination by Pitch Publishing

Printed by Bell & Bain, Glasgow, Scotland

Contents

Introduction

'On Starting'

21 August 2015

STARTING IS difficult. As is ending. The key to any story is knowing which part to relate, telling the most important part of your character's life. Not the whole life, simply the crucial, life-changing part.

What if your character isn't a character, though? What if your character is *you*? What if you're writing in the present with no idea of where the story will end? We're covering a season here. Covering, roughly, a year in a life, with all the unexpected moments that entails. The end is a long way off and totally unknowable. The beginning, though? Could be here, could be further back. If we're honest, it's further back, possibly somewhere in 1986. Possibly further back than that.

The other difficulty in starting? Writing involves work. Why work when you could be trawling Twitter, checking whether the world has 'favourited' and RT'd the 140 characters that you moulded so carefully, this one linking to a piece by a journalist who advises that the Amazon workers having issues with their employers and the level of physicality and target-setting involved in their work should be glad that they don't work for Jose Mourinho. He then goes on to invest further in his Mourinho love-in, defending Jose's public slating of his medical staff after the first game of the season. Hopefully, one of the sub-plots of this year will be the further unravelling of Mourinho's galactic-sized ego. Couldn't happen to a nicer person.

And, yes, this rambling *is* part of the avoiding starting. It's also emblematic of what you'll find in the following pages. If you know any of my work at all, you'll know this. Let's indulge my own ego here. You possibly know this already, possibly from *The Anfield Wrap* to which I contribute, possibly via my theatre work. That will be mentioned as well. Along with family, friends, music and politics. It won't *all* be football, you know. It *can't* all be football, football's part of life, intertwined with everything else that we do. You can't avoid it creeping into everything else any more than you can avoid everything else creeping into *it*.

Starting then. Since we've established that we don't need to think about how it ends – maxim for life right there, kids – let's look at other ways to avoid starting. Figure out what music you need in the background. Playing with the iPod wheel, flicking through Spotify, both so much more enjoyable than actually *doing anything*. Talk Talk, since you were wondering; *The Colour Of Spring*, the point where they're still *nominally* a pop act, before they go all free jazz and become something incredibly 'other'. That's probably the soundtrack to the rest of the day, which might alter the speed of the writing considerably. Pastoral, bucolic, dream-like. You'll spot the moment when that happens: the sentences will grow longer, more random. It'll be glorious.

Let's start then.

And here's a good place to take a brief aside and acknowledge the whole 'without whom' etc....

The Anfield Wrap, and particularly Neil Atkinson and John Gibbons' splendid *Make Us Dream*, the story of the 2013/2014 season's almost absolute glory, for the idea that a season review written as it was happening could be valid and compelling.

Sachin Nakrani and Karl Coppack's *We're Everywhere, Us* (full disclosure, I have a chapter in there) for showing that the personal was the key to the football.

John Graham Davies' magnificent play *Beating Berlusconi* for inspiring me to work in theatre and genuinely changing my life.

And last but not least, our kid, Keith Salmon. His self-published book *We Had Dreams and Songs To Sing,* which he worked so hard to sell to like-minded fans, for charting the way the game is so much a part of our family's life.

One last thing. One last thing that I'm adding here on 24 May with the season ended. Everything that follows is what I thought as it happened. I've changed nothing, no matter how stupid I might look. And there are moments where I'm going to look pretty stupid.

The Start

(still 21 August 2015)

THE START isn't 21 August 2015. The start is July 1986. The two are linked. The dates 5 August and 15 August 2015 as well.

I've been thinking about 1985/86 a lot over the last couple of days. A special on that season for *The Anfield Wrap*, they needed somebody old, somebody who could remember that year. I'm old. Old enough that I needed to research the season as there was no way that I was trusting to memory on that front.

1985/86 is a weird season. There's no TV coverage for the first part: the league was demanding more money than the TV companies were willing to pay and, at that point, the TV companies held the power in any deal. Seems absurd now, doesn't it? You realise how long ago 1985 is. You realise how much of your memory is visually based, that much of that memory is reinforced by revisiting events over the years. You don't really remember the video for The Cure's *Inbetween Days* from watching it at the time, you remember it from seeing it repeated and repeated. Liverpool's games from 1985/86? They're a blur to me. I genuinely don't remember which games I was at. Even after reading up on them, even after watching the footage that *is* available on YouTube, I don't remember much.

I do remember two games, though. I remember two games and I know one thing.

I remember Liverpool winning at Goodison. I vividly recall Kenny Dalglish scoring in the first minute. I remember the vantage point that I watched that goal from, to the right of the pitch, close to Dalglish as he ran. The problem is, that doesn't work, there's no way that I could be there. It was a 52,000 sell-out away game (even if 'away' in this case is a walk across Stanley Park and closer to my home, both then and now – though thirty years and four houses separate us – than Anfield is) and my remembered view is somewhere among the Everton fans. Perhaps I've imagined this, though I've no idea how I'd invent a whole new camera angle for it. Perhaps I had a ticket through a friend. Perhaps it was a dream.

I remember the FA Cup Final, the all-Merseyside FA Cup Final. Travelled down, and back, with an Evertonian friend. Didn't get a pint all day. Remember being very calm when we were behind. The first half lasted for about five minutes. I've never seen forty-five minutes pass so quickly. Remember falling backwards down the Wembley steps, holding on to our mate, Fleety, screaming: 'We've done the fucking double.' Still didn't get a pint all day.

And I know this: I know that I'd seen enough football that year to decide that I was finally buying a season ticket. I think that's how season tickets worked in the eighties, you just decided that you were buying one and bought it. I don't remember the waiting list being about three million deep. Sure, you could just rock up at Anfield on the day of the game and pay to get in. Winning everything in sight but not selling out. Attendances were in the mid-thirty thousands. Football was different.

So, I was buying a season ticket. And then I found a new job. I'd been working for an insurance agent in County Road. It closed on Saturday afternoons, so heading to the match straight from work would have worked. Hated the job. Wanted to work in a record shop. So I got a job in a record shop. And worked Saturdays. For the next twenty-seven years. Which kind of inhibited me from going until Sky invented Sunday afternoons and Monday evenings and we were back in Europe – and I was back in Liverpool after four years in Yorkshire – and match-going became a thing again (I had access to a season ticket, but let's not talk about how).

It took me twenty-seven years and, after the world decided it didn't really *need* record shops, redundancy to achieve two things,

1. I became a writer. It was what I was always supposed to be, although I'd always sort of thought that I'd write comics, never thought that I'd find my way into writing about football, didn't occur to me for a second that I'd become a playwright. An award-winning playwright, he adds hastily, got certificates on the wall and everything.
2. I finally have a season ticket. That's where 5 August comes in.

On 5 August 2015, I headed to Anfield. Fresh from a week in Gran Canaria (part one of the holidays, the family bit), fully refreshed and nicely tanned carrying a letter, a bill for proof of address and my recently used passport as identification.

The letter was from Liverpool Football Club instructing me that my season ticket was ready for collection. 1986 to 2015. The blink of an eye and a lifetime. I present the letter, the passport, the bill and the girl behind the window reads the seat details to me and asks: 'Is that right?

My first reaction is: 'No, that's my dad's seat.' Nothing computes. I can't understand how my season ticket can be in my dad's seat. For a second.

Since we lost dad in November 2014, I'd been using his season ticket. People had whispered to me that I should just keep using it. Not say anything. Stories held that there were people sitting in the main stand at Anfield who were 125 years old and still, miraculously, attending games on a regular basis. Stories held that, if you requested a ticket changed to your name, the ticket would (at best) head towards somebody on the waiting list. More likely still, they claimed, was that it would head to the corporate sector, becoming another space given to tourists with plastic bags full of souvenirs.

Stories get it wrong. Whispers aren't always accurate. Anfield might have taken some time (the second half of the 2014/15 season), but they did it. They transferred the ticket. My dad wanted me to carry on his season ticket, I'm carrying it on. I sit in his seat, I talk to the guys who sat by him, I see the match from the angle he did, I probably complain about the same things he did. I swear much less than I did in the Kop. I'm carrying it all on, but I'm creating a season of firsts. Everything's new, everything changes.

And it's the new that we're here to talk about. The new for Liverpool after a crushingly disappointing 2014/15 season, new signings, new coaching staff, what seems to be a new approach to the media by the manager in terms of him just getting on with the job without trying to be liked any more, and the new for myself as this new career moves ahead.

Which is where 15 August comes in.

We were in Santorini, myself and my wonderful wife of twenty-five years (intelligent, beautiful and an Evertonian; this detail will undoubtedly arise during the year). Second holiday in three weeks, this one being for our silver anniversary, in an unbelievably beautiful hotel in the unbelievably beautiful village of Imeriviogli. Three hundred metres up on the edge of the caldera of a volcano, clouds (when they appeared) below us, helicopters passing beneath, boats vanishing to dots on the horizon, sunsets spectacular.

In amongst the peace, the grandeur, the innate romance of the locale, we spoke about the 'what's next?'

I'd finished my fourth play and was looking for the right idea for the fifth. I had something, ran it past Jeanette (we'll call her J from here on, it's what she prefers) to see what she thought. My best sounding board, my wife, the perfect audience. If it works for her, then it's going to work for others. The idea worked for her. 'And I've got another idea,' I said. I knew that the chapter in *We're Everywhere, Us* would be available on our return to Liverpool, thought of that as a starting point, thought of the sheer quantity of writing on Liverpool's season that I'd put out online and not brought together. Thought of missed chances, thought of the year-long blog that I had published, thought 'here's something'.

We talked, we refined what it could mean, how it could feel, what was important, and I came home with something else to do. This is that something else.

To start, now that we've spent the preceding pages talking about starting but not quite managing it, we need to move back a touch, to 5 August again. On the day I picked up my season ticket, my own season ticket, I wrote a piece for Neil Poole's fine *We Are Liverpool* fanzine, a rallying call, a statement of intent, an attitude for a new season, a new start.

Here it is, let's start.

We're Going To Win The League

5 August 2015

WE'RE GOING to win the league.

I know I have a tendency to ramble, waffle, meander, throw in tons of preamble before I get anywhere near a point. Not today. Not now. Not here.

We're going to win the league.

That's the point. That's what we're here to discuss. Say it, believe it, we're going to win the league. Feels good, doesn't it? Say it again. Feel it. Send a message to the universe and believe it, make it happen. We're going to win the league.

You thought it was mad at first, didn't you? Thought I'd lost it? But the more you're saying it, the more you're thinking it, the more you're feeling it.

And you want to know what makes me believe that we're going to win the league? Alberto Aquilani.

We were on holiday in 2009 in Rhodes or Kos or Crete, somewhere Greek. It was the summer when my youngest son fell off a church. Long story and he's fine, so we won't go into it in any detail. I spent the entire holiday waiting for the English papers to show up so that I could trace the progress of the transfer of this lad that we were buying to replace Xabi. We know what happened, but that's not the point. The point is this: I've just come back from a week in Gran Canaria, where I idly flicked through the papers without a care in the world, safe in the knowledge that we were waiting on nobody, on nothing, all our business done. It felt fantastic.

It felt assured, confident, professional. It felt everything that last season didn't. It felt decisive. It felt like we knew what we needed to do, we made the decisions and we did it. Didn't talk about it, just did it. And after we'd done it? Still didn't talk about it. Not Ian Ayre, not John Henry, not Mike Gordon, not Brendan. Nobody. It was right. It was the right way to do things.

Were they the transfers that I wanted, the transfers that were designed to excite me? No. Not even close. I didn't want Benteke, Ings, Origi, Milner, Bogdan. I wanted Kovacic and Reus and Lacazette and Cech. Same as everybody else. I wanted names, I wanted marquees, I wanted statements and glory. Am I disappointed? Not even vaguely. Di Maria was a name, a marquee. Falcao too. They worked brilliantly for the Mancs, didn't they? I wanted statements? Here's a statement: 'We've bought these lads who know what they're doing.' Maybe the blokes who run the club know more than I do.

Did I want Brendan still here? No. After Stoke, I was as anti-Brendan as anybody on the planet. I wanted him sacked. I wanted Klopp. Same as everybody else. Instead, Fenway Sports Group pulled out a robust review and backed their manager. And then BACKED their manager. Figured out what he wanted and went and got it. Ian Ayre has said that they 'set out a plan with Brendan at the start of the summer, and identified the objectives the manager wanted to achieve' and, crucially, added 'we've achieved all of them'. That's a statement. That's what we wanted the club to do.

We've rebuilt. Again. This time, though, we've mostly done it with lads who know the English game, who won't take time to settle, who can make the impact we need, give us options. The options are the important thing. The options we didn't have to change games at the end of the season before last, that we thought we had at the beginning of last season but turned out to be illusions. This time? These are real options, options that show a bit of a threat.

Mignolet, Clyne, Skrtel, Sakho, Moreno, Milner, Henderson, Coutinho, Firmino, Benteke, Lallana. You having that as a starting eleven? Tweak it if you want but come on....there's threat there. Add Ibe, Can, Markovic, Lovren (no, go on, add him) Bogdan, Ings, Origi and you've filled your bench. Add Lucas, add Gomez, Toure, Ilori (maybe), Teixeira, that Alexander-Arnold lad that none of us had heard of a week ago. Add them all. We're on twenty-five already. Anyone missing Sterling yet? We've got threat, movement, pace, goals. And we've got one other thing.

We've got Daniel Sturridge coming back for the United game and we don't need him to be a saviour this time. We've signed a guy who cost more, who scores one in two, who can pull off THAT kind of a volley. The pressure Dan had last year? Gone. All he needs to do now is score goals. He doesn't NEED to score goals, there's a hell of a difference.

The opposition? Chelski got Falcao. That's just Jose's ego at work. City got Sterling and Delph. I mean, I loved Raheem and all that, but is he really the game-changer City need? Delph? This year's Rodwell. United? Schweinsteiger and Schneiderlin. Gives them a better midfield than they've had for years. Still, no defence and only Rooney in attack. Arsenal? They'll do the usual Arsenal thing, start brilliantly then fade out.

Us? Alternatives, options, threat, movement, goals. Rebuilt with confidence and purpose and belief.

Feeling it yet? Believing it? Say it. Say it again. Keep saying it. We're going to win the league.

Stoke 0 Liverpool 1

9 August 2015

I'M USED to the idea that Liverpool kick off the Saturday after I return from holiday. Holiday is always planned so that our anniversary falls in the second week. The league starts the Saturday after we return. Always has, always will do. Not this season.

This season, the league starts absurdly early. Having to plan a family holiday and an anniversary holiday and somehow fit in our kid's fiftieth, the first match of the season drops handily into the end of a four-day period where we're actually in the country. I know, world's smallest violin and all that.

Wife and youngest son, also blue, both season ticket holders, get to see their lot draw two-all with Watford. The first-half performance is, apparently, awful. I manage to fit in watching our game on TV, picking up the cases and heading out of the door seconds after the final whistle for Manchester Airport and a flight to Greece. It's a way to live, nobody's complaining.

Stoke obviously needs context. It's unlikely that any of us are forgetting the context, but context always helps.

In the aftermath of the last game of last season, the game that saw Steven Gerrard's last appearance in a Liverpool shirt, the game where we realised that the semi-final loss to Villa wasn't the most spineless performance that we'd ever suffered watching, I recorded an *Anfield Wrap* where, in the most incensed manner possible, I demanded to know why Rodgers hadn't been sacked yet.

I'd moved into the #RodgersOut camp after the Palace game. I'd been wobbling for a while, his 'the occasion was too big for us' comment after the Villa semi-final (while my eight-year-old nephew was still in tears, although obviously Brendan couldn't know that) had appalled me. We're Liverpool. We 'do' the big occasions, that's what we're there for. We'd just watched a seventeen-year-old that none of us had heard of six weeks earlier run the game and we were being told that the occasion was 'possibly' too big for us. Palace had tipped me over the edge, we sat in the courtyard of the Lady of Mann, drank, and discussed the possibility of Jurgen Klopp, how he could improve this squad, how Brendan had 'gone'. How we'd clearly reached the end.

The post-Palace sad resignation became the post-Stoke fury. Six goals conceded. One Gerrard consolation which I'm sure even he won't count as his last Liverpool goal. Five goals down at half-time. Not on TV, not at the match, no reliable stream to be had, I listened on the radio. The first forty-five minutes done with, I sat, at the age of fifty-one, almost in tears over a game of football, and prayed for more goals. I'm not happy about this but I prayed for humiliation so that the manager would be sacked. It was the last days of Souness again, Hodgson again. It was too much. I needed change. I wasn't alone in this. Doesn't make me right. So, the next day, I wanted to know why nothing had happened.

Nothing had happened because nothing was going to happen. Liverpool Football Club had become very, very quiet. Coaching changes were made, assistant manager and first-team coach departed, new incumbents arrived. Explanation? Justification? Nothing. The club made changes, although not the change many wanted and expected, and carried on. We bought players. And none of those players were the big European names that we demanded, none were the names that Twitter's 'In The Know' accounts linked us with. They weren't the signings that we wanted but *were* the signings we expected. And, as the section on winning the league indicates, I'd come round to the idea that this was okay, that this would work. They might not be the 'right' signings but there was every possibility that they were the *right* signings. You can see the subtle difference that demands italics.

On the pitch, though? On the pitch at Stoke where we demanded retribution, a new start and a fresh approach? We didn't see the subtle difference that demands italics there. Instead, we saw, *I* saw – let's keep this purely personal – the same problems which were so upsetting last year repeated.

The 4-2-3-1 formation with Henderson and Milner both pretty much holding. Lovren chosen over the superior Sakho – the fact that his wife had given birth not seeming sufficient explanation for his absence; after all, Henderson had arrived at one game last season direct from the delivery room. The idea that young Joe Gomez, an eighteen-year-old centre back, was in at left-back ahead of the older, more experienced, more expensive and long-sought-after Albert Moreno? I was okay with that. All indications were that the lad had something. Pre-season word was spectacular. I might not have seen a great deal of this pre-season, but I was willing to take literally *everybody's* word on this. The fact that Benteke was a lone striker and seemed as isolated as Balotelli had been last season? That worried me. That we were already resorting to pumping long balls over the top of the Stoke midfield and defence, albeit not as brutal now that they've decided to reinvent themselves as an actual football team? That was terrifying. That seemed desperate. Questioned later, Brendan said that we intend to be unpredictable this season. Hopefully the unpredictability involves not repeating the long ball tactic too frequently.

The ball went up, the ball didn't stick, runners to accompany Benteke were notable by their absolute absence. It was everything that we'd feared a Benteke- fronted Liverpool would become. All we could do was pray that this wouldn't be the shape of the future, as a tedious game of post-summer football played out, all sense of invention and creativity as scarce as the low moments in the first and last thirds of the previous season.

Ultimately the game was settled by yet another slice of Coutinho brilliance. This description was questioned by a City-supporting friend on Twitter. "Can brilliance come in slices?" he asked. Yes. Yes, it can. From nowhere, with nothing on, cutting in from the left and suddenly the ball is in the back of the net and we can ponder tactics later. The little Brazilian magician starts the new campaign in the way he spent much of last season, embarking on his own, one man, goal of the season competition.

And with that, with the game settled, with no time for inquest, with no need to worry about the form of the victory or the shape of the manager's post-match comments, I'm off. Cases in the boot of the car, heading for Manchester, then a Greek island.

The season's here and I no longer need to worry about it.

Interlude

9-17 August 2015
Somewhere in the Cyclades

YOU WANT to talk about bliss? Not the football-related Istanbul/Cardiff/The Glory That Was Rome bliss, wonderful as all that obviously is, but the real stuff, the stuff that you presume you only get every so often, if at all. Real bliss consists of moments in baking sunshine, in a suite in a ridiculously good hotel with your own swimming pool on the balcony, high on a caldera overlooking an active volcano. So high that there is genuinely only one room higher than you on the entire island, so high that you can wake one morning to find that you occupy the interior of a cloud.

True bliss is lying back on the deck of a semi-private yacht trip, looking up as the engines cut and the sails unfurl, perfectly white beneath a blue sky.

True bliss is spending these moments with the woman that you have loved for the best part of thirty years and remembering, realising, that you're still the people you were when you met, when you married.

True bliss is realising that silver anniversaries aren't things that happen to 'old' people. They can't be because you know for an absolute stone-cold fact, with every fibre of your being, that you're both still young, that you're still the people you were when you met at twenty-three and twenty and married at twenty-six and twenty-three. It's knowing that your best friend is still your best friend and that you're both still together because you want to be and that you're still *you* and not just 'mum and dad'.

It's a fantastic thing to realise. What's it got to do with football, though?

Absolutely nothing. I said there would be diversions, didn't I? Warned there would be sidebars. Football's nothing if it doesn't fit as part of the rest of your life. Nothing in life sits as a thing to itself. We take our emotions into the game and the game colours our emotions. Everything's linked. I'm very chilled, I'm expecting this mood to rub off on the lads in red. Let's talk Bournemouth, shall we?

Liverpool 1 Bournemouth 0

17 August 2015

THE FIRST home game of the season just happens to coincide with the last day of my holidays. It's all part of that 'the season's starting early this year, isn't it?' feeling, the 'is it because of the Euros, is it because of the World Cup in 2018 sitting in a country that nobody wanted to go to because FIFA are basically – don't say it, there are libel laws and stuff – and everything else moving round to accommodate it?' feeling.

Could have been disastrous. Could have meant me missing the first two games of the season, one on TV, one in real life. Could have meant myself and my Evertonian wife missing two games each. Substituted for a glorious holiday, obviously, but missing the games is missing the games. Something to thank Sky for, then. They give us the Stoke game on a Sunday afternoon with one eye on an embarrassment that doesn't arrive and they give us Bournemouth on a Monday night for probably the same reason.

(As a connected aside, J only misses one game, Southampton away, and we catch the goals from that on a YouTube clip at a hotel bar overlooking the sea with cocktails in front of us. You'd take that, wouldn't you? Shutting up about the holiday now.)

At noon, I'm in a car to the airport. By one, I'm stood behind a Manc lad who has decided to complain about everything to everyone in that way only the most English of the English abroad can, bitterly and loudly with a misguided sense of superiority. The queues for the check-in are too long, the queues for the gate are too long, the queues for the gift shop are too long. These are evidently the first queues that he's ever encountered and they puzzle and perturb him. He's a lovely individual, I wish I'd had the chance to get to know him better, I'm sure he'd have had some entertaining opinions about.... well, everything basically.

I'd say 'C'est la vie' but I'm fairly sure he wouldn't approve of the sheer foreign-ness of the phrase.

Me? I'm the most chilled man on the planet. I've had my holiday, I loved it, nothing will ever upset me again. Nothing trivial anyway. I will queue, I will queue as long as I need to and I'll be cool with it because life is basically brilliant.

Which obviously isn't how I feel when Manchester airport is failing to come to terms with the concept of delivering our bags, forty-five minutes after we touch down. 'It's as though they don't realise that we kick off in two hours' I tweet before complaining that, 'if Manchester bloody airport can't sort out the whole baggage thing then they should at least set up decent Wi-fi while we wait.'

And the big hole that had opened up on the Mancunian Way no longer seemed as amusing as it had when the news originally broke once we realised the effect that it had on traffic around Manchester and, seemingly, on Thelwall's gorgeous viaduct. Delay upon delay upon delay. The minor collision that jammed the traffic thirty yards from our house seemed a particularly sarcastic, needless punchline.

Six-thirty. Half an hour of tidying the beautifully minor kitchen carnage incurred by two teenage sons looking after themselves for seven days and back into the car. Ten-year-old Renault Scenic, handles like a tank, absolute nightmare to drive. A drive through Walton, past the *Famous Blue Star* chippy (never entirely sure where it feels that fame came from) and along the edge of Walton Hall Park, where we watched The Farm support The Mighty Wah! back in '84, parking in one of those back roads around Goodison that you're really not supposed to, chips from the best chippy in Liverpool (honest to God, Goodison Fish Bar, try it sometime) and I arrive at Anfield with five minutes until kick-off.

The warnings had been there, the e-mail had been sent by the club in the week. Leave extra time for your journey, building work will cause delays. Sorry lads, couldn't have left much earlier. I was in a different timezone at lunchtime.

The queues outside are merciless, the back of the main stand's a building site, we've a new 'spar'. It's a beautiful thing, ready to support the roof that will appear sometime before next summer to transform the stadium's exterior appearance, add new corporate areas and do almost nothing to alleviate the length of the season ticket waiting list, allow younger fans the chance to enter the ground, or improve the atmosphere. It's a nothing answer to a big question:

'What do we need to do?'

'We need to extend the ground, the whole ground.'

'Will this bit do?'

'Yeah, go on then.'

I've no idea how anyone's getting into the Kop, hitting the Anfield Road or the far end of the main stand. There appears to be one gate which has little or no queue. It's one of the gates listed as entry on this shiny new season ticket that I have in my pocket, all safe and secure in its leather holder. All safe and secure in dad's leather season ticket holder, one pocketed side decorated with the club crest carrying my ticket, the other carrying dad's ticket from last season. It's the ticket that I started using in late October, which became mine in November, that I carried on through the season as he'd wanted. I'm carrying it with me, I always will. I'm taking him to the match, I always will.

And this is the real start, isn't it?

Greetings to the guys that I sat by last season, quick catching up, You'll Never Walk Alone ringing out – George Sephton on DJ duties as ever, fading out Gerry Marsden and his lads so that the Kop can take it and make it special, make it ours, the song we played to dad in hospital, the song we played at his funeral. There'll never be a moment that it isn't his. His and our uncle Len's and our granddad's. Same as it is for so much of the ground. The history of the song goes with us every time we sing it. It's not about the football, it's about everything else.

But the football's what we need to talk about, it's what we're here for.

And the football's doing that 'game of two halves' thing. In the first we're fast, tricky, inventive, there's creativity all over the place. The midfield is impressive, Henderson sits behind Milner, who sits behind Coutinho and Lallana and Ibe, with Benteke as the front man, but with runners getting a damn sight closer to him than at Stoke. Coutinho links with him, Lallana runs off him. There are flicks and tricks, balls are passed around corners, triangles happen. Benteke looks impressive. Looks extremely impressive, slimmer than you expect, more mobile than we'd thought, offers far more than just the 'big lad up front' that we'd feared. Long balls still find their way to him, but they seem to do it with reason, with purpose. It might be that Mignolet's distribution has improved dramatically over the summer, it might be that Benteke makes him look good. Wherever the long kick is going, Benteke is going to win it. There are no aerial duels. The opposition haven't got a cat-in-hell's chance. Benteke's going to win a lot of 50/50s this season. He's going to make a lot of people look good. I think I might owe him an apology. Consider this to be chapter one of that apology. There might be many more. I'm impressed.

That said, his goal's offside. His first goal in front of the Kop, in his first game in a red shirt, not the thunderbolt that we expected, not the sublime chest-to-volley into the top-left corner of the net that we saw in pre-season, but a tap with the studs from six inches out. Scruffy but it counts. Counts despite the fact that it's clearly the most obvious offside ever. Not Benteke, Benteke's run is fine. It's a lovely run, the timing's gorgeous. Coutinho's offside, though, and he challenges for the ball as it swings in from a well-worked corner.

This well-worked corner? Most of the ground groans as it's taken, treats the short corner as a wasted opportunity.

Approves slightly more once the ball is nestling in the net and our new number nine is leaning into the Kop celebrating. We're showing real invention on set pieces already, sure we'll see more. The crowd might have to accustom itself to the unusual, the unexpected.

So, this unusual corner. Coutinho challenges despite being roughly as far ahead of the last defender as I am, sitting here, at the moment. Which makes him offside. A few days later, the Premier League takes the step of confirming that the goal shouldn't have stood.

'We don't usually do this,' they basically say, 'but thought we'd have a word on this one as it all needs clearing up.'

Cheers lads. Can we expect you to clarify every decision that a ref gets wrong from now on? Can we go back and discuss that Sterling goal at the Etihad that would have won us the league? No? Thought not. Just when it suits you then? Cool, nice one, thanks for that.

The second half, we just kind of disappear. We lose Henderson to a foot injury after ten minutes, take the chance to reshape and then stop doing all the good stuff that we were doing in the first forty-five.

Obviously we need to accept that those eleven lads in the Bournemouth shirts quite fancied the idea of winning their first ever away game, quite fancied having a crack at an Anfield victory to start their top-flight tenure. They're not lying down, they're going for it. And they're playing nice football. They're playing the football that brought them up to the Premier League in the first place. And we're standing resolute. Our new full-backs look excellent. Clyne looks quality, Joe Gomez doesn't look like an eighteen-year-old centre-back playing out of position at a higher level than he's ever encountered before, he looks like the answer to the decade-long left-back issue. He looks born to the role. And smack bang in the middle, Dejan Lovren looks suspiciously like he might well be turning into a 'second season player'. He looks like last year's nightmares might be behind him. His manager's belief in him looks as though it might be well placed.

So, obviously, all you can hear on the way out as we skirt the skeleton of the new stand is: 'Same shite as last year,' 'can't keep playing like that,' 'disgraceful display,' *ad infinitum, ad nauseum.*

Two games, lads. Two games, two wins, no goals conceded. Five points better than Chelsea already. Not entertained? Do you actually remember how the Suarez season started? Three one-nil wins on the bounce. New players learning how to play with each other, pre-season turning into the season itself. Takes a while to kick into shape. Anybody else looking superior to the rest after two games? There isn't, is there? Get a grip. Ta.

Arsenal 0 Liverpool 0

24 August 2015

ANOTHER MONDAY night. A week of decompressing and returning to the grey reality of the English 'summer'. 'We're okay with going home,' we'd said. 'It's been fantastic, it's been perfect, we can deal with being back home.' It took two days until we were saying: 'Wish we were still on holiday'.

The problem with this part of the season is there's just so much time between games. A week? A full week? Really? We've only just got it back and you're making us wait an entire week until the next game? In October, you'll be giving us games every other day because you wasted a fortnight letting Roy Hodgson convince the southern media that he genuinely *is* an England manager despite all evidence pointing to the fact that he's a chancer whose main qualification for the national job is not being Harry Redknapp.

And I was one of the idiots who thought he might be a calm hand at the tiller when he was appointed Liverpool manager. That foolishness lasted slightly longer than the 'we're okay with being back in England' illusion but only very, very, slightly.

Perhaps this time round, Roy won't break one of our players and derail our season for us? One can but hope.

That, from here, is the future. From where you are, it's the past. Hopefully you're not looking at this going 'yeah, but if only Clyne hadn't broken both legs in that pointless bloody friendly'.

This is where we are before the third game of the season. The last team (last two teams, obviously) to play. Only

City, who had looked a class above Everton on Sunday, with maximum points. United looking extremely ordinary, midfielders bought but still soft at the back and pointless up front. In a few days' time, Louis Van Gaal will reveal that he intends to use Marouane Fellaini as a striker since all he has otherwise is a far from convincing Wayne Rooney. It does beg the question, why bother sacking Moyes if the next bloke is going to use the same tactics? Wherever we finish in the top four this season, and we will, trust me on this, it's going to be United that we displace. Their top four finish last season had less to do with their abilities than it did with our failure to convert the run of form of January to March into a rhythm which would carry us through to the end of the season. Make no bones about it, they were in the Champions League this season because of our inadequacies.

Arsenal away. One of the seven hard away days that the fixture list threw in front of us, one of the seven challenges to start the season. It would be easy to be despondent in the face of your first seven away games of the season being the toughest aways in the league, but let's look at it from a positive point of view: you've got to play them all at some point, might as well do it straight away. Positivity, we're doing positivity.

Thankfully, so are Liverpool.

And we're doing the two halves thing again. Not necessarily our doing, there was this other side that quite fancied having a go, a very good side, one of those sides that are good at the whole footballing side of things.

Arsenal was the test, the first real, proper test. Don't get me wrong, Stoke was a test, always a nasty place to go and last season to get out of our systems. Arsenal, though? Arsenal is a *statement*. Arsenal wasn't the *start* of the wheels coming off in the spring of 2015, but it was the point that we realised that they'd possibly, maybe definitely, gone. The week after losing to United at Anfield, in their first actual United-like performance of the Van Gaal era, and we were at the Emirates without our captain after that *interesting* thirty-second cameo that he gave against our neighbours from the other end of the

M62, charging around the pitch desperate to rectify the lack of resolve demonstrated by his team-mates in the first half for just long enough to garner a straight red. We were almost surviving at Arsenal. Almost getting through with minimal damage and then they scored three against us in the ten minutes before half-time and that was it, season over. The belief gone and us finished.

This Liverpool isn't *that* Liverpool. This Liverpool isn't carrying the hangover from last season. Half the starting eleven isn't even thinking about last season and the hangover, they weren't here. Clyne, Gomez, Benteke, Milner and Firmino, who's making his first start for the club, none of them were here to suffer that destruction, to experience an incisive Arsenal shredding our hopes. Clyne, Gomez, Benteke, Milner and Firmino, this is their Liverpool now. This is the Liverpool of O'Driscoll, McAllister and Lijinders rather than Pascoe and Marsh. Crucially, this might well be far more the Liverpool of Brendan Rodgers than last season's meek mirage. The manager appears to have been given the power that he needed to make decisions. He appears to have been backed by the board. There appear to have been no qualms from FSG when it came to deciding whether he should stay and have more time to complete the job. They've been convinced of the veracity of there being extenuating circumstances and they've backed the man they appointed three years ago. Suddenly, nobody is talking about transfer committees. This is the manager's team, the team that he will stand or fall by.

At the time of writing this – and God knows, I reserve the right to change my mind as we progress – I'm saying he's going to stand. This Liverpool has two sides to it, each neatly demonstrated here, a half at a time.

Brendan had spoken before the game about the idea of dominating the space. He'd looked at the last ten teams to win at Arsenal and noted, publicly and loudly so that Arsene and his boys knew that we knew what we were talking about, that each had low possession rates. For a team which has prided itself on possession, for a manager's ethos supposedly built on retention of the ball, this seemed an unlikely scenario. For a team which had historic issues with the concept of defending, this seemed an *exceptionally* unlikely scenario, Liverpool were going to go to Arsenal after last term's decimation and *defend?*

Well, no. Not really, not entirely. We would have to, and we would undoubtedly have known that we would have to, but it wasn't necessarily our intention. Our intention at the moment is the unpredictable.

No Henderson, Lallana or Allen. Firmino making his first start in the toughest game possible. An eighteen- year-old at left-back. Let's attack, shall we?

The first ten minutes are odd. Coutinho hits the bar within the first three, Arsenal rally and push. We look susceptible, it looks as though Sanchez and Cazorla can cut through us at will. For ten minutes. And then we decide that we're going to kick on. And we push forward and keep pushing forward. We have more shots on target in the first half than any other side has against Arsenal in an opening forty-five minutes since, ooh, the Boer war or something. We're everywhere and we're pushing and probing. Lucas, supposedly Besiktas-bound at the start of the day, is back and crucial as the holding midfielder in front of the back four. He's a platform for the five lads in front of him to push on from.

Benteke does the Benteke thing that he did against Bournemouth again. He pulls others into play, wins the ball with his head and his chest and his feet, picks the ball up, carries it. You can claim he should score when Firmino plays this gorgeous cross into him in the six-yard box. You can claim that he puts it too close to Petr Cech. I'll argue that he puts it where no other keeper is getting down to, but Cech picks this particular Monday night to demonstrate why Arsenal thought buying him might be a really good idea. Two poor games on the bounce, obviously he picks us to show form against. The save is magnificent. It's equalled by the finger-tip diversion of Coutinho's shot on to the post shortly after. We have pace, momentum and we don't want the half to end. We should be three up. We're not. We won't argue about Ramsey's goal for the hosts being incorrectly ruled offside. I'm obviously not even vaguely bothered about that. I'm happy with that one.

The second half is Arsenal, as it probably should be. They're a quality football team. They pin us back, threaten, show their quality, show all the quality that we scared out of them in the first half. And we stand firm, resolute. It's a nice thing to be, resolute, feels good. Feels amazing after last season, when the chances not fully taken in the first half would have been exposed as wasteful in the second. Skrtel is at the heart of everything we do defensively. Nothing will pass. Clyne is rock solid, Gomez a revelation again, and Lovren faultless. Mignolet? Mignolet is to our second half what Cech was to Arsenal's first, world-class saves all over the place.

As we tire, as our legs start to show the strain of the pace, our character remains, the concentration is unbelievable, we are a thing of wonder and determination. We have a new mentality and that seems to come from the man who captained the side here. James Milner has come in from a side that has won titles and has brought a title-winning mentality with him. He is sure, confident, professional and those around him are feeding from this feeling. Tonight is a captain's performance. It's everything that you want. It's the longest game of football that you've ever seen. It seems to go on for weeks and the stress levels are ridiculous. It's gorgeous. It's the start of a new Liverpool. It's that simple.

It's not often that you can come away from a nil-nil draw simultaneously relieved that you didn't lose, distraught that you didn't win and delirious at the idea that you've seen something special from your team.

Three games, seven points, no goals conceded. If you offered us that at the start of the season...

Yeah, I'll take that. This is a start.

Interlude

Liverpool City Centre

25 August 2015

SO, I'M on an *Anfield Wrap* podcast on the Tuesday afternoon following the Monday-night game, five of us in a darkened studio, talking about the game and, moments before the recording starts, news breaks that Mario Balotelli has passed a medical at AC Milan and is on his way back to Italy on a season-long loan. As we're leaving I ask Gareth, editor of the TAW website, if anybody has filed a piece on Mario yet? 'A sort of "cheers Mario, do one" piece?' he kind of says.

'Yeah, that kind of thing,' I say.

'No.'

'Cool, I'll have one for you later on,' I say as we part.

And this is what I wrote:

Mario Balotelli

The End Of An Error

The Anfield Wrap 25 August 2015

I'M GOING to let you in on one of my (many, very, very, many) idiosyncrasies: I like order. Specifically, I like order in terms of dates, in terms of history. I like things to tie up, to be neat and tidy and… well, orderly.

I used to have this history teacher, let's call him Mr Roarke — as that was his name — (it's okay, he was a blue, probably still is, no way he's reading this) who always liked to point out that he loved the way that any nineteenth-century British Prime Minister died shortly after losing office as it kept history tidy. Doesn't work so well in the twentieth and twenty-first centuries unfortunately. We'd have been rid of her quicker if it did. Still, you get the idea — neat, tidy, story told, all tied up.

I like coincidence, serendipity, synchronicity. I like the things that are clearly meant to coincide. I love the fact that I can tell you the date I met the girl that I'd marry as we married on that very date four years later (romantic as well). I love the fact that our eldest son was born on his granddad's birthday. Meant to be. Obviously meant to happen that way. It's great when dates give history a sense of meaning, of importance.

Can you see where this rambling's going yet?

Mario. One year ago today, we signed Mario Balotelli. Today, he's gone-ish. Sort of, kind of. We'll come back to that. The idea that Mario was with us for exactly one year just seems right, seems like the proper way to end things — yeah, yeah, if we have actually ended it, coming back to that — seems neat, tidy, planned, organised. Seems like all the things that his time at the club wasn't.

I'll admit it — I kind of have to, it's in print and, if you were bothered to, you could probably Google it and throw it back at me — I was all for the idea of signing Mario Balotelli.

In the wake of losing Luis and after the seeming sterility of the first couple of games last season, I wanted some madness in the team, some unpredictability, some chaos. Be careful what you wish for and all that. Go on, I thought, sign Mario, it'll be a laugh.

It wasn't, was it? We didn't get the rockets set off in the bathroom or the driving round, dressed as Santa, giving money to the homeless, the going the supermarket for food but coming back with a trampoline and a train set. We got none of the fun. Crucially, we also got none of the football.

There's this myth that Mario Balotelli is a major talent just waiting to explode, with the right guidance. We've all believed it at some point. Brendan clearly believed that he was the man that could tame Mario. And we — okay, I, I'll talk for me, nobody else on this one — went for it. 'Yeah, you know what, he might do this. Look at what Brendan did with Luis last season, lad's on the verge of going to Arsenal so he bombs him out, makes him train with the kids, sorts it, gets him back on board and he gives us *that*. Yeah, he can do this, it'll be great.'

He couldn't. It wasn't.

I should have known really. I should have listened to the sensible side of my brain, whispering on the day we signed him: 'Think, just think. When we played City, you were always relieved when Mario came on because he was never any threat. It's going to be that again.' I ignored that voice, that horrible, smug, reasonable bit of me that talks sense and takes away all the fun. 'It'll be fine, it'll be better than fine, it'll be great, sod it, it'll be fantastic, we're going to win everything.'

His debut was good. Let's give him that, shall we? Looked good next to Danny, then Hodge broke Danny and Mario had nobody else to play with and he just wandered round looking lost. For the rest of the season.

I could list all the things that were wrong with Mario, the complete lack of any tactical understanding, of an ability to read a game, of any kind of partnership with any of his team-mates. We've all seen Simon Hughes' fascinating piece in The Independent *by now, all aware that he didn't know his team-mates' names by Christmas (even a player with a really short first name), all aware that he was disruptive in training sessions. We all know the 'own goal from the halfway line in training' story. There's no real need to repeat them.*

What I will say is this: I've no ill will to Mario Balotelli as a person, he's not El-Hadji Diouf. He's done me no wrong. I just don't think he's a very good footballer. I think the myth that he's this rare talent, this maverick genius, is just that, a myth. There's no real proof that he's ever going to come good on any potential that he might possess. And, yes, I am taking into account that his goal record prior to coming to Liverpool is basically verging on one in two, but I'm balancing it out with the fact that I've seen him at close quarters now. For a year. An entire year.

It could be an attitude thing, it could be that things came so easily to him so early in his career that he doesn't see any need to try and can't see that there's anything wrong with what he's doing. Better men than I have tried to analyse the workings of Mario's mind and failed.

Here we are, though, one year down the line and another club has decided that they will be the ones to finally harness the maverick magic of Mario. Strangely, it's the club we bought him from a year ago. AC Milan are willing to take Mario back, to attempt to tame him or at least harness the madness more capably than we were able. They're not confident enough to pay a fee for this privilege, it's a one-year loan deal with no compulsory purchase clause. There's a possibility that he could well be back at Anfield in a year's time. To be loaned out again, in an almost Aquilani-esque manner obviously, but still back at Anfield.

What does Mario think of all this?

'I always had Milan in my heart and always had hope that I would return one day. Will I end my career here? I just have to start to work and have a good year. I'm looking forward to training and

proving my worth. I have a lot of motivation but I just have to work and not speak.'

Good luck with that, Mario. Training? Working and not speaking? Good luck. No, seriously, good luck. I genuinely hope it works out for you, I do. A year was enough, thanks.

One year, not too long in history. Neat, tidy, orderly. And hopefully over.

Interlude

A Field In South Liverpool

31 August 2015

I STEPPED off the train at Aintree station, signage proudly proclaiming its status as 'Home of the Grand National'. I walked the steps to the main road and that is when the rain started. Not small drops hinting at a downpour to come, not that really fine rain that gets you soaked, which helped to provide Peter Kay with a public identity, but real rain, the sort that De Niro promised us would 'come and wash the scum from these streets', the type of downpour that appears suddenly, unexpectedly, from nowhere, utterly torrential. It's a twenty-minute walk to ours.

Small mercies. Other than a light spattering around three in the afternoon, the rain managed to avoid us all day. Which made the last day of the Sefton Park-based third annual Liverpool International Music Festival (LIMF) much more comfortable than could have been the case.

I'd considered the Saturday line-up and its adoption of Basement Jaxx as headliners but had declined on the grounds of …well, Basement Jaxx basically. Good festival band, know how to put on a show, but write such terrible songs. I wasn't prepared to travel across town to watch them. At a free show. North Liverpool to South Liverpool?

A rare journey to an alien place. Sunday was denied to me by my fourteen-year-old son's desire to watch Labrinth and

Katy B with his mates. The idea of running into his dad at a festival? Not happening.

And, in fairness, Labrinth and Katy B? Not fussed, if we're honest. Silent Sleep tempted me, but I've done the two-hour journey to see twenty-minute sets before. Too old for that now.

'How was Labrinth, Matt?' I asked him when he returned.

'Not that good,' he reckoned. 'Bit boring, played too many new songs that were rubbish.'

'You won't be impressed by this photo of my mate with him then?'

'No.'

Never try to impress a fourteen-year-old son with loose connections to the famous.

The Bunnymen, though? The Bunnymen with the Royal Liverpool Philharmonic Orchestra? That's designed for my age. That's my record collection (and CD collection and bootleg cassettes and mp3 files and everything) live on stage before me. It's not like it's a novelty, it's not like I haven't seen them since the mid-eighties, since they last played Sefton Park in August 1982, as was the case for many around me. Once a year, twice most years, all the way through. Every line-up, the Royal Albert Hall, the Duchess of York in Leeds, Marsh Lane Community Centre in Bootle, I've done the miles on this band. There's a period of two to three years in the early eighties where they're not just the best live band on the planet, they're the best live band that the planet's ever seen. Their shows were a religious experience, Mac blessing the crowd with a swinging spotlight while Will made his Fender Jag sound like metal being ripped from walls and hurled across the stage. A visceral, unique, gloriously savage experience and the rhythm section of your dreams.

They could have been bigger than U2. The Edge knows this to be a fact and, deep down, Bono probably knows it too. They could have straddled the globe (although it would have to be a much darker, more intelligent world that would accept *Over The Wall* filling enormodomes rather than *New Year's Day*). They just couldn't be arsed. Simple as that, really. Didn't want to waste time messing around the back roads of America. Do things their way or not at all. Motto for life, right there.

So, I've got the background. I know that we're not doing the nostalgia trip, not watching a band going through the motions for the payday. What we're watching is a band who remain vital, remain powerful, still instil wonder and awe.

The set is short, less than an hour, and perfectly measured. It's the songs that everybody there will know, that the casual punter will have heard of, can't have fail to have heard of. It's the classics that you might not even realise are classics until they step up and slap you, and you realise that somewhere deep down you've always known all the words and that this orchestra behind them are adding another level to the sound that you'd forgotten that you remembered.

That sound is massive. Glorious and beautiful, rich and deep and filling the field. It's like floating. It's the singles, short, sharp, shockingly timeless. No between-song languors, no mid-song diversions, every song hits you where it's meant to. It's a band knowing the job it has to do to entertain every section of an audience and then going out and doing that very job. It might hold nostalgia but it's far from being a nostalgia act. It's a reminder of how glorious our shared youth was and how young we all still are and as the last chorus of *Ocean Rain* ('The second greatest song ever written' according to its creator, with the greatest having already appeared in the form of *The Killing Moon*) swells and then fades and the fireworks burst from behind the stage. It's impossibly gorgeous, perfect and timeless.

Which is good as it rescues the weekend from Saturday's football.

Liverpool 0 West Ham United 3

29 August 2015

I HADN'T meant to be late to the game, to walk in as *You'll Never Walk Alone* started, clutching a hastily bought sausage sandwich to ward off the hangover. I'd meant to arrive early, stroll casually to my seat and relax. Hadn't planned for the hangover, though. We were out on Friday night. Unusual for us and pretty much unplanned. And all the better for that fact.

J's cousin and her husband, a meal, good conversation and some wine. Some wine. It's the some wine that does the damage. Those nights where the offer of the refill arrives before the glass is empty and you feel that refusal would be impolite. I hate to appear impolite. So, I keep saying 'yes', which is all fine and good until Friday night becomes Saturday morning and coffee with J's mother and a splitting headache and the idea of food sits badly and you think that you'll get a bacon butty in the cafe behind the Kop, but you're too slow leaving the house and hit the cafe at ten to three for a three o'clock kick-off and there's no bacon left, so you settle for sausage and eat as you walk and as you sit. Eat as everybody else sings *You'll Never Walk Alone,* but no flags wave.

We're in protest mode today. The lads who organise the flags have been in discussion with the club, attempting to negotiate some level of accommodation for fan interest at a club that is becoming more and more business based by the day. The discussions weren't working. The flags, the show of unity and pride that the club partly sells its public image on, weren't present. A blank Kop. Hopefully the gesture will work.

Certainly the removal of the usual flags last year to facilitate a show of plain black replacements and banners, protesting rising ticket prices at a time when television deals are reaching new levels of insanity, brought attention to the cause.

Perhaps it was an apt day to highlight the reality of both the club and the game's current situation. It was certainly the day that the early-season bubble burst in the most dispiriting manner. The forthcoming two-week break I was bemoaning in the previous pages currently appears to be a blessing. Seems to be the time that we will need to recover from the humiliation of 29 August.

The two slim victories that had started the season, a world-class goal and an offside decision or two being all that separated us from scoreless draws or a draw and a loss, had promised little. The Arsenal game, scoreless as it was and dominated in the second half by whatever Wenger's half-time team talk had provoked, had promised much. It had spoken of invention and resilience. It had indicated a new mental strength to this Liverpool team. It spoke glowingly of bright futures. It seems to have lied.

The Liverpool that faced Slaven Bilic's West Ham was toothless in every possible area. The selection was odd, the tactics were either misguided or badly followed, possibly both.

The idea that we would need a defensive midfielder at home to a team that had not managed to beat us at Anfield since 1963 was... interesting. The idea that we would start with a 4-3-3 formation that would quickly change into a 4-5-1, with that '1' being a very long way from the '4' and the '5', wrongheaded in the extreme. Suddenly, the promise of Christian Benteke looked very, very similar to the inadequacies of Andy Carroll and Mario Balotelli, a big lad up front who we'll pump long balls to so that he can flick them down to... bugger, forgot to tell the others to get close to him. Not Benteke's fault, the tactics were completely at fault. Bilic outwitted Rodgers over two games with Besiktas to put us out of the Europa League last season (after everyone else had put us out of the Champions League) and yes, it took the hapless Dejan Lovren to absolutely 'sky' a penalty in the shoot-out for that to happen, but Bilic's tactics over four hours of open play had been perfect. Here, he did it again to greater effect in just ninety minutes.

West Ham knew when to sit and when to go, when to chase our flanks and when to confront us head-on down the middle, when to run at and panic us. Their first goal, destroying any game plan that we *might* have had within three minutes, was facilitated from the flanks and helped by Joe Gomez, otherwise a revelation this season, choosing that exact moment to switch off completely. Their second came from the return of Lovren to last year's disasters.

Three games. Three games of Dejan doing the simple stuff. Three games where little was expected of him other than the basics, heading out, getting rid, giving the ball to a more talented lad in front of him. Suddenly Dejan decided that he was possessed of a Messi-esque level of invention, beauty, poise and control. 'Cruyff-turning' a forward in the vicinity of our own corner flag? Yeah, why not? 'Now I've done that, now I've done the difficult bit, what shall I do? Pass to their forward? Yeah, that'll be a laugh. Two-nil.'

The bizarre thing is that it wasn't our defending that was the problem at that point. Our problem was our attacking prowess or lack thereof. The gap between Benteke and the two supposedly supporting him, Coutinho and Firmino, was growing by the second as the two dropped deeper to retrieve the ball and hoped to make something happen. The three behind them stopped being a holding midfielder and two creators and became three holding midfielders. At home. Against a side we're *supposed* to beat. Against the kind of side that you think will ship several goals. We knew what we had to do in the second half, we had to score more goals in forty-five minutes than we'd managed in the preceding three games. We didn't. You know we didn't. The fact that there was one shot on target from the home team in the entire game, and that from the ever-hapless Dejan, is damning.

The fact that West Ham scored a third in injury time simply inevitable.

I'm fifty-one years old. West Ham had never won at Anfield in my lifetime. I appear to have accidentally entered a brave new world. I don't like it.

Liverpool left the field at half-time to a chorus of jeers, not something I subscribe to but I 'get it'. They left at full time to virtual silence. The third hit the net and the exodus started. Then, of course, the 'fume' followed. The calls for the manager's head, the cry that he had learned nothing from last season, that the summer transfer business had been as appalling as last year's, that we were further away than ever.

This is how we are now. More amplified, more exaggerated than ever. The Suarez season has shown us how close to glory we can come. The fact that first the season then the player were taken from us has shown us how much despair a simple result can provide. We no longer know if a bad result is simply a bad result or the sign of a much worse malaise. Arsenal was good, West Ham was bad. A two-week gap now. Two weeks to seethe and fester. Two weeks of international interruption and then United at Old Trafford. That's United who are now a million miles above us in people's minds while simultaneously managing to be beneath us in the table, playing as badly as ourselves, if not worse, and having the most bizarre, nightmarish transfer window that you could imagine.

The Transfer Window

1 September 2015

I'M JUMPING the gun on this one a little. It's 5pm as I write, the transfer window is due to 'slam shut' (never simply 'close' always 'slam shut') in an hour and I feel relatively free to talk about it, as though I were some sort of authority on how everything will sit in the very near future.

The transfer window as a concept seems to become more ridiculous with each passing year, more pressurised, more panicked. Sky Television's co-opting of the period into a last-minute circus show is either the cause or the best representation of the desperation of the day. We might have thought that the stupidity had peaked with the appearance of a bright purple dildo in a reporter's ear live on air but it hadn't. It simply gave Sky the chance to sanitise the proceedings and further glorify the ego that the channel had created for Jim White. Any amusement factor that the presenter had once represented on 'deadline day' faded long ago.

The Bank Holiday Monday has given us an extension on the carnival this year. Instead of slamming shut at 11pm on the Monday night, we now have until 6pm on Tuesday. Let joy be unconfined. The reason for this nineteen hours extra? Not a clue. Nobody has bothered explaining.

I know this, though: I know that the Spanish window did its slamming at 11pm last night, their time. I know this because it created, from a Liverpool vantage point, the most amusing moment of the window.

David DeGea saved United loads of points last season. Loads of them. Player of the season by the proverbial country mile. Without him, they don't finish top four. And Real Madrid wanted him. We knew this all summer. Real want him, he wants to go to Real. Done deal. Louis Van Gaal isn't talking about it, but DeGea's not in the team and LVG's face is telling us everything we need to know. The deal's done. It's done on the last day, in the last hour, in the last minute of the Spanish window. David DeGea is a Real Madrid player. He's a Real Madrid player for nowhere near what he's worth and Keylor Navas. Except he's *not*. Somebody has made a mess of the paperwork. Something hasn't arrived in time. Real say it's not them, United say it's not them. Whoever it is, Manchester United have a goalkeeper who doesn't want to be there. What they don't have are strikers. RVP goes, Falcao goes home and then goes to Chelsea, United pay £36m for Anthony Martial and the whole world says: 'Who?'

Elsewhere, all the real fun is in the teams that are refusing to sell. Tottenham want Saido Berahino from West Brom. They want him to the point that they put in four offers. West Brom say no to all of them. Good on West Brom, basically. Except Berahino tweets that he'll never play for West Brom again as long as Jeremy Peace is in charge of the business. So, no money and a player who doesn't want to be there.

Everton are more impressive on this front: Chelsea want John Stones. They want him to the tune of a £30m offer, then £35m, then £37m. Everton say he's not for sale. The player puts in a transfer request, Everton say he's not for sale. And keep saying it until Chelsea sign some kid for £2m and go chasing a PSG defender only to be told 'he's not for sale.' Chelsea: not winning games, not signing players, it's a beautiful thing.

From Liverpool's point of view, we can ignore the whole thing. Like it or not, and after the West Ham mess there are plenty who don't, we've made all our signings. The Balotelli experiment has ended with the loan deal, we've somehow managed to sell Fabio Borini to Sunderland for actual money and Jose Enrique has gone to… no, sorry, Jose's still there/here.

Going nowhere. We have at least another three months of his Instagram updates to look forward to until the whole circus starts again.

Although there are still ten minutes to go…

International Interruption

Let's call it 13 September, shall we?

SO, WHAT happened in the eleven days between then and now?

Well, Wayne Rooney scored his fiftieth goal for England, breaking Bobby Charlton's record courtesy of a fairly soft penalty against Switzerland at Wembley. In fairness, the record would quite possibly have been broken the best part of twenty-five years ago if Graham Taylor hadn't made the bizarre decision to substitute Gary Lineker while England were chasing a goal and a result. (This is from memory, it might have happened differently, and it's England, so who's really interested enough to Google the details?)

Other than that, David De Gea, after supposedly being on the brink of leaving United for Real before paperwork/files/ whatever they use now went astray, suddenly signed a new deal. On the eve of Liverpool visiting Old Trafford. There was no way that could be a good thing.

And somewhere in all this, I was asked if I would write another piece for the fine *We Are Liverpool* fanzine. One issue in this, the deadline for the piece, for the issue that would appear at Liverpool's next home game, was Friday 11 September. Nothing to talk about. West Ham was ten days in the past, Manchester United at Old Trafford still in the future. Ah, if we could only keep United away at Old Trafford in the future, if we could make it *not* have happened yet.

I went out on a limb. I wrote this. Wrote a piece that critiqued, some might say criticised, the knee-jerk reaction to the West Ham loss, in the hope that I would be right, in the hope that the side would come good, in the hope that the manager would come good:

Come On Lads

GOT IT. Got the 'in'.

Sometimes you need an 'in', that bit where you start talking, start writing. You might not know where you're going, might only have the vaguest idea where it will all end, but you've got faith that it will sort itself out and everything will fall into place before you hit the finish line. That, in case you were wondering, is a pretty clumsy metaphor. It didn't start out as one but I realised halfway through that what I was talking about mirrored the shape of the season. I really AM making this stuff up as I go along. Like you didn't know.

What are you supposed to write about when it's nearly a fortnight since the West Ham game and the United game hasn't happened yet and the only football we've seen is Wayne Rooney getting a soft penalty to break Bobby Charlton's England record? Congrats and all that Wayne but... England? Arsed.

And then I saw it. Trawling back through Facebook, I came across a sign. That's not a metaphor, it was genuinely a sign. Words on it and everything.

Remember the day that the Nazis didn't show up in our lovely city centre? Not the first one where a handful got off the train and ended up locked in left luggage for their own safety having warned that 'only bullets will stop us', but proved that bananas and eggs would do the job. Bunch of meffs. No, the second one. The one where they got off at Widnes – not a euphemism — and just didn't show. Bad, bad meffs.

They're not the point, though. The point is the sign that the anti-fascist demonstrators brandished outside. In the tradition of Father Ted's glorious 'Down with this sort of thing/careful now' placard, this read simply: 'Come on lads, stop being divvys'.

And this is relevant in what way?

We're being divvys. Tons of us, full on divvy-ish behaviour. We're four games into the season and the lads who rent out the planes and print up the banners are rubbing their hands in glee at the potential earnings they stand to make from our divvyishness (think I just invented a word). The #RodgersOut brigade is carrying out thumb exercises readying itself for the next full on Twitter fume. We're four games into the season and writing it off. Because of West Ham.

Yeah, West Ham was appalling. Embarrassing, shameful, pathetic. Brendan got his tactics wrong. Badly, badly, badly wrong. Let's be honest though, Bilic? He's a pretty decent coach, isn't he? Pretty experienced by now. Came with a gameplan and made it work. Helped by Brendan deciding to play with two lads holding and one up front. At home. Before the game, though? Before the game, I didn't see many complaining about the team selection. Same team as Arsenal? Cool. I'll have that. Did well at Arsenal, should walk over West Ham. That first half destroyed us. Awful first half, shameful, shoddy. Second half wasn't much better. Flashes from Ings and Moreno but overall... nah. Rubbish.

Which doesn't excuse the fact that we booed the team off at half-time. And I'm calling it as 'we', 'us', all of us.

Three games down. Two of them 1-0 wins, neither of them particularly inspiring but let's be honest, the first few games of 2013/14 weren't that hot and the season turned out okay. Not setting the world on fire, but shall we make a list of all the teams that have looked impressive so far this season?

City.

There you go. Quite concise that wasn't it?

So, we have one bad day. An appallingly bad day, no escaping that fact, but instead of looking at it and going 'this might just be a one-off', we're calling it as the end of days and further proof that Brendan must go and FSG are killing this club. It was one day. It might be part of a larger trend, but we don't know that yet. By the time you read this, we might be basking in the glory of a fit-again Daniel Sturridge's second-half substitute appearance inspiring the still-mighty Reds to an 8-0 victory over our friends from down the M62. Or not. We don't know yet.

And while we're waiting to find out, while we're waiting to settle, while we're still having a better start than Chelsea, let's get behind our lads and against the other lot. Let's not boo our own team off the pitch at half-time.

To put it another way: Come on lads — you, me, all of us — stop being divvys.

And then *this* happened

Manchester United 3 Liverpool 1

12 September 2015

AND THE day had started so well.

I'll be open about this. In the Labour leadership elections, I had pinned my colours to Andy Burnham's campaign very early on. Early enough that Jeremy Corbyn hadn't entered the race at all. As the campaign progressed, I quickly saw enough of Corbyn to feel torn. Old school Labour, proper socialism that believes that hospitals and schools carry more value than a nuclear deterrent which, if it could be argued that it had ever held a place in the world, certainly holds no value now. The war that we've been dragged into with a previous Labour regime's 'sexing up' of dossiers and unsubstantiated claims of weapons of mass destruction isn't a war against a location that can be targeted, attacked and annihilated, it's a war against a philosophy with a changing face. The money that the Tories are willing to invest in the American-controlled Trident could be diverted to so much good elsewhere.

Which is wandering from the point somewhat.

I felt Jeremy Corbyn to be the leadership candidate who most closely reflected my own views, but I stayed supporting Andy Burnham. My allegiance was stated and I kept it there.

I kept it there for very obvious reasons.

I was at Anfield for the service commemorating the twentieth anniversary of the Hillsborough disaster. I was there when Andy Burnham, then a serving minister in a Labour government that had denied a new inquest, stood and took the massed criticism and protest, nodded, agreed and went and did something about it. The power of the supporters influenced one man to ensure that the Hillsborough Independent Panel happened. It's the most impressive individual demonstration of the politics of conviction that I have ever seen.

Jeremy won, though. A landslide. Sixty percent share of the party vote in the first round. And the acceptance speech was glorious, thanks to those who had supported him, an attack on the Tories and their pet rags, who had slandered him and attacked his family throughout the campaign, and a clear affirmation of all that he believes to be right. Everything that all people with compassion for their fellow man should believe.

It felt like a rebirth, a revival, a return. It offered hope, there might be four more years of Cameron and his politics of entitlement to suffer, but there is hope that there is now a convincing alternative. Later than we needed it perhaps but there at last.

And then there was the Everton game.

The fact that I'm married to an Evertonian makes me (I think) more accepting of the blue half of town. My youngest brother hates Everton with a vengeance. Me? I'm okay with them. More than happy for them to come second to us in anything. And it probably goes without saying that, on a day where it's Everton against Chelsea and the chances of Mourinho's lot continuing their poor start to the season seem high, then we're all slightly bluish really.

Everton were excellent. Everton had everything that Chelsea lacked. Speed, power, skill, invention. A hero emerging from the bench to score a hat-trick. A true hat-trick, left foot, right foot, head. A proper hero. Steven Naismith, unheralded, under-appreciated but a player who never gives less than his best, a player with the sort of personal convictions that prompts him to buy match tickets to donate to the poor. A decent pro, a decent bloke. Everton were the better team. Ignoring Jose's obvious, ungracious post-match comments, Everton deserved their win. Everton were genuinely impressive to watch as they took a major scalp in a fine performance.

All of which merely emphasises the levels of sheer misery that we had to endure from 5.30pm onwards.

The absence of Rooney – hamstring, post-England or in training, depending on your chosen source – meant that Van Gaal decided to play without a recognised striker of any kind. At home. Against your most fierce rivals in the most viewed Premier League game of the season. A five-man midfield behind Marouane Fellaini as your choice of attack? As somebody on Twitter phrased it, given Daley Blind's presence at centre back, 'a midfielder behind a midfielder behind a midfielder'. There for the taking.

That we approached this game, this opposition, still far from being anywhere near a good United team, with such caution, such negativity, such lack of adventure, rankles.

Lucas sitting in front of a four-man defence, Ings and Firmino bizarrely utilised as wide men and Christian Benteke somewhere in the distance for long balls to be aimed at. I'm sure that this isn't what he saw in the brochure before he came to Anfield.

The first forty-five minutes might be the worst half of football that I've ever seen. Ever. Anywhere. Two poor teams refusing to trade blows, both sides more concerned with not losing than with winning. It was clear within the first ten minutes that our lack of shape and shambolic approach to both defending and passing the ball to another white shirt would cause us problems. The fact that the manager could look at the opposition on the field and not attempt to press them in the way that we had Arsenal felt nervous, felt cowardly, felt like a man who was scared for his job, a man who knew that pressure was coming and that this might be the only way to avoid it. Note to Brendan: Caution only keeps you in a job if it works.

The second half was better. It had to be. The shackles were forced off when we conceded from a well worked free kick, three minutes into the half. The fact that it wasn't a free kick, the fact that we should have had somebody watching Blind on the edge of the box, the fact that Schweinsteiger was dragging a player away in the box? None of these matter. All of these matter but none of these matter. We shouldn't have put ourselves in a position where United had the chance to take the lead. We could have/should have shown initiative in the first forty-five minutes, we could have imposed our will on the game. We didn't.

We woke up after the goal. Amazing how often we wake up after a goal, isn't it? Speed suddenly became a conscious decision instead of a vague rumour. The shape didn't change, that would be far too much to hope for, but the urgency did. We pushed, made chances. De Gea saved from both Ings and Ibe. And then Joe Gomez gave away a penalty. All he had to do was stay on his feet and shepherd Herrera out of play. He didn't, he's eighteen, he'll learn. And the insurmountable became ever more so.

Until the Benteke goal, obviously. The Benteke goal, which Sky Sports' commentator compared to Rooney's overhead kick of a couple of seasons ago. It was infinitely superior. Rooney shinned his, Benteke hit it clean. Gorgeous, the kind of goal that deserves to win games, not sit within a two-one defeat. 'Hell of a goal' I tweeted, 'now make it f***ing count'. I take full responsibility. Three-one down within minutes. The £36m teenager on the bench? The one that I'd previously referred to as 'who?' Allowed to waltz through our defence and slot home. A new Mancunian hero, first shot in the shirt sinks Liverpool. He might never do anything else. They'll love him forever anyway.

And that was that. Three-one. Blown away, ripped apart, embarrassed. By a United team whose first shot on goal from open play was in the 87th minute. Many have pointed out that on another day we win the game, we created more than United did, had more shots on goal, were more threatening. The reality is that two very poor teams faced each other and the *less* poor of the two won. The reality is that we got it wrong.

And the specific reality is that our manager got it all very, very wrong. The wrong shape, the wrong passion, the wrong intensity. Players out of position, a complete lack of joined-up thought. For me, that's the reality.

Twitter, inevitably, exploded. The '#RodgersOut' brigade raised their heads and roared. Sane voices added themselves to the clamour: last season was bad, Stoke was awful, this season had, bar the first half at Arsenal, been poor rising to ordinary at times. This was the killer blow. To go *there* and do *that*? Too many had had enough.

So we split. We split into the 'sack him now' and the 'don't sack him' and sub-divided into 'it's the manager's fault' and 'it's the players' faults, he can't control them once they're over the line' and we argued. This is where we are now. We argue with each other all the time. We're divided, conflicted. I tweeted my view, just my view, no more than that, I don't claim any authority, and became trapped in an argument which was curtailed by the other party's decision that my opinions hold no validity as I don't have a coaching badge. Apparently, I'm not allowed opinions without appropriate qualification. That's really going to limit the rest of this book, isn't it? On so, so many subjects.

Which only adds to the pertinence of the following question:

What happens next?

FC Bordeaux 1 Liverpool 1

17 September 2015

THURSDAY NIGHTS. The result of last season's appalling run in is Thursday night football. The Europa League. Not Champions League Tuesdays and Wednesdays, not real glory. Thursdays and then league games on Sundays. The whole week slightly skewed, not the pattern that you either want or expect.

The obvious question following from that situation being 'how seriously are you going to take this competition?'

Me? I'd take it very, very seriously. Not for the 'winning it gets you into the Champions League next season and we might not qualify via the top four' argument, but for the simple fact that it's the UEFA Cup and always will be, and we have a fine tradition with that gorgeous old trophy. I grew up watching Liverpool win that competition and I'd love to see us win it again. Even apart from the obvious 'you should aim to win every competition that you enter' argument, we're Liverpool, we exist to win things. Best make that 'existed to win things' – we don't do it very often now.

I genuinely don't know how Brendan feels about that concept. He'd said at the start of the season that he intended to use the Europa as a chance to give game time to fringe players and youngsters, which doesn't usually signal either the intention or the possibility of winning the competition as being too likely.

I was about to defend Rodgers' stance as that of a man 'already being described as beleaguered', but that description has been solidly in place since the turn of the year. Even in the period when we were playing attractive football and putting together a ridiculous level of unbeaten games and not conceding goals, that concept still lurked, waiting for the next opportunity to raise its head. There's every possibility that, should Rodgers ride out the current revisitation of the twitter fume/bookies' odds storm, that he'll always be beleaguered. This is his being now, it's attached to him. As long as he's at Liverpool, he'll always be one game away from a crisis.

We (me and J) had to be somewhere at the start of the game, the other peril of Thursdays being 6pm kick-offs – thanks to 'the telly' for that – so I followed the game on Twitter with the box set up to record for watching once home.

Twitter made me not want to watch. The 'fume' was terrific, a fume of almost galactic proportions. The lads tweeting were in bits. We were terrible, we had nothing, we were dreary, there was no threat, we couldn't defend. Adam Lallana was the devil incarnate.

The side was, as promised, fringe players and youth team prospects. Simon Mignolet giving Kolo Toure seemingly the worst dead leg in the history of mankind meant the insertion of Emre Can into a three-man defence and the introduction of Pedro Chirivella for his debut. With Jordan Rossiter already on the field this meant that, against FC Bordeaux's first-choice eleven, we had two eighteen-year-olds running our midfield. With an eighteen-year-old Joe Gomez central behind them. And a twenty-year- old Divock Origi as our attacking threat until he was replaced by the twenty-two year old veteran Danny Ings. A ridiculously young team by any standards.

You know what? They did okay. They were okay. Didn't really threaten, but weren't really threatened. A sublime Lallana goal (see that, Twitter? That's what he can do) gave Liverpool the lead that we possibly, just possibly, deserved. The seconds that Joe Gomez spent watching a Bordeaux forward ball-juggle in the area provided Emre Can with sufficient time to make a crucial tackle, crucial in the fact that it worked as an assist for the Bordeaux equaliser.

The returning Sakho was a plus. We suddenly had authority at the back. Rossiter was a plus. Disciplined and effective in the middle, doing the simple things well, an undervalued attribute in a midfielder, until replaced, cramped up, by Cameron Brannagan towards the close of play. Chirivella, as effective and uncomplicated as Rossiter, yet another plus. Origi, carrying out the thankless lone role inhabited by Christian Benteke this season, offered little. Very, very little. Still no idea whether the lad has anything. The jury might remain out on this for a while yet.

Ultimately, in a match where very little happened, we came away from the French team's ground with a fairly stale draw. Want to know what we called that in the seventies and eighties when we were winning these things? A European away, simple as that. Job very nearly done but not quite, nothing dangerous, nothing damning. Except for the fact that everything is damning at the moment. Nothing sits in the story of the season without context. This game had to be the reply to the West Ham embarrassment and the United humiliation. It wasn't. It was just a game. Just a very ordinary game of football.

In terms of context, of the narrative of the season, the important thing here was that so many of the first-team squad hadn't travelled to France, that both Sean O'Driscoll and Gary McAllister had been left at home. There had been time to work with the eleven who would start against Norwich on the Sunday afternoon. Planning and preparation were everything, all was in order. All would be well. Wouldn't it?

Liverpool 1 Norwich City 1

20 September 2015

WE'RE TALKING context again, the context of the last few times that we've played Norwich, the number seven we had who seemed to take personal pleasure in torturing this team. We're talking hat-tricks, three hat-tricks against the same team, we're talking four goals against them in one game, goals from the halfway line, the moment where he flicks the ball *around*, not over but *around* Leroy Fer before volleying his own flicked pass into the Norwich goal and wheeling away in front of the Kop, laughing hysterically at his own audacity and ingenuity. That's what we're talking about. We're talking about how long ago that all seems and how far we've fallen in eighteen months.

We knew we were in the presence of genius, we're not stupid, we *knew* that. We knew that we had one of the greatest players in the world in our team. More precisely, we knew that we had one of the *three* greatest players in the world in our team. Only Ronaldo and Messi were breathing the same rarefied air. Specifically, for three months in early 2013, we knew that we had the single best player in the world playing for us.

We knew it when the supporters of every other English team, particularly the ones across Stanley Park, were deriding us, denying us, ridiculing the belief. Incredible the way they agree now that he's at the Nou Camp, isn't it?

What we didn't know, what I don't *think* we knew, what *I* definitely didn't realise, was exactly how far we would fall without him. On the last day of the 2013/14 season, I stood outside the King Harry pub and argued that *it wasn't over.*

Fleety: 'What if this was the only chance?'

Me: 'It won't be, we'll build on this. We've come close, all we need to do now is take the next step.'

Yeah, we know how that turned out. The loss of Suarez compounded by the injury to Sturridge, by Raheem's end-of-season circus, by Steven Gerrard's farewell tour. Everything went to hell. All of which left us with no idea of what we were any longer. This August's Arsenal game pointed in one direction, both halves in their different ways. Everything else pointed in another.

That's the context. The detail goes like this:

Sturridge is back. Back from the first minute, back in the starting line-up, not the 'sitting on the bench, ease him in with the last twenty minutes' comeback that you or I – definitely I – might have expected.

Three at the back, full-backs moved up to the wings to sit alongside Milner and Lucas, with Coutinho, Benteke and the aforementioned returnee in front. A 3-4-3 or a 3-4-1-2, however you want to look at it. A welcome change in formation, a positive thought. None of which actually meant that we could be creative enough to break down Norwich's defence in the first forty-five minutes. Any move which didn't break down at James Milner's feet broke down at the eighteen-yard line.

That's not to say that Benteke and Sturridge weren't connecting: there were definite signs of a partnership which might explode into creativity given the chance and if not denied by injury.

The fact that Benteke was withdrawn at half-time with a hamstring issue might indicate that the fates don't intend to be kind to Brendan on this one, no more than they had been when Henderson's heel injury suddenly transformed into a fracture *in the other foot* on the day before the game. It doesn't matter, it's the job of the manager to deal with fate's conspiracies and make the most of what he has available.

That availability includes Danny Ings. Here, today, he was exactly what the team needed, a player who was willing to define himself with the passion that fans require. He was tireless, determined, frustrated when events didn't run his way. Three minutes into his afternoon and he's scored Liverpool's opening goal. Liverpool's only goal. We try for more, we move, we probe, nothing happens. And then we concede yet another soft equaliser, another corner not defended, another dead-ball situation for the opposition to capitalise on, another squandering of two points which seemed sewn up.

There's a smattering of boos at the final whistle. There's frustration. These are the games that you need to win, the days where Anfield is supposed to be a fortress, the longest ninety minutes of the visitors' lives. Today was no such thing. Liverpool weren't necessarily *bad* they just weren't very good, weren't *good enough*. There were moments, flashes, but not enough to actually pull together and convince anybody that there was real hope. We look limited, like we lack invention, like we lack depth. Circumstances might have conspired. Clearly the plan was to remove Sturridge at sixty minutes and not to lose Benteke at half-time, but only having one recognised striker on the bench would indicate that precautions might not have been fully thought through. Sturridge leaves the field as planned and suddenly, already without Benteke, we have midfielders all over the place and our threat has receded again.

And, once again and very obviously, the manager is being questioned. A statement of intent was needed. It didn't arrive. Six games into the season and we have won two, drawn two, and lost two, scoring four goals in the process. It's not good enough by any standards and particularly not in light of the history that we grew up with and the challenge so recently witnessed. We're missing genius and it shows.

Current form is woeful and we're not even talking about those six games that matter most immediately. If we run the rule over the last eighteen games, then Liverpool have won five, drawn five and lost eight, only scoring more than one goal in two of the last twenty games. To describe this as 'relegation form' is a very, *very* minor exaggeration. It's the form of a team that survives relegation in the last week of the season. It is *not* the form of a Liverpool team.

The clamour grows, the questions are asked, the bookies shorten their odds, everything is tenuous, the question is still 'which is the real Brendan Rodgers?' Is it the man lost on the line at Wembley, changing his formation with the wind, reaping no benefit? The man who has persisted in playing players out of position? Or is it the man who harnessed the genius of Luis Suarez, allying him so well with Sturridge and Sterling and making him into the best footballer on the planet for those three blissful, dreamlike months that suddenly seem so long ago?

Liverpool 1 Carlisle United 1

23 September 2015
Capital One Cup
Liverpool win 3-2 on penalties

I REALISED the date at some point in the first half. A month until I turn 52. As ages go, that one seems fairly absurd. I realised something else as I started to type that sentence. This will be my first birthday without my dad. November 9 will be the first anniversary of losing him. It will also be our youngest son's fifteenth birthday. From this vantage point, I'm not entirely sure how I'll deal with any of those things. As they happen, I suppose. It's all you can do really, isn't it?

There was another thing that came to me at some mid-point between those two realisations, as the news came through that my uncle, my dad's younger brother by two years, had been hospitalised again. I reflected on the fact that the wallpaper on my phone is of my dad and two of my uncles in Trafalgar Square, heavily over-coated on an unseasonably cool May afternoon in 1965 before our first FA Cup triumph. It hit me at that moment that these three were vital young men out at the match, same as us. Nothing new in that realisation, I've reflected on it before. The fresh aspect was this: I'm now old enough to be the father of those men in that picture. The oldest is thirty years old, the youngest still in his mid-twenties. Odd, the things that hit you about the ageing process.

I realised my age at the match last night. Realised as I leant forward to discuss yet another wayward shot, another easy opposition attack through the heart of our defence, that I was now talking to these older men as an equal. I wasn't a kid anymore, no matter how much I might imagine myself to be. Realised that, to the young bloke next to me, I am one of the old guys now. I also realised that I sound a lot like my dad when I speak. That was nice.

We despaired at what we saw in front of us. We took the 'here we go again' stance. And in the midst of this stance, I realised something about this Liverpool.

Watching this Liverpool fail to cut swathes through a team from the current second division as we heard that Southampton had put six past MK Dons, United had eased through, and only Newcastle were making us look good –and that's kind of their job – I realised this: I don't know who this Liverpool are anymore. So I wrote this for *The Anfield Wrap,* with its title taken from one of the evening's many contentious moments:

Liverpool – Who Are Yer?

LOOK, I'LL be honest with you from the start, I don't know where I'm going with this. I haven't got a piece (article, comment, whatever) plotted out. I'm not entirely sure what my point is. I'm not entirely sure I actually have *a point. I'm just writing because I bloody have to, because I feel the need to get this out, because I'm sat at a keyboard and I* need, *absolutely* need *to talk about Liverpool.*

I honestly don't think I've ever been as depressed about Liverpool Football Club as I am at the moment. Honestly. Even in the dark days at the end of Souness's reign (and that was a far worse team than this), even in the utter horror of Hodgson, I don't think that I felt this lost, this adrift. I could see ends to those, could see change. At the moment, all I can see is this going on forever, gradually getting worse. I don't see anybody arresting this slide any time soon. I don't see action being taken. I could be wrong, I hope I'm wrong, I don't feel wrong.

I looked at the pitch sometime in the second half – God knows when, it seemed to last forever – and thought, 'Mid-table.' For the first time ever, I looked down at a Liverpool side and thought, 'we're mid-table, that's what we are now.' And the worst part? I resigned myself to it, accepted that there was no way back, came to terms with the fact that we were now, and probably always would be, ordinary.

It wasn't the team that I expected. In theory, it was stronger. There were more seasoned professionals on the pitch, more senior players. There wasn't the emphasis on youth that I expected from this competition. It looked like Brendan had decided to go pretty near full strength, strong enough to show that we intended to take care of this Carlisle team, make a statement that we're Liverpool and we take things seriously. That's what I thought. It's not what I saw, just what I thought.

I expected Bogdan. I got him. Fair enough, good on the pens and all that. I expected Rossiter to start, Chirivella. Both had played well enough against Bordeaux to feel that they deserved a start in a lower-profile competition than the Europa League. They wouldn't, after all, be playing a team that had just drawn with PSG, they'd be playing a team with the worst defensive record in the universe. I haven't got the stats, I don't want them, they'll only make me sad. If I were Rossiter, I would understand not getting on the pitch. The way the game unfolded, it wouldn't have been right. I'd possibly want to know how badly James Milner has to play before I get on, though. If I were Chirivella? I'd want to know why I couldn't get on to the bench. Surely the lad deserves that.

Expected Gomez. Started well this season, got a little exposed, taken out of the firing line. Surely this was the game to put him back in that line? Expected Ibe for exactly the same reason. Are these lads better than old fourth division standard? Of course they are, well better. So was that lad with the mad parrot haircut for Carlisle. In fairness, didn't look fourth division. Whole team didn't.

So I don't know what Brendan was trying to achieve. Play some of the lads that he needs to do the job in the league into something that looks like form? Didn't work. Sweep away the opposition? Didn't work. Build confidence? Get the crowd back on side? Did. Not. Work.

I liked the fact that we were keeping the ball. Ings keeps the ball, Lallana keeps the ball, Allen keeps the ball. Possession's good, possession's cool, the other lot don't score when you've got all the possession. I liked the fact that a decent cross into the box gave us a decent header and the lead. I like the fact that we went for a second. Appetite, I like appetite.

What I didn't like, then? We allow an attacker to charge through the middle of the park. Again. We stand off said attacker. Again. We concede. Again. Dejan Lovren is at the heart of the problem. A-bloody-gain. Wish the lad well and all that, hate seeing anyone stretchered off with the oxygen mask going, but he was abject last night. Can't stand his opponent up, can't head at the back, can't head at the front but we keep lumping it to him at corners. Truly terrible. We concede. And then our heads fall off for five minutes and only one team looks like scoring and it's the team with the lad who looks like a cockerel in the number ten shirt.

What didn't I like? The lack of speed, incision, decision, sense, in-game intelligence, thought. We have two things out there. One is receiving the ball and moving up the pitch slowly enough that Carlisle can put every man behind that ball before we hit the halfway line so that they can watch us run round the edge of the box, turning and twisting and passing and never actually achieving anything at all. And doing it again and again and again for two bloody hours.

The other thing is shooting. All the time. From miles away. Shooting wide and over and over and wide and straight at the keeper who we managed to not actually trouble once all night. Forty-eight thousand shots on goal and we didn't stretch a keeper who plays in the old fourth division. Coutinho comes on and it appears that his instructions were 'You know that goal you scored, Phil? Do it again. Just keep going until it happens' and 'See that Lewandowski lad last night? Five goals in nine minutes? How great would it be if you scored the same goal five times in one game?' Hitting the same point in the Kop fifteen times isn't the same. I love Phil but I dearly wanted him to stop shooting and actually make something happen.

Was there anything I liked, then? Liked Emre Can, that's his position. Doesn't like it there? Keep using the word Beckenbauer at him until he's convinced. Liked Joe Allen, thought he had a good game. Like Danny Ings. Danny Ings has become the 'us on the pitch' that we need. There's the passion, there's the desire, there's a lad who wants it, really wants it, who gets it. There's a lad who'll bleed for the shirt. On his arse after seventy minutes, like. Ran himself out. First name on the team sheet for me.

That's the only thing I know. Everything else, I just suspect. I suspect that Brendan's done. I suspect he doesn't know where he's going any more. The fact that he didn't put himself in front of the cameras last night, whether Gary Mac had been doing all the pre-match media or not, whether Gary had actually run the whole thing last night and it's all actually down to him, Brendan should *be putting himself in front of the cameras and talking about it. He's the manager. However it was set up, it's his responsibility. Letting somebody else stand as the face of that game? Shameful, that. Soz Brendan, but there you go.*

I don't know what Liverpool Football Club is any more. But there's this as well, I don't know who we are any more. That's the we in the ground, the 40,000ish. The die-hards who are always there and the guys who got hold of tickets just for that game. We're split. We're really split. There were tons of songs from the Kop to start off with. There was backing, hope, belief and support for the team. There was support for the pens. There was a brief rendition of 'Brendan Rodgers' Liverpool' and it sounded halfway convincing, as though there are some of us who still believe in him. Probably less this morning.

And there was booing. Too much booing. Any booing is too much but last night there was too much of too much. There was booing at the end of extra time. These lads are about to take penalties in front of the opposition fans and we're booing them? Really?

And there's that whole 'Who are yer?' bollocks. Yes, you can claim that the Carlisle fans started it and it was a reply to that but they're Carlisle, they're a small club coming to a big club and taking them to the wire, they get to do that. We rise above that. Do it to Chelsea, do it to the Mancs. Doing it to Carlisle? That's bullying. We're better than that. They're Carlisle, these are as big as their days get. We're Liverpool, we win European Cups. We used to win European cups. And leagues. Seems so long ago now. The Suarez season seems so long ago. The glory feels like ancient history.

Who are we now? Haven't a clue. Don't think anybody has. Maybe that's my point. Maybe the point is there isn't a point any more.

If there's anything to add to that, it's this: We progressed to the next round of the Capital One Cup (least attractive name ever) through the lottery of the penalty shoot-out. Three penalties converted to Carlisle's two. Coutinho and Lallana's efforts were weak, tired and saved. Adam Bogdan made up for his culpability in Carlisle's goal by saving three from their lads.

The whole keeping tally of who had scored, who had missed and what it meant illustrated beautifully by Bogdan's lack of immediate realisation that he had won the game for Liverpool after his final save on the fifth of the Cumbrian side's spot kicks.

Judgement is further out on the manager than ever before. The situation seems utterly irredeemable. Obviously, from your vantage point, you know how this all ended. From mine (3.50pm, Thursday, 24 September), I can't see an end.

Oh and an addenda — the guy who sits in front of me compares Ings to Roger Hunt. 'Never the greatest footballer in the world' he said, 'but he'll work for us.' Notably the only player to have his name sung with any conviction, this is how heroes are created, through hard work, determination, self-belief and honesty. Standing up to be counted is a wonderful thing.

Liverpool 3 Aston Villa 2

26 September 2015

IT'S WEIRD. It was all so vivid on Saturday afternoon. I'm two days on now, the result of an excellently busy Saturday and a wonderfully lazy Sunday where I refused to look at a computer screen, and summing up the match has become ridiculously difficult. I've started this three times (there you go, that's the 'pulling back the curtains on the Great and Mighty Oz' moment for you), and deleted the whole thing each time.

I think the problem is this: I finished the first draft of my latest play on Friday afternoon and I'm pretty much 'worded out'. Nothing's flowing. Add to that the simple fact that I basically never warm up until about five in the afternoon and it's currently twenty past four, and surely nobody can expect good work from me under these conditions?

An 'additional addition'. Last night was a Supermoon eclipse, probably the last of my lifetime, and I was pretty desperate to make certain that I saw it. Eclipse due at roughly 3am, alarm set on phone for about 2.15am, alarm sounded and duly turned off as I slept through the whole thing. Unlike my wife. The alarm worked on her. And she sat and looked at me as I snored. But I dreamt that I saw the eclipse and that's pretty much the same thing. I think.

On top of that, NASA have found proof of actual flowing water on Mars, which is pretty cool, very focused and makes my whingeing look slightly pathetic in comparison.

Shall we talk about the football, then?

We all know how the previous meeting with Villa played out: score first while playing badly, fail to threaten further, surrender meekly, Brendan panicking and making formation changes every thirty seconds, with the end result being that our only day out in London was for a semi-final and not the 'it's Stevie's birthday, let's win the FA Cup' party that we'd all been planning.

Villa had lost players all over the place since then: Delph to City, Benteke to us. Benteke was injured, though, a hamstring issue putting him out for 'the foreseeable future', which could mean a week, could mean forever. Still, Villa struggling, new players bedding in, on a bad run. Exactly what we needed.

Denials were flying everywhere. The club hadn't, definitely hadn't spoken to Carlo Ancelotti. Weren't saying they hadn't spoken to Klopp, though. Or DeBoer. Nobody was making statements that Brendan Rodgers was safe. Nobody was making statements about anything. Complaint was rife, 'fume' everywhere.

Everyone was being asked what they would accept from the Villa game. The idea that any victory would be satisfactory was put forth by some. Others – I'm one of those – were going with the line that we needed a victory *and* a performance. Nothing less would do. We needed a statement that we still had a Liverpool that we could believe in. Revenge for the semi-final wasn't an issue, we just wanted the here and now sorting out.

Villa is the sort of team that you expect a 'sorting out' to be possible against. Unless you look at statistics. At which point you realise that we tend to perform very, very badly against them at Anfield and have done for quite a while now.

So what did we get?

This: One-nil up after a minute thanks to James Milner.

One nil up after a minute is always a dodgy position. You never know whether it's a good thing or not, whether it's to be the precursor of a glorious rout of a quickly demoralised opposition, the prelude to ninety minutes of utter tedium as the gameplan heads out of the window and nobody is entirely sure whether they should stick or twist, or an invitation to a spirited fight back from the other eleven lads.

What we got was *all* of the above.

The first half showed as little invention as the rest of the season. A lot of play across the edge of the box with no real breaking down of a defence that had decided it would place ten men behind the ball at all times and not really try to get back into the game, but simply play around with defining the concept of damage limitation. The second half might have indicated to the lads from the Midlands that running at our back three and slinging crosses in might be a more beneficial strategy.

The dull first half gave way to an invigorated second, and here we might finally need to give some credit to the beleaguered manager. The 3-4-1-2 formation employed in the first forty-five minutes, with Coutinho passing the ammunition to Ings and Sturridge in a not overly successful manner, was tweaked to become a 3-1-4-2, with Lucas holding the midfield behind a more advanced line of four. Suddenly, there's movement and creativity. Suddenly, we look threatening.

Which is where we start to talk about the single most important difference in the game: Daniel Sturridge. Sturridge, let us never forget, was (and, at the time of writing, still is) Liverpool's most clinical striker. Ever. Best conversion rate of any striker that's ever worn the red shirt. Which is one hell of a stat. There have been a few decent names in there over the years. He puts us two-up with a sublime volley, stroking a dropping Milner pass with the outside of his left foot into the Kop net. The reaction is joy and relief, for both player and fans. The anticipated demolition is back on.

Until it's not. If we're going to enjoy the positives of the 2013/14 season, then there's the very real danger that we might also have to endure the insanity of its defending. This is where Villa might have come to rue their cautious approach to the game. We're unpicked far too easily, we allow Villa the ball, give them time to pass their way up the field, space to deliver a cross from their right and Rudy Gestede – who is, by quite some distance, the biggest man you've ever seen — appears to power the ball in. Comeback, apparently, on.

Except we score again within a minute. Not the kind of thing that you expect from us, not the kind of defiant mentality that we've shown a great deal of over the last year or so, 'You've scored? Fine, we'll score again.' It's Sturridge again, neat little triangles with Coutinho on the edge of the box and slotting home with that right foot that he supposedly doesn't have. It's the best few seconds of football, actual genuine football, that we've seen at Anfield in quite a while. The comeback is over, the rout is back on.

Until that's also not the case.

The second Villa goal is probably something that you don't deal with, there's no real apportioning of blame. The cross is from deep on the left and Gestede's header is of the 'textbook definition of towering' kind. There are twenty minutes left and anything could happen.

Nothing too drastic does. We hold out. It's not the most convincing win of all time, but the second half has displayed the fact that we can still produce entertaining, flowing, creative, attacking football when we have a focal point hitting form. Without Henderson, Benteke and Firmino, we still looked convincing. Going forward, the future might possibly look bright. At the back, though? Still all over the place. That Gestede was able to penetrate our defence so easily twice doesn't fill you with hope for their chances with the superior Romelu Lukaku at Goodison next week.

The mood afterwards is positive. None of us looking at the table, none of us worrying about points totals. A win is a win, three points, three goals, we're in the King Harry pub for a while and we're okay. Nothing can go wrong.

The day that had started with friends in The Sandon, in sunshine and hope, had ended with family and positivity about our team. The night was a thoroughly splendid show by the (kind of, sort of) reformed Icicle Works, two hours of excellence spent, accidentally, in the company of old friends that I rarely see. All is good in the world. Nothing can go wrong.

Brendan Holds Forth

27 September 2015

SO, WE'VE established that we were good. Established that, for forty-five minutes, we looked like a Liverpool team. That's won three, lost two, drawn two, eighth in the league, not something to crow over. It's the kind of situation where you keep your own counsel, speak with modesty, if at all.

Brendan, apparently, according to the media, according to Twitter, goes on the attack after the game. Talks about the hysteria around the job. Pronounces it as 'high-steria', which is odd. Insinuates that there is a plot to remove him from his job, seemingly makes reference to a shadowy cabal who want him gone.

Mentions the 'high-steria' again. Says there's obviously something behind that. Won't say who he means. Pundits? Ex-players? The majority of Liverpool fans? He's talking about the fact that we've lost as many games as United, fewer than Chelsea, City, Arsenal, in all competitions, that we're only five points off the top. Most notably, he talks about the fact that he's a manager who is able to manage big players. Given the tools, he'll do the job.

The media narrative loves it. This is the arrogant Rodgers pushing his own claims on the back of one win, ignoring the appalling form that we've shown to date and concentrating simply on the fact that we've managed a good half of football, concentrating on the fact that Daniel Sturridge is fit, keeping him that way has tended to be an issue, so let's hope that's changed, shall we?

Twitter predictably explodes. Even the reasonable half of Twitter explodes. Points out (correctly, in fairness) that the reason that so many of us wanted him sacked at the end of last season, and might still want him sacked at the moment, is nothing to do with those forty-five minutes and all to do with the simple truth that we're looking at a run of appalling form that started against United at Anfield last season and has continued with very little interruption until 4pm yesterday. We're thinking about this, Brendan isn't. Brendan's talking about the now and how others are struggling this season while ignoring the concept that those 'others' won things last season and are present in the elite European competition that we're missing out on.

Brendan has blinkers on and is thinking about nobody but Brendan. He's reverted to his inherent 'Brent-isms'. The ego has, very definitely, landed. He's talking about himself as a better manager than he was in 2013/14 despite it being obvious that the team that we've been watching for the last year isn't even on the same planet as that one.

We don't like this. Even after a win, we're all (not all, obviously, but that's the impression the world is given by the social media folk) screaming for Brendan's head. There is no other reading of this.

Except there is. Reading in the cold light of the next day, the quotes aren't that bad. It's possibly just a man defending himself having suffered intense pressure. I thought that I would be going into today writing about Brendan's arrogance and idiocy and tagging that to the end of the piece on the match itself. Then I read the report in the Liverpool Echo and I thought, 'yeah, so what?' I watched video footage from the press conference and had the same reaction. The 'rant' simply wasn't there. You can see him thinking before he very deliberately pops in a contentious point, but he's measured, calm, not particularly arrogant. There was nothing there that was shocking, the idea that he can manage well 'given the tools' could be construed as an attack on his employers not giving him those tools or could equally be a simple stating of the fact that last season we didn't have a striker who could do what Daniel Sturridge does.

The stating that he took the team from eighth to second? No matter how much that concentrates on the past, I think he's got a right to put that out there once in a while. If we're subjecting him to pressure, then we should expect him to reply at some point.

But.

It's a timing thing, isn't it? The timing is all of the problem here. This weekend wasn't the time to do that. This weekend was the time to say nothing, be bland, offer platitudes. Give out nothing that can be used as ammunition. The media love ammunition, Twitter loves ammunition, don't give them ammunition. You've won one game, played well for half of that game. There's a European tie to be negotiated with Sion on Thursday and then the small matter of the derby on Sunday lunchtime. And as we all know, the derby is a game where anything, absolutely anything, can happen. Rhyme and reason don't belong in derby games.

For me personally? Brilliantly, the first derby of the year, the one where the blue side of the city hopes they can get our manager sacked, *has* to fall on my Evertonian wife's birthday, doesn't it? Fate could have been a bit kinder to all sides there, thanks. Not particularly conducive to having a great day, that.

Sorry, digressing, won nothing yet, Brendan. That's one game. Everton to come. Get through that before saying anything. Get through the next before saying anything. And the next and the next and the next and so on. Keep your head down, keep your mouth closed, keep your opinions to yourself and see what happens at the end. *That's* when you make your statement. When it's done.

Liverpool 1 Sion 1

1 October 2015

AND THIS is why you don't open your mouth before your point has been made, and made silently, completely, beyond discussion, beyond argument, incontrovertible.

We're going round in circles at the moment, the only difference being the volume of the dissatisfaction at the end of that particular rotation. What was it? Two games ago? Three games ago? The game where the booing arrived at half-time, then full time, then halfway through extra time – Carlisle, must have been Carlisle, extra time being played after all – the only thing that prevented the boos arriving at the end, post-scraping through, was the fact that thousands had already departed. Doesn't feel like it was Carlisle, feels like it was one of the others. I could go back and check. I'm not checking, I've lost the will to check. I'm dispirited. Let's let this suffice? Liverpool have now been booed at home in three of the last four games. I'm not even sure that this happened under Hodgson. And last night's booing was the loudest by quite some distance despite the fact that thousands had gone before the final whistle, sure and firm in their belief that nothing was actually going to happen that would result in a Liverpool win. The guy who exited before me, older than me, white hair white beard, definitely Scouse, screaming 'F*** off Rodgers' at the top of his voice, seemed to sum up the mood quite well.

It wasn't supposed to be like this. A fourth-minute lead against a side who finished seventh in the Swiss Super League, whose own chairman described them as 'pathetic and awful' and has employed thirty managers, including himself twice, in twelve years should herald a canter. For thirteen minutes, it seemed that would be the case. And then Sion equalised and everything stopped. Again.

On paper, the side looked strong. Surprisingly so. The talk in the papers' match reports the next morning, *this* morning, is of 'fringe and youth players' but when those fringe players include Kolo Toure, Joe Allen and Adam Lallana, when the youth comprises Gomez, who started the season, Ibe, who impressed last season to the point that the anti-Sterling contingent (and I include myself in their number at that point) of the fanbase acclaimed his move to City as no loss as 'Ibe will be better than him anyway' and Divock Origi, who cost £10m, when the other berths are occupied by Mignolet, Clyne and Ings, who are all first choices, then the only 'weakened' choice is Jordan Rossiter, who deserves the chance anyway. Hard to argue against the idea that this side should be strong enough to deal with Sion.

It wasn't, though. Chances were squandered, finishing was wasteful. Statistics will show creativity in the opposition penalty box, will show shots on target, will show *things happening*. Things didn't really happen, though, not often enough, not with enough urgency, not with enough conviction. Circles. We're going round in circles and it seems never-ending. We're complaining about the same faults again and again and again and they don't seem to be something that anybody at the club either can, or will, rectify.

The manager came out afterwards, did the press conference spiel, talked about the fact that we should have won four-one, should have put Sion to bed early, mentioned the fact that Origi showed movement but 'at this level' needs to finish his chances. 'This level' in this case being against the side that finished seventh in the Swiss Super League last season. Not really a level that, to be honest, not a level which should be troubling Liverpool in the way that it did, in the way that so many sides 'at this level' continue to do. Brendan mentioned Origi's wastefulness in his chance-taking and highlighted the mistake that brought about Sion's equaliser. 'The mistake?' Pick any one of three, Clyne's bizarre pass to a yellow shirt, Ibe's positioning far higher than you would want your wing-back and Mignolet quite simply opening his legs to allow the Sion player to pass through them.

Three problems here:

Nathaniel Clyne. He's a right-back, he's not a wing-back. He *must* have been bought for a more orthodox back four. The lad that plays wing-back when we have three central defenders? His name's Lazar Markovic. We sent him out on loan.

Mignolet. His head's gone again. His upturn in form last season was attributed to a conversation he had with his girlfriend at Christmas, when she pointed out to him that he was overthinking his game. Between the nutmeg invitation and this bizarre habit that he's developed of punching balls which could have been more easily caught, he could probably do with speaking to his other half a bit more often.

Jordon Ibe. God knows what's happened to this lad. It looks as though somebody has taken the decision to coach all the adventure, fun and joy out of his game. The idea that he's an explosive winger with pace and power who can take on a defender seems to have entered the realm of myth. He's become cautious, timid, unconvinced. His confidence is non-existent. And the worse that he gets, the worse the crowd react to him. And the worse he gets. And so it goes.

More problems, then?

Us. The fans, we're a problem. We're edgy, nervous, as unconvinced as any of the players. We're simply waiting for the next disaster. We don't believe in anybody or anything and we're turning on each other. This morning's Twitter fume is an ongoing narrative of locals blaming tourists for the lack of atmosphere at the ground, the result of the club chasing 'glory hunters' who will shell out on kits and souvenirs. I can't see it. There were people close to me who aren't usually there. They were singing. They might have been tourists, they might have been more 'up' for the occasion than the locals were, they might have been making their only trip to Anfield, they might have been fulfilling a lifelong dream, determined to enjoy it no matter the quality of football on show. Obviously they stopped when they realised how grim it all was, but until that point they were possibly less jaded than those of us with the letter 'L' in our postcode, less likely to loudly criticise any mistakes made by the players, less likely to fill the rafters with disappointed groans.

And there are those who argue that we need to be behind the players, need to provoke them into action, act as the fabled 'twelfth man' in order to gain a response. They're opposed by those who counter with the idea that 'surely earning a living through playing football is enough motivation for anybody?' Stick me in that last bracket. The result is that we're arguing with each other: endlessly and publicly. Unity seems a long way off, a memory, a fictional concept.

The big one, though? As ever, the manager. Obviously. His public criticism of Origi's finishing, undoubtedly in response to a question, might be accurate but doesn't address the real issue that everybody else in the ground can see: everything is too slow, too cautious, our approach too mannered, too obvious. We simply don't move up the pitch with enough urgency, we don't combine our midfield with our forwards, we don't combine our forwards well enough, we are a set of individuals, a long way from a team at the moment.

Our manager's response to this? We're rebuilding, he relishes the challenge. He's in his fourth year and he's rebuilding the team for the third time, which indicates that last year's rebuilding didn't work. We're aware of that fact already, it's what's worrying us, making us nervous about the idea of this year's rebuilding. It's tied to the fact that we're already seeing unexpected change, nervousness, a lack of conviction. The idea that we're rebuilding again isn't washing, the idea that we're always going to be 'in transition' is becoming more terrifyingly real by the second. It's becoming increasingly difficult to see how Brendan Rodgers is the man to turn the situation around, improve things, pull a rabbit out of a hat and suddenly give us *our* Liverpool back again. There's a long way to go but I (and this is obviously all about the 'I') can't see how he can last, can't see how he is the man for the job.

And on Sunday we have to travel, with our fragile egos and shattered confidence, across the park to a buoyant Everton in a hostile Goodison.

The blues must be bloody terrified.

Everton 1 Liverpool 1

4 October 2015
(and everything that came after)

WELL, AT least nobody ruined my wife's birthday.

The game itself was as perfect an illustration of Liverpool's season as you could wish for. For half an hour, we looked magnificent, far and away the better team, taking the game to an Everton side that might have been missing three of their first-choice back four but were still far from weak. Coleman, Stones and Baines missing, but Galloway, Browning and Funes-Mori more than capable in their place. In comparison, we were missing Henderson, Benteke and Firmino, and the energy and threat that they would carry, even if Firmino has shown little of it to date. Let's call that balance, shall we?

We played *all* the football, we looked superior. We didn't actually threaten, though. Same old same old. Everton looked limited in comparison but threatened. Mignolet did that thing where he'll punch a ball that could and should be caught but then pull off a world-class save seconds later. By the thirtieth minute, we were in fairly complete dominance but could have been behind. That was the point when Everton chose to finally start to push us. When a team starts to exert some pressure of their own, the best thing that you can do is score. So, for a change, we did. From, of all things, a corner. We don't score from corners, it doesn't happen. Today, we did. Danny Ings' hand placed lightly in the small of Ross Barkley's back, not a push so much as light guidance. Ings stands alone in space, the ball drops, he connects. It's genuinely that easy. Tim Howard needs questioning, Everton's otherwise solid defence need questioning. We're ahead, all we need to do is protect this lead.

Which we do. For nearly three minutes. Yet again a simple ball into the area causes absolute, undiluted panic in our back three/five/however many shirts we have hanging around at the time. The ball drops, Can clears it, as far as Skrtel. It's harder to hit the lad than to miss him, there's an entire side of the park to put the ball in but, instead, Can puts it on a plate for Lukaku to equalise. And, yet again, our heads go. It's that easy. If you're an opposition team then you simply wait for Liverpool to commit a mistake and then capitalise.

The second half is all the other football that we've played this season. It's all the moments where we haven't pressed, haven't dominated, haven't created, haven't looked like scoring. Everton are, and it pains me to write this sentence, the better team.

We emerge from Goodison, from a fairly entertaining game of football, if you're a neutral, which I'm bloody not, with a draw. If you were offered a draw before the game (and nobody actually ever offers you results before a game, that would be weird, but if they did), then you'd take it. This one's odd, though. You're left feeling absolutely gutted about only getting a draw that you probably didn't deserve anyway.

This is Liverpool as of 4pm on Sunday 4 October, dispiriting. We're no fun to watch, there are no expectations of success, no light at the end of any hypothetical, illusory tunnel. The idea of change seems a long way off.

The rest of the afternoon went like this:

I left the house the second that the final whistle blew, all pre-arranged, drop off J and youngest son at Goodison at lunchtime, head home to watch the game on telly with standard rules applying: 'If you're three up with five minutes to go then I'll leave early. Anything else and I'm watching the game till the last second', pick them up, sit in post-match Queen's Drive traffic by The Mons, try not to discuss the game.

We'd done the sensible thing, we'd 'had' J's birthday on the Saturday, been shopping, had lunch (excellent tapas place in town, thanks), had a good day, all just in case the game had gone drastically either way. A large win for either side would slightly cloud one of our days, a contentious win would basically wreck it. We both feel strongly about our own teams. Results affect us in the way that they affect everybody else. The fact that there's somebody else in the house who has just watched their team win when yours has lost isn't great. When yours has lost to that actual team, everything's magnified. An irrefutable, inarguable win with absolute conviction is the easiest thing to take. Nobody can dispute the fact that the other team deserved the victory if they have clearly run rampant. An incident-filled match where the team with less chances, less possession somehow flukes a narrow win totally against the run of play with a lucky deflection or a hotly-debated penalty? Horrible, although, obviously, highly amusing if it's *your* team that's benefitted from that.

The 4 October draw suited neither party. J and Matt thought we were there for the taking in the second half. I was basically moaning about how bloody depressing watching Liverpool was at the moment. Liverpool were now seemingly more than capable of bringing my wife's birthday down by not actually winning. This was a new one.

The sight of Arsenal dismantling United in the first twenty minutes of the day's second televised game was amusing but didn't lift me. It had absolutely nothing to do with us any more.

And then it happened.

Brendan Rodgers

4 October 2015
End of a brief era

LET'S BE honest here, shall we? Going into this whole book thing, there was always a chance that I'd be documenting this happening. The end of last season, coupled with the fixture list that the Premier League computers had thrown up (yeah right, they're dead random those computers, aren't they? That's how you get Everton vs Liverpool and Arsenal vs United in the same weekend, coincidence and kismet), indicated that a poor start could see Rodgers in trouble. Obviously, we were getting to the point where many of us wanted it, saw it as necessary, knew who we wanted in his place. Rumours were circulating, the papers were talking about who Liverpool were talking to and the club *hadn't* moved to quash the idea that they'd spoken to Jurgen Klopp. Nobody knew what this meant, significance was being read into everything and, as ever, Twitter was arguing with itself over what was to happen. All this *before* Liverpool sacked their manager.

Let's rewind a little. Southampton dismantle Chelsea at Stamford Bridge on Saturday evening in the way that nobody ever does. They put three goals past Abramovich's lads. You've seen the post-match interview, it's a thing of beauty. One question, one answer. One *seven-minute-long* answer. There's a moment at the beginning where you think Mourinho is finally going to hold his hands up and take some blame. He says that the time has come for him to be honest, he breathes in for a second and you think 'he's going to admit they were poor, he's going to admit that he made a mistake, chose the wrong team, set them up badly, prepared badly' and he breathes out and blames the referee. And the media and the rest of the world and everybody else that's ever watched a game of football and the guys who employ him, everybody that isn't Jose Mourinho. He talks about being sacked and says that 'if they want to sack me then they'll have to sack me because I don't walk away' and the subtext is clear. I turned to J and said: 'He's been told he's getting sacked'. It's all over his face, conversations have been had, threats have been made, this man's goading his boss into sacking him *very* publicly. It's brilliant, astonishing, reckless, insane and compelling in equal measure. It's good enough to stop us turning over to Strictly Come Dancing. I turn to Twitter. 'We'd better sort Klopp out now,' I tweet, 'before *Chelsea* do.'

That was Saturday, let's hit Sunday again, shall we? The Arsenal/United game has ended as a three-nil Arsenal saunter and I'm still not amused. And then the yellow band pops up. The 'Breaking News' band. And the Sky presenter stops talking to Souness and Carragher and Henry about the 'top-of-the table clash' they've just witnessed, because they have 'BIG NEWS' (their capitalisation) 'JUST BREAKING'. Two things, it can only be one of two things. Advocaat left Sunderland at lunchtime and everyone knew that was coming and it's only Sunderland so it doesn't really matter. This could only be Mourinho or…

'Brendan Rodgers has left Liverpool'.

Relief. That's the first reaction, relief. The owners have acted. We didn't think they would, we didn't think they had the kind of ambition that provokes that kind of reaction, but it seems that they have.

There had been debate in the previous week: if we were to lose to Everton then there was every possibility that Brendan would lose his job and there were plenty of us who wanted that to happen. The fact that he would be losing his job over a defeat to the club on the other side of Stanley Park, though?

The fact that there would be Blues gloating throughout the international break, throughout the two weeks of an enforced lack of actual football, was bad enough, the reality that they would gloat about having cost one of our managers his job *forever* was much more hideous. Would the forcing of the necessary change be consolation enough for the years of abuse?

Yeah, go'ed. We'll have that.

It doesn't matter now. We all know that it wasn't the result that cost him his job. The timing was more to do with the natural break point in the season. There had been speculation for a few weeks that the international break would be a crucial moment in Rodgers' tenure and that speculation seemed to have been very informed. Two weeks gives you a chance to recruit without appearing to have already put a plan in place, gives your new, not hastily appointed, manager time to prepare for the next/his first game. Brendan Rodgers didn't lose his job due to the derby draw, he lost it on the back of Carlisle, West Ham, Sion, every performance dating back to the moment that Manchester United signalled the end of last season at Anfield. He lost it on the fact that he had lost his way. The owners clearly looked at it through the eyes of the fans and saw no prospect of improvement.

All of which obviously begs questions about their summer support. If you think that you're going to remove the manager from his position, if you are even vaguely considering that he might not reach the second week of October, why back him? Surely the immediate aftermath of the Stoke six-one is your moment to act?

We'll never know, will we? There's a book to be written here, an expose from Brendan's side that would explain everything that he went through over the year-and-a-bit since we didn't quite win the league, of how he didn't have the power to get the players he wanted, how he was saddled with players that he neither wanted nor rated, with Mario Balotelli basically at the front of that list. Hopefully, he'll never write it. It'd be a great read but he's left us with dignity. His statement was broken but dignified and it said everything that needs saying. He'll work again, so he might as well keep a reserved silence over the whole thing. The seven million quid that he's supposedly getting to pay off his contract will probably help on that one.

And that adds to the question, doesn't it? FSG are paying Brendan to go after shelling out for what were supposedly the signings that he, not the much-spoken-of transfer committee, wanted this summer. This either smacks of utter indecision or absolute ruthlessness in adjusting a long-term business strategy. I'm going with the latter. I'm going with the idea that Brendan, very legitimately, convinced his employers that last season was the result of him not having the control he needed to build on the work that he had already carried out. I'm not a subscriber to the theory that 2013/14 was purely the result of having a genius in our midst, more that it was guided by a manager who was able to combine maverick talents to an incredible end. Brendan Rodgers needs to take the credit for bringing us closer to the title than any other Liverpool manager in the past twenty-five years. He gave us a hell of a season, facilitated some of the finest football that we've ever witnessed and he should go with our thanks.

But the key is that he *should* go. If the owners had been persuaded by the argument that he had simply not had the tools to work with the previous year, then they had acted swiftly during the transfer window to ensure that he would have exactly the tools he requested for this season. That he was still using those tools in the wrong way could only be attributed to his own abilities. All the bad habits that were witnessed last year were still present: changes of formation, indecision as to who constituted his most effective defence, square pegs in round holes – Ings and Firmino as wingers against all common sense — a lack of organisation, motivation and urgency, all still there, all still his.

There's a further argument here, the idea that the players who were least impressive in a Liverpool shirt (Allen, Lovren, Lallana – though I personally rate the lad – Borini etc) were those that were chosen by Brendan and the players whose abilities the fans have most belief in (Sturridge, Coutinho, Sakho, Firmino *et al)* were purchased by the maligned transfer committee. The theory, which seems to carry the weight of credence from journalists who are actually 'in the know', is that Brendan has handled talented players badly because they weren't his choice whilst also buying very badly. We're all holding this to be true now, another symptom of the general issues behind the fall from 2013/14.

The Everton result wasn't the cause, it wasn't even the top hat, the full stop on the cause, it was just the game before it would happen. All informed opinion seems to indicate that the decision was made before the game, the information relayed immediately afterwards, the manager unaware, the intention being not to disturb preparation for the match itself.

If nothing else, it was worth sitting through that whole day just to see Thierry Henry's shocked grasp at Jamie Carragher's thigh live on Sky as the news broke. And on Twitter every twenty seconds for the next few days.

So Brendan was gone and the 'search' was on for the new manager, a man the board intended to identify and appoint with appropriate speed. By the time Brendan left his house the next morning for a Malaga-bound plane, we'd already forgotten him. We already knew who we wanted and we were pretty damn sure that we were getting him. And soon.

Things That Rhyme With Klopp

9 October 2015

THE WEEK kind of went like this:

The rumour mill swaps between the names Klopp and Ancelotti all night and into Monday morning. The majority of fans seem as though they would be happy if we could attract either, both being huge names with huge CVs, but are definitely leaning towards one man.

Carlo Ancelotti would bring experience and surety, he'd be a safe hand on the tiller, but that's not what we want. We've had a safe hand on the tiller before or at least we've had a hand on the tiller that was *supposed* to be safe. His name was Roy Hodgson and he was bloody awful. Brendan has moved on after eight games, with us six points behind the leaders in the midst of a run of our toughest games. Hodgson went in January with Liverpool mired in a relegation battle playing the worst football that we had ever seen. Brendan leaves behind Benteke and Sturridge and Coutinho and Firmino as his legacy, Hodgson left Poulsen, Konchesky and Cole. We don't need a safe hand to settle things down, we want somebody to push forward, to get us playing football again, to get us enjoying ourselves, to get *the players* enjoying themselves. We don't want safe, we want mad. We like mad. Jurgen Klopp looks like he's our kind of mad.

Klopp has seemed a Liverpool manager in waiting for a long time now, packed with charisma, getting his teams to play with passion, building a bond with his fans, creating a dynasty, building something. We *knew*. Knew that he understood

Dortmund as a city, as a people, so he'd understand Liverpool and the peculiar demands – and God, they're demands – of the fan base. Knew that when he touched the sign in that pre-season game, he knew what he was doing, knew he was sending out a message, knew as he stood and watched the Kop that one day he was coming to us. We wanted Klopp, simple as that.

By Monday night, the media were convinced that it was Klopp. By Tuesday morning, they were reporting talks being 'positive and ongoing'. By Wednesday, it was a done deal, with the announcement due on Thursday and an unveiling on Friday. By Thursday, he was telling Sky that 'from tomorrow I will be Liverpool 24/7' via his intercom and then on a plane that was being tracked in a 'Santa's Sleigh' manner by so many, then at an airport and a hotel and then announced, pictured, signing.

This was FSG 'walking the walk' in a very big way. In the way that we'd conducted the summer's transfer business with little fanfare or comment, just going out and getting the players that the manager wanted, we now conducted our negotiations for our new manager. We said nothing, we got our man.

The man that any major club with genuine ambitions would have on their list: Chelsea, Arsenal, United, Barca, Real, Bayern; his accomplishments with Borussia Dortmund are genuinely of that level. The most coveted man in world football. And he came to Liverpool. I don't know how many of us thought that we were still in a position where we could attract a manger with pedigree, a manager with a very current, very impressive CV. The last time we managed this was the day that we unveiled Rafael Benitez. A man that wins things. Replacing him with Roy Hodgson was a comic epilogue on a par with the Hicks/Gillett era, replacing Hodgson with Dalglish was inspired and romantic but not long term, no matter how many of us feel that he deserved longer. Most of us were of the opinion that we could only attract, that the owners would only ever look at, up-and-coming coaches, 'yes' men, pliable, inexperienced coaches who would be moulded into the shape that FSG planned for.

Instead, we were presented with the signing of a genuinely world-class manager. And we fell in love.

Opposition fans ridiculed our instant adoration, headline writers looked for every way that they could possibly substitute the word 'Klopp' for the word 'Kop', both positive and negative but all equally cliched. Suggestions were put forward that we were deluding ourselves, heading for another fall, readying ourselves for another 'slip' (witty that one), but does anybody really believe that we were listening to any of that?

All we wanted now was to see him unveiled. All we wanted was to hear him speak.

The press conference. 10am Friday morning. Jeans, jacket, open-necked shirt. Beaming, grinning, apologising for his faultless English. Scolding photographers for the noise they made as a journalist asked her question. Telling the journalists that he had heard so many bad things about the English media and that it was up to them to prove him wrong. Praising the level of the squad that he had inherited while noting that they looked as though they were playing with no enjoyment. Stating that he had watched our last three games, thereby giving an idea of when conversations started, pointing out that by Saturday night he would have watched every game played so far this season. Giving the TV lads the quote that they wanted. Pressed on Mourinho's 'Special One' nonsense, he said that he was normal 'There you go, you can have that if you like, "the normal one,"' letting them know as he said it that he knew it was all a game, that the term was ridiculous and would only be used by the ridiculous themselves. Obviously everybody used it and saw nothing but the words, the surface, missed the meaning, missed the subtext, including the club, which printed up frankly absurd shirts carrying that phrase within hours.

Every sentence engaged, every grin enchanted, every comment drew you in, every word *convinced*. And that's the difference. There were those who *never* took to Brendan Rodgers, not even in the 2013/14 season. To many, he seemed too middle management, seemed to be a collection of coaching platitudes, underlined, highlighted in training manuals. When he was at his peak, we were still slightly divided over whether he was any good or not. When he was failing, we were as torn a support as you could imagine. You don't need to imagine it, you lived it and it sits in the preceding pages.

All that bitter atmosphere has gone. One man has united the entire fanbase, given us a belief, a hope, that we thought unlikely to come back. We feel like *Liverpool* again. We have a *Liverpool* manager again. Everything is wide open. Jurgen has told us that the players need to go from doubters to believers. They'll start that path in training, either on Monday or when they return from the latest set of pointless international qualifiers, but we started it at 11am on 9 October, eight days until Spurs and nearly a fortnight before we'll see Klopp at Anfield against the 'might' of Rubin Kazan.

From the post-derby moments, where I was grateful for the fortnight's respite, to the point where, once again, I can't wait for the next game. And the next. And the next. We're going to win the league.

Spurs 0 Liverpool 0

(and everything that comes before)
17 October 2015

A WEEK is a long time. When all you've got to see you through is the hope that your players will return unscathed from whatever pointless, unnecessary, unwanted at the best of times friendly they've racked up the air miles for this time, it's bloody endless. We've got to the point where we've heard everything that we can hear about the new boss. We were experts before he hit English airspace. We'd read everything, You-Tubed everything, were fluent in the concept of *gegenpressing*. We wanted to see action.

Clearly, so did Jurgen. His pre-Spurs press conference indicated as much. In the space between the two pressers, he'd been seen all over the place. If he went to a bar, he was photographed, if he went to a restaurant, he was photographed. House hunting? Having a crafty fag on his hotel balcony? Cameras clicking from afar. He had to point out at the conference that he'd quite like to do his job if that was okay? Without his space being invaded by selfie demands. He'd been to a restaurant with his assistants and all their respective partners. There for five minutes, asked for a photo, had to decline, had to ask if the photos could be done at some other point as the whole world seemed to think that he was out all the time. Pointed out to the still massed ranks of the press pack that he had met a guy for thirty seconds while looking for somewhere to live (as you do) and the next morning it's all over the news. The message was clear: he wanted to crack on with his job. There was less laughter, less throwing out quotes, more determination.

And the players that he had at his disposal? One less at that point, actually two but we didn't know that yet. Joe Gomez suffers an innocuous challenge in an England under-21 game, innocuous enough to damage his anterior cruciate ligament (ACL) and put him out of action for the rest of the season. Not the last time that we'd hear reference to an ACL that day.

Danny Ings. The Danny Ings who had been one of the few bright points in the early part of the season. ACL. An innocuous challenge in training. How come they're always the result of innocuous challenges? How does innocuous manage to cause so much sodding damage? He tried to walk it off, which is pretty cool. It's like Carra trying to walk off a broken leg at Blackburn. Ings, out for the season.

Still, answered one question. We knew, absolutely *knew* (and were wrong in that knowledge) that Jurgen was going to play 4-2-3-1. The identity of that 'one' was clear now: it would obviously be Daniel Sturridge.

Saturday morning hits and word breaks early. Sturridge is injured. Again. Nothing serious, an 'impact' with Jordon Ibe, some swelling, something that they don't want to risk straight away. It's sensible but it's disappointing. It's just another thing and it adds to the list which goes Sturridge, Ings, Firmino, Benteke, Henderson, Lovren and is added to by Jordan Rossiter returning from England duty with a hamstring problem and Jon Flanagan still, *still*, a long-term issue. Options aren't limited, they're non-existent.

All of this is put into perspective at around 11am. We're sitting in a cafe in our local Marks & Spencer's when the news breaks. 'We' being me, J, our youngest son, mother-in-law, auntie, sister-in-law and a couple of cousins. I get the news. I'm not being ignorant, I just happen to be checking Twitter. I draw breath and I turn to J.

"Howard Kendall's passed away."

'Passed away'. I can't say 'died'. I have enough trouble typing it. It's not even a year since we lost my dad. I can't say the word yet. The fact that this is a figure from our fathers' generation hits both of us. We can't avoid the fact that he was young and vital and notable at the same time that our fathers were young men going to the game, mine to Anfield, J's to Goodison. Kendall was one of 'the Holy Trinity' alongside Alan Ball and Colin Harvey, a midfield that those of our generation didn't see but have been told so much about. We know him as a manager, we know him as Everton's greatest manager, we know him as a man who won things. I didn't even realise until this week that he was the last English manager to win a European trophy.

We saw him one day a couple of years ago. Walked into a cafe bar in Formby Village and he was sat having a quiet drink. My first thought was 'I should buy him a pint, he was brilliant.' It didn't matter that he was the very successful manager of our biggest opponent, he was part of the 'Merseyside, Merseyside' final and he put out teams that played good football. We left him alone, didn't interfere with his day. Everything you hear about him says that he wouldn't have been bothered by the interruption of strangers, but we didn't feel right so we moved on. There have been many days where I'd wished I'd bought him that pint. J is just glad that she saw him once, close up and in real life. We were both devastated. J was, very understandably, the more shocked but I was genuinely taken aback by just how saddened I was.

All of which makes the transition into talking about a game of football all the more difficult, but let's go with the idea that the best way to pay tribute to a footballing man is to talk about football and crack on from there, shall we?

The gaggle of photographers that surrounded Klopp before kick-off is hopefully the last that we, and he, will see of such over-zealous media attention. Hopefully, from here, it will all be about the football and nothing else. Clearly, that's exactly what Jurgen wants. So, post-international-nonsense, post-injury, post-Rodgers, let's kick off the new era, shall we?

Obviously he's had no time to spend with the majority of his new squad and has a sizeable portion of that squad unavailable. He's dealing with what he's got, the team is picking itself, the idea of Divock Origi being our only fit striker is terrifying, but that's where we are. We deal with it.

The formation is unexpected. It's a 4-3-2-1 with Milner and Can accompanying Lucas in the middle, Coutinho and Lallana playing in pockets behind Origi but with a twist: Origi has license to drop into a false nine role to allow the others beyond him. It's a tactic that almost works at times. Jurgen (and I'm really enjoying typing his name, there's a joy in putting it on the screen, still a disbelief that he's ours) has said before the game that we won't play in the way that Spurs expect us to and we don't. The shape isn't what they anticipate, the pressing might be – God knows, it's been spoken of often enough – but the ferocity seems to take them by surprise. Liverpool are hunting in packs and at pace, closing down, intercepting, tackling. Speed is everything. For twenty-five minutes, it's absolutely glorious and then the fact that the manager has only had three days to teach them this stuff sinks in. They get it. Their heads get it but their legs don't seem to be up to it just yet. The pressing feels like the 2013/14 season but faster, stronger. It takes more out of them, and earlier. Jurgen's legendary double-session approach to training is going to come into force soon. It's going to have to in order to allow the team to play in the manner he expects. Half an hour in and the sobering revelation hits you that 'these lads just aren't as fit as we thought'.

That first half hour, though? It's all pace and forward think-ing. It's moving the ball up the pitch quickly, which we're really not used to seeing. It's not passing the ball to the keeper every ten seconds to invite pressure and allow opponents to regroup. It is, crucially, one-touch passing, such a gorgeous concept. The ball zips. We'd forgotten zip. It's ages since we saw a bit of zip. Love a bit of zip, love watching the ball actually move.

Origi has the best chance of the half, our best chance of the game. He heads against the bar, the ball drops and he tries to chest it. There's an argument, a bloody good argument, that he should just stick his head in where it hurts and think about the consequences once the ball's in the net. He doesn't, though, and that's kind of it for attacking threat. From here on, it's all about defence. It's about the fact that Martin Skrtel is repeatedly turned far too easily, that the space between him and Clyne is exploited and it's about Mamadou Sakho proving yet again that he's far and away the best central defender at the club and, despite opposing fans' claims that he's clumsy, awkward and unreliable, one of the best in the league. It's about Simon Mignolet making three outstanding saves. It's also about the hitherto unforeseen spectacle of Adam Lallana running himself into the ground for the cause. Best game in a red shirt by a country mile.

By the end, we're the only team to run further in a single match than Spurs this season. And no, running around doesn't win you matches and, yes, Brendan went to Spurs in the last two seasons and won 3-0 and 5-0. This season, we've managed a 0-0 draw without really threatening to score, but we're pleased with the fact. It's the manner of the draw, where we've come from to get that draw against a Spurs side who are now looking solid under Mauricio Pochettino, who work hard, score goals, finished above us last season and who ripped apart Manchester City three weeks ago. We've gone to White Hart Lane, worked and showed signs of what our new manager wants from a team. With half that team missing.

No matter what the result of the last few meetings, it wasn't *that* history we'd have been taking into this game under Brendan Rodgers. We would have been taking the history and the mindset of the first portion of this season. That history, that mindset, wouldn't have been good enough. You can't escape the idea that we might have drawn Jurgen Klopp's first game in charge, but under Brendan Rodgers, under *this season's* Brendan Rodgers, we'd have lost.

Klopp will have more time on the fields of Melwood to get his ideas across, he'll have players coming back, he'll have options. This is a start.

Liverpool 1 Rubin Kazan 1

22 October 2015

EVENTUALLY, THE circus will subside. The wall of cameras are here again tonight at Anfield. We've had the first game, tonight's the first home game, European rather than domestic, and Sunday will give us the first home league game. Hopefully, after that one, the media lads will get bored and wander off realising that taking shots of a guy who's looking straight ahead isn't actually that interesting.

There's no ceremony tonight, no unveiling, no fuss other than that presented by the camera crews. There's just a team walking out, their manager taking his place in the dugout and waiting for kick-off with what appears to be, from the vantage point of the main stand, an intent stare on his face. There's a playlist from George Sephton, the wonderfully ever-present *Voice of Anfield*, which pulls together every possible German-themed disc that the Anfield vaults hold, tied together with the metal that our manager seemingly loves. Having a bit of trouble with him liking metal, to be honest with you. Can't stand the stuff myself. I'm taking the report that says his favourite song is *Halleluwah* by Can and holding on to that for comfort. *That's* a cool manager. Still, George gives us a spin of Bowie's *Helden,* so it's worth it all for that moment.

The game? You probably want to know about the game, don't you?

The game's okay. The speed that we saw in the first twenty-five minutes at Spurs isn't really there. It's all a bit slower. It's positive, though, the movement is still forward, the intent is still fine. The fact that Kazan score first is obviously a long way from ideal. They're kind of raining on our parade here. Don't they realise we're supposed to be having a party? Can scoring our equaliser seems apt: German manager's reign starts with goal from German player. We're still playing a 4-3-2-1 and the midfield lads still look pretty solid. There's a mistake or two for Kazan's goal that you'd want ironing out quickly, Can charging into space and allowing a lad to slip past him, Clyne sitting on the wrong side of his attacker as the ball drops and completely failing to defend the inevitable goal, but there's promise elsewhere. The cutting edge isn't really there. Origi moves around fairly well but doesn't make things happen. We look sharper when Benteke makes his return from injury on the hour mark, but still not sharp enough to break through the now massed ten-man ranks of Rubin. With their captain yellow-carded for the second time before the half-hour mark, they close up shop and do that whole 'sometimes it's harder to play against ten men' thing. It's frustrating but not terrible. You can see positive signs.

I leave the ground relatively okay with the whole evening. Thirty yards outside Anfield and I recover some kind of phone signal, the ground itself being a horrible big black hole for telecommunications. I hit Twitter and realise that I'm in a minority here. The world hates tonight.

One upshot of this? I hadn't written anything new for *The Anfield Wrap* since the Klopp unveiling. I'd needed an angle, needed an 'in' that nobody else had used so far. Now I had one. Here's what I wrote:

We Want The World And
We Want It Now

Part One

WANT TO know what I don't get?

Okay, first, preamble as per always. I haven't written anything for a few weeks. Here, that is. Tons of other stuff but nothing football-y, nothing here. Nothing since Jurgen got the job. Two reasons for that:

One) All the other stuff. Takes time, you know. All that staring at a blank screen trying to come up with some kind of clever? Time consuming.

Two) All the Jurgen stuff. I mean, seriously? Have you read it? All of it? It's incredible. There's been some amazing stuff written prior to his arrival on what this could mean in terms of the pulling power of the club, and post his arrival on what he can actually do with those lads on the pitch. Tons of stuff, brilliantly written. On here, that is. I'm sure there were other people writing stuff, but here's the stuff that matters. Genuinely nothing that I could add, everybody had it nailed down perfectly. And they all felt the same way that I did or I felt the same way they did. Basically we all, all of us, – total unanimity amongst the fanbase on this one – had fallen in love with Jurgen Klopp.

I love his attitude to just about everything, love the laugh that he throws out there when something genuinely amuses him. I love the fact that I was slightly shocked when he moved from speaking pretty damn fluent English into answering a question in German.

The German shouldn't really have surprised me, what with it being his actual language, but it did.

I love the fact that the madness of the first press conference gave way to absolute common sense very quickly. I love every single appearance that he's made, hang on his every word. I'm willing to watch him sit and listen in the post-Rubin Kazan presser as somebody translates his answers into Russian. I might be obsessed but we all are, that's why I had nothing new to add. We all know all this stuff.

I'm happy with the Spurs game. 0-0 away after what they did to City when he's only had three days with the team and suddenly we're pressing higher and faster and with more energy. We look goosed after twenty-five minutes, look like we desperately need these double sessions at Melwood to get as fit as he wants us, but can see that it will come. I'm happy with the Spurs game.

And this is where we come to the crux of things, the 'want to know what I don't get?' bit. I'm happy with the Rubin Kazan game. Genuinely happy. No problem with it at all. Only managed a draw against a ten-man team who are sitting twelfth in their league? Yeah, fair enough, that ten-man thing can be more issue than assist most of the time, we know that. A million shots but very few on target? Fair enough. Not ideal, obviously, but I'll take it at the moment. Would I have taken it under Brendan? No, but Brendan wasn't in the middle of changing things after a week's worth of training. Not changing things in the right way anyway. Tons of changing but nothing changed, if you get my drift.

I sat in the main stand last Thursday night and I saw lots of good things. I saw an organised defence that stood its ground pretty damn well. I saw Mamadou Sakho carve his name into legend letter by letter with every take, with every pass. I saw Skrtel do good things. I saw Moreno and Clyne pick up the ball and run. I saw Emre Can basically be Emre Can all over the place.

Milner, I'm not sure about. He's going to work hard, he's going to redefine workhorse, but I'm not entirely sure what he does. Not sure what he gives to the team. Certainly not corners. Think he needs to be looking at Jordan Henderson. I know there's loads that disagree on this one, but not as many as disagree on the next one.

Joe Allen was good against Kazan. He genuinely bloody was. Worked well as the pivot, burst through men on a couple of occasions, won aerial duels. Joe Allen won aerial duels?. *You see that coming? Me neither. Joe Allen was good in the first half. Lucas was better in the second, like, but still, doesn't alter the whole 'Joe Allen Was Good' argument. Lallana was excellent. Again. He's basically being Adam Lallana but at speed with some bollocks and he's turning into a proper little nark as well. I like that.*

Coutinho's struggling but that's okay, Bobby Firmino's being reintroduced and he showed well in his European twenty minutes. Wanted the ball, popped it round, talked to midfielders, favourite moment was the one where he clearly told Milner 'give it to me and I'll give it to him' while pointing at Can and then did it perfectly, all in less time than it takes to describe. And that turn? That turn? Jesus. The lad's got something. It'll happen.

Origi toiled, worked hard, threw some nice turns in. If we can find him a killer instinct then we're laughing, but that's okay, Christian Benteke's being reintroduced and, no, it didn't quite happen for him against the Russian lads but there's that movement for the chest-down about thirty seconds after he comes on, there's the space he makes on the left to pop that shot in that hits the post. On another night...

And Big Si makes another cracking save.

And yeah, there were too many hopeful crosses low into the box and high into the box, but next week there'll be a lad there who meets those things and he'll have been back from six weeks out for more than ten minutes.

So, pretty much okay about the whole thing really. The result might have felt like a Rodgers result, but the performance felt far from it. The performance kept going all the way to the end.

And then I turned Twitter on and realised that we were actually shite. Clearly deluded in my belief that I'd watched a pretty okay game of football, where all that was needed was a cutting edge that would come with time with the new boss, it appeared that what I'd actually witnessed was evidence that the malaise was far deeper than we had thought. It was evidence that this was a very poor squad and that Jurgen was in for a much rougher time than any of us had thought, that the rebuilding job was immense. I'd like to apologise to all of Twitter now for quite enjoying the game, if not the result, which I was merely okay with. I'd also like to thank them for putting me right and for their sterling efforts in tempering everybody's optimism. Equally, I'd like to thank all those in the ground who started screaming at Coutinho the second that he misplaced his first pass to Emre Can. It's a good job that those guys are there to point out that the ball was shit as he wouldn't have realised otherwise. He might have laboured under the misapprehension that he and Emre have only played in that combination a couple of times and possibly don't know each other's preferred runs as yet. He might have thought 'Next game, I'll know that he wants it three yards that way and then we're laughing'. Possibly in Portuguese, that last bit but that might have been where his mind is. Thank God people were willing to put him right and let him know that he'd fucked up. That'll help the lad sort it out.

You'd hope that we'd develop a bit of patience on this one, wouldn't you? We realise that Brendan was sacked because it was going wrong and we needed someone to put it right. We know that we appointed the single best candidate for the whole 'putting it right' job in all of world football. And it hasn't all become the 1988 team in the first three hours of football, so we're throwing doom and gloom all over social media and criticising loose passes from the stands. It might not have been a masterclass but it wasn't the worst day of my life. A bloke that knows more about football than I do said that.

Which isn't quite where it ended. There was a final line or two summing everything up in a pithy manner, but I loaded everything up on to the website (as you do) and dropped an e-mail to let the guys know it was there. Which promptly landed in the junk file. By the Monday morning, when it was found, an article which ended there was clearly outdated, what with playing Southampton on the Sunday and everything. Could I update it as the themes had stayed horribly valid? Of course I could. And you'll get it in a bit. First we need to actually talk about Southampton.

Liverpool 1 Southampton 1

25 October 2015

FULL DISCLOSURE, between those two matches I had a birthday. My fifty-second. Had a nice day, thanks. Quiet. Went on the live version of *The Anfield Wrap*, broadcast from a big tower in the sky overlooking Liverpool, didn't mention my birthday. Fifty-two is a ridiculous number, I'm maintaining that I'm thirty-six or twenty-seven. The grey hair's an illusion, your eyes are playing up.

The cameras are still there, still documenting Jurgen Klopp's every step, still covering all the firsts. They might have to come back, they didn't get his first win. We draw again. That's roughly thirty-eight years of one-all draws. At least it feels that way. It's actually eight out of the last nine games drawn, all but one of them being one-all, the other nil-nil. This is without checking any actual details or anything. It's all too depressing to go checking stuff at the moment. It's not Klopp's problem (it's his to sort but it predates him), it's a *Liverpool* problem, a weakness in mentality somewhere. As the manager points out after the game, it's a lack of belief on the part of the lads who have to kick the ball around for a living. They don't believe that they can protect a lead, that they can survive setbacks. Their mindset expects disaster. Accordingly, so does ours. There's a vicious circle going on at Anfield from stands to pitch to stands to pitch and all the vice-versas that you want to run from that.

Which will bring us to the '*want to know what I don't get*' conclusion fairly shortly. First though, the match:

The first half is absolutely awful. Southampton are well set out, well marshalled, well drilled. They're dropping to five at the back when they need to, but springing forward to hit us on the break when given the chance. We're slower again, we're static and we're lacking creativity. Divock Origi is a passenger, utterly unencumbered by involvement in the game. The ball doesn't come anywhere near him and it's hard to tell if that's because he's not showing for it, or if the lads behind him aren't willing to play it forward, or if the opposition are cutting off channels.

It's not happening, though. That he doesn't emerge for the second half is unsurprising and, quite frankly, very welcome. Being on the field is doing no good for either him or us. Christian Benteke offers more in the first two minutes than Origi managed in the preceding half. He's moving, he's a target, a threat. The Southampton defence finally has something to occupy itself with. We're much improved, movement is better, pace is present. We're still not cutting through but it's looking more likely. The introduction of Firmino for the tiring Lallana makes us more threatening still. When our newest Brazilian settles, he's going to be something to see. His movement is wonderful and surprising. He gives us an edge of unpredictability that no other player is offering at the moment.

The goal, when it comes, is gorgeous. James Milner swings in a deep cross from the touchline just as I'm screaming 'don't throw in another long ball' and Benteke rises higher than anybody you've ever seen to power, genuinely, really, honestly *power,* home. It's a proper, old-fashioned centre-forward's goal and deserves to win the game. All we need to do now is take the sting out of the game, stay calm, see it out.

It doesn't win the game, we don't take the sting, we aren't calm, nothing is seen out. Panic arrives at exactly the moment we put ourselves ahead. Panic arrives at exactly the moment that you would least expect it. Jurgen has only just landed from a wild, delirious leap of celebration and we've gone. We're chaotic, haphazard, terrified. We've given up, we don't expect to pull ourselves back into the game. There are ten minutes to go and the whole ground has decided that the game will end in a draw. Which is where we go back into part two:

We Want The World And
We Want It Now

Part Two

IT'S NOT the moment when Southampton equalise that knocks our heads off, it's the moment when we score ourselves. We score, we lose our heads, the pattern's self-fulfilling at the moment. The players become anxious, the stands become anxious, the players feel the anxiety in the stands and become more anxious. Anxiety is all, equalisers are inevitable. The boss has said it, we're not calm, we don't defend the free kick calmly. I'm blaming the free kick, the act of conceding it, others will blame the defending. The free kick is, it can be rightly argued, forty yards from goal, there's a lot of defending that can be done between point A and point B. It feels ingracious criticising Milner for conceding a free kick there when he's put in that cross for the goal, feels equally ingracious criticising Benteke for not clearing the first ball into the box when he's put us in the lead with that bloody header.

I'm going with the Milner option, then. We all know that we're not going to defend that free kick particularly well, so don't give it away. You're a senior pro, you're the captain, you're the calm, experienced head. Be calm, be experienced, be senior, be pro, stand your man up, close him off. All we had to do was take the sting out of the game for five minutes. All we had to do was know that we could take the sting out.

We couldn't, it's a learnt behaviour. Our heads fell off as soon as we scored, because we know for an absolute, stone-cold certain fact that when we score, we concede. So we did. That's what we do at the moment, that's *what Jurgen's seeing in the players' eyes. That's what he needs to deal with.*

Which still isn't the 'know what I don't get' bit. That bit's the bit he can't deal with. Not immediately. It's the bit that he's dealing with bit by bit by bit by bit. It's the long-term bit. It's the tempering of us, it's the dealing with our *reactions.*

It's the comments from the stands. It's the criticism of Sturridge for being injured again. As though it's the lad's fault. Pretty damn sure that what he wants to do is play football. Pretty damn sure that he doesn't want to go from private hospital to private hospital getting scan after bloody scan after bloody scan and having blokes in white coats stick sharp things into various bits of his body that aren't doing what he wants them to.

Bit of sympathy for the lad might be nice. Bloody Sturridge. We should get rid. Waste of space, waste of time. Origi. Waste of a shirt. Should be changing it now. He's shit, why haven't we started Benteke? Errrrr.. .because he's been out for weeks and had half an hour of football so far and might break down and then we'd be buggered? Just a thought, like, just throwing it out there. Origi doesn't look very good at the moment but he's our fourth-choice striker and our only choice. I have vague memories of a young Thierry Henry not being very good in his first season in England, a young Ian Rush being unremarkable at nineteen in his first Anfield season. Thank Christ they didn't have Twitter to pass judgement on them.

It's this as well. It's the reactions. It's the online shite where we all tell each other stories and they become truths, where we all look at people who portray themselves as experts and believe them and pass it on. I'll hold my hands up on this one – I'm not *an expert. I'm a bloke who goes to the game and has a keyboard. Feel free to agree, feel free to tell me I'm talking shite, all opinions are valid on that one. What's not valid though? This: clickbait sites with teaser tag-lines like 'Liverpool Fans Destroy Player after Southampton Performance' to drag you in. They snare you, they pass on the tweets that you've already seen and they reinforce the idea that Divock Origi is the anti-christ instead of a lad who's just had a really poor forty-five minutes of football.*

And the opinions go round and round and we take them as fact because the website has nice graphics and looks like it knows what it's doing, but all it gives us is what we've already said. It's not giving an opinion, it's not presenting argument, it's re-presenting public opinion, nothing more. And this which follows is opinion, nothing more: Divock Origi had a really poor forty-five minutes on Sunday afternoon. It happens, deal with it, get some perspective, move on.

It's the exodus. Eighty-five minutes gone, the other lads equalise, and thousands stand up and head for the exit. Some of that I get. The bloke next to me, I get. He's eighty, walks with a stick, getting out before the bulk of the forty-thousand is pretty advantageous. And there are many in that position.

Everybody else, though? 'They've equalised, there's no way back, I'm off' – I don't get that. That's nine minutes to go, we've been pushing all through the second half, Benteke and Firmino look good, there's a chance, you can't see it coming but you couldn't see that bloody header coming either, could you? This is the bit where we can do things, this is the bit where the miracles happen and the legends grow, this is the bit where you sing, where you scream, where you support. We've been doing it all through the second half, silent in the first but pretty much 'us' in the second, showing belief, showing desire, showing passion. Less of the getting on to the lads and more of the getting behind the lads going on, much more us. And they equalise and thousands go 'nah'. Seriously, stick around, see what happens, it could be amazing. It wasn't, like, but you didn't know that, did you?

That's the problem, we think we know. Nobody knows. They think, they expect, they assume, they don't know, not know. The sooner we all, players and fans alike, stop thinking that we know it's going to go wrong, the sooner it'll stop going wrong. Law of attraction and all that, I could do a couple of thousand words on the law of attraction. Take this as a taster, expect the best and it'll happen. Believe in the best, it starts heading towards you. Jurgen needs to have the lads in the red shirts believing that and we need to start showing the patience and understanding that gives him the time to alter their mindset. We need to alter our mindset, big style.

We want the world and we want it now. Jim Morrison said that.

We want everything immediately and when we don't get it, we can't figure out why it hasn't happened. We might accept that we're in this for the long haul, but we're all convinced that it's far worse than it is and can't see the good because we expect, because we condition ourselves to look for the bad. I said that.

We've got a new dawn and we're still playing with pessimism, the players <u>and</u> the supporters. That's what I don't get.

Liverpool 1 Bournemouth 0

Capital One Cup
28 October 2015

I WAS in the car. Approaching 10pm, approaching Queens Drive. No extra time, no pens, no repeat of the Middlesborough 'are we ever going to be allowed to go home?' situation that saw the clock edging to midnight as I arrived home, the result of both teams going through sudden death twice. Not now, not tonight, one of the few games in this last sixteen which didn't go all the way. Chelsea out on pens (hilarious), Everton through on them (first time they'd won a shoot-out at Goodison in forty years), Arsenal embarrassed (brilliantly) by Sheffield Wednesday. The only obvious problem with that last result was that, amusing as seeing Arsenal lose three-nil to a Championship side was, it threw up the frankly hideous prospect of seeing us draw Wednesday in the next round and having to play at Hillsborough. Apologies to the team and their fans, but I'd be happy with them spending their entire existence in the lower leagues just to avoid the need for Liverpool to visit their ground ever again.

But we were talking about the car, let's do the car bit first.

I was in the car, had the radio on. Five Live were covering the United game as it petered out towards penalties, discussing the fact that Rooney doesn't have the effect that he once had because the players around him now are of a lower calibre than they used to be. And holding up Nani as an example.

Genuinely. Nani. I do wonder about commentators, about their connection to the world that the rest of us live in and how they manage to be paid for the nonsense that they spout. I can spout nonsense, I can sound disinterested, pay me. Rooney was dropping deep to get the ball and nothing was happening. The nothing happening made me turn to Talk Sport. Turning to Talk Sport is like going into a pub and asking everybody to offend you with bizarre opinions then screaming at them for doing exactly what you requested.

"Jurgen Klopp finally gains his first win as Liverpool manager."

Finally. Finally gains his first win. It's been a fortnight, lads, try and get a grip on reality, stop being the verbal equivalent of clickbait. It's frankly sad.

Three games in, three draws, two goals conceded, no losses. I like the no-losses bit, you can build on no losses, what with Jurgen currently being on a better unbeaten run than LVG, Arsene and Jose and all that. First win, though? First win's a genuinely good thing and the nature of this one is pretty satisfying.

It's the fact that we've scored our only goal early on and we've defended it. We've defended it past the thirteen- minute mark that's been pointed out as the point that we can defend up to and no further. We pass the thirteen minutes and we keep going. For an entire seventy-five minutes. There are moments, of course, moments where Adam Bogdan, looking more secure, more solid in all departments than Mignolet has in quite some time, is called on to make a couple of excellent saves. Other than those, though? Not really troubled by a Bournemouth team who start brightly with their own high-intensity pressing game but are hugely hampered by a lack of quality, with their every major summer signing subject to long-term injury. They work hard but lack a cutting edge. Sounds familiar that one, doesn't it? They sound like us, sound like the old us while we're watching a new us starting up.

The manager's the difference here, the clear difference. Brendan Rodgers seemed intent on treating the Capital One

Cup as a competition for a first-choice team and the Europa League as a place to blood youngsters. Jurgen Klopp seems to take the opposite stance. No, the results might not have shown the difference between the two approaches yet as all we've done to date is keep on drawing but last night is a signpost, a signpost that we can change shape, change formation, change personnel and, most significantly, change attitude.

That change in attitude isn't just in the defending the lead, it's all over the field. Nine changes from Sunday afternoon, only Origi and Clyne retaining their places. Origi as there's genuinely no other striker to take his place, and God knows he needs to play himself into some kind of form at some point, Clyne as we're short of cover at full-back so he finds himself at left-back for the night. Jose Enrique, perhaps sidelined by some selfie-inflicted injury. (See what I did there? Selfie-inflicted as he's always all over Instagram and all that? Never mind.)

There's a mix of fringe players and lads from the under-21s. Lovren, Allen, Toure, Ibe and Bogdan all step up from bench duty, Connor Randall, Cameron Brannagan and Joao Teixeira all make full debuts. All emerge with credit.

Toure lasts about twenty minutes before his hamstring ends his night and in that twenty minutes he shows very little other than the fact that his time's probably up. Can't criticise the lad, his job in 2013/14 was to bring spirit, confidence, experience, professionalism and attitude to a young team. His first week with the squad and he was telling all and sundry that we could win the league. We nearly did, so we can only thank him for what he brought to the table there. Gone now, though.

Lovren has one of his better games, looks strong, comfortable, does nothing wrong. Origi does that thing that he's been doing all season where you look at him and think 'I know he's got something, I know he must have, can't see what it is.' He's instrumental in the goal, though, winning the ball deep, bursting forward, pulling back for Firmino to slip to Teixeira, who attempts an audacious back heel. Goal-line clearance, Clyne pounces, a natural predator at left-back apparently.

It's only the next morning after a phone call from my mother that I realise my mum and dad know Connor Randall's grandfather and have watched his career progress for years now. The lad's exposed throughout the first half, targeted by Bournemouth as a possible weak link and he struggles to deal with a lot that comes his way. Something clicks on sixty minutes, though, and he starts to play with real confidence, bursting forward. It's nice to see.

Brannagan's tidy, neat, does what's needed in the middle next to and in front of Joe Allen. We appear to be playing something like a 4-1-4-1 with Allen sitting in front of the defence, pushing forward to free Firmino. There's natural width from Ibe and Teixeira, there's movement, there's options. Teixeira's done his Anfield career no harm tonight. Three years in and the promise looks like it might have some fruition. He might not be a first eleven player, but he looks like an option from the bench. He'll try the outrageous, he's nothing but confident and he's got the arrogance to take a free kick away from the lad that we paid £29m for this summer.

But that lad? The lad from Hoffenheim? The lad that Klopp had described as the best player in the Bundesliga last year? It's his night. Firmino conducts everything, wants the ball all the time, wants other players to respond to his instructions, not bad for a lad who doesn't do English yet. He's full of flicks and tricks and gives us the unpredictability that we've been missing since that little Uruguayan went to Barca. He's a proper *footballer*. He's exactly what we need. He's bringing the best out of others as well. Ibe has his best game in a long time tonight, linking with Firmino, running at men, going inside, going outside. The caution that he showed in the first few games of this season, when it looked like all the joy was gone from his game, has vanished. He looks like the player we thought he was, dynamic, pacy, creative.

It's all change and you can argue that it's not a big deal. We only beat Bournemouth 1-0 in a cup that doesn't really matter, but our manager says it matters. He says that he doesn't change teams to experiment, to look at players, to give players a rest, although the lads who've done four games in eleven days clearly needed it. He changes teams to win games and he wants to win every game. This team did that, it's a first win. A second on Saturday against a Chelsea team who are wobbling like crazy at the moment would be a glorious thing. The idea that it might seal Mourinho's fate? Not interested at the moment – although I'll be gloating in the next few pages if it does. I just want to watch Liverpool keep winning.

Chelsea 1 Liverpool 3

31 October 2015

WHICH IS what I did, watch Liverpool keep winning, that is, just in case it's a while since you read the last line of the previous chapter. I watched them keep winning in the most glorious, most beautiful, slightly unexpected way.

It's Monday morning as I write. Mourinho remains in work. Not what people expected at all, that. Everybody thought that he'd go straight after the game. The songs were circulating the ground as we pulled his team further apart, 'sacked in the morning' and all that. The meltdown was continuing as he deemed the Sky cameras worthy of his attention. "I have nothing to say," he said. Repeatedly, turning the phrase into a mantra made from his own madness, "I have nothing to say, I have nothing to say, I have nothing to say."

And what did he have 'nothing to say' about? Lucas not getting a second yellow card, Coutinho scoring our first-half equaliser after two minutes and *twenty-eight seconds* (the twenty-eight seconds is the important bit, it deserves italics) of a minimum of two minutes added time.

Shall we deal with these two, first? Yeah, let's.

The two minutes and twenty-eight seconds of added time at the end of the first forty-five minutes? That's to do with the fact that the referee instructs the fourth official to signal a 'minimum of,' no let's stress that one, a *minimum of* two minutes added time. Could be two minutes dead, two minutes and ten seconds, two minutes and fifty-eight seconds, anything that's less than three minutes, basically.

So, we score in the time that the referee has added and is playing. Mourinho won't whinge because he'll be fined. Might be worth pointing out that the last time that he was fined, it was because he'd claimed in his ludicrous seven-minute rant that every referee in the country was biased against Chelsea. If you don't want to be fined for saying things like that, don't say things like that. Simple solution. Play to the whistle and all that.

The second yellow? Yeah, Lucas is lucky. Not as lucky as Costa was a minute earlier when he kicked Skrtel in the chest. If Skrtel rolls around and screams a bit, as Costa did, holding his mouth after Skrtel put an arm across Costa's *chest* in the first half, then Costa receives yet another thoroughly justified red card. Obviously I'd love Costa if we'd had last season's version playing up front for us but we didn't, so there you go.

There's another point to make on the second yellow, though. Ramires is on his way down before he's touched. He's looking for the foul and most days he'd get it. Today, he didn't. Them's the breaks, lad.

So we expected Jose to be out of a job. A friend on Facebook had it on 'good authority' from two different sources that Jose was gone, announcement to be made on Monday. It's noon and it hasn't happened yet.

I'm sat, writing this, and I'm partly glued to Twitter. I'm following rumour, gossip, stories of press conferences and impending announcements, but none of them concern Mourinho. They're all very, very much Stone Roses related. Twitter is buzzing that *something* will happen today, that some Roses-related announcement is heading our way. After two years of post-Heaton Park silence, there is news. People are gathering outside the Hilton Hotel in Manchester, posters with the legendary half-lemon image are appearing mysteriously in sympathetic Manchester shops. I'm fifty-two years old and ridiculously excited.

Which has nothing to do with the match at all and should really appear as a separate chapter with the heading *'Interlude'*. And might do so yet, once the actual story breaks. It feels inevitable. If not now, then soon. He can't transition teams, can't rebuild. He can come into a club, spend a lot of money, buy players and build a team, but he can't rebuild that team when it starts to age. He can't do more than three years. Never has, probably never will. He might criticise Arsene Wenger but he'll never achieve his longevity, never play attractive football for as long as Wenger's teams have. He managed three months of expansive, entertaining play at the beginning of last season and then pulled the hatches down once again, returning to the 'anti-football' that he does so well. Except even that's deserting him. Now, it appears, his team have given up on him.

It would be entertaining to have seen Abramovich once again sack Mourinho after this loss, would have felt like glorious, exceptionally cold, revenge after his running down the line beating his chest in the wake of Gerrard's slip and Torres' assist for Chelsea's second goal as our title hopes faded.

In fairness, with every word that I write on the subject, I take more delight in the idea of the egotist losing his post at our hands but I don't want to go with the media narrative, don't want to give any indication that Halloween 2015 was concerned with something that Mourinho either did or didn't do. This game was to do with us.

That Chelsea managed to score within four minutes, a Milner non-tackle allowing a cross into the box, a Moreno 'I'll look at the lad charging in, where did he come from?' moment allowing Ramires to head into the net, was obviously a blow. It felt like the honeymoon had ended, felt like some reality was returning. The script was writing itself anew, Mourinho, with calm arrogance, acknowledging the fans' joyous receipt of the goal, Klopp now certain to witness his first Liverpool defeat, the goals to rain in, the media to fall back in love with Jose and his cheap and easy quotability.

I love it when a plan goes awry.

Our performance was immense, beautiful, compact, perfect, everything you would want from an away performance, everything you would want from a Liverpool team playing a Chelsea team. There might have been unease, caution, nervousness, but these all came in the first ten minutes. From that point on, through, every second that the referee chose to add to the day, we played, we performed, we battled, we dominated.

No recognised striker in the first half. That's what the commentators and 'experts' on BT television insisted on telling us. A front three that moved like liquid, though: a line of Firmino, Coutinho, Lallana switching, interchanging, combining, contrasting. A midfield three of the utterly imperious Lucas and the workmanlike Can and Milner. I'll be honest, shall I? Watching the game live, I thought that Milner was woeful, thought that Can was slightly better but less influential, wanted Milner pulled within the first ten minutes, wanted Benteke on immediately, wanted change, wanted threat. Viewing again this morning (hold on, just going to check on the Roses again, no, nothing, still quiet), I realised that Milner was working. Working hard. He was deep, he was forward, he was central. I think we're beyond the point of talking formations here. I think Jurgen's inventing new stuff as he goes along. As long as the pressing happens, everything else can flow, change, develop. We're swapping formations, we're swapping who the deepest man is, Adam Lallana's playing centre forward, everybody's a false nine. Coutinho's everywhere, Firmino's linking with him, feeding him and the end result is the equaliser. It's gorgeous and very, very Coutinho.

A shuffle, a small gap, a curl into the top corner. Very him, very us.

The second and third, after the Costa controversy, after the lucky Lucas moment, are all about Benteke. They're about the header down for Coutinho to collect (after Lallana can't quite connect) and hit the other top corner of the net via John Terry's midriff and they're about Benteke himself collecting an Ibe pass, dummied by Lallana, and being able to walk around the Chelsea area for what seems to be about fifteen minutes, weighing up the ineffectual Cahill and Terry before shooting through Cahill's legs.

The celebrations are as they should be: Klopp pictured in mid-air as he leaps with joy, the players in with the fans as they should be. There's a movement starting and this is how it starts. It starts with the first win in eight games over an enemy that has only really existed in this form for a decade, with us scoring three goals instead of drawing one-all. It starts with us having the confidence to not give up after conceding an early goal. Last year, that would have been a major loss. Two weeks ago, we wouldn't have come back from it. We might have only lost one-nil, might have conceded a second, probably wouldn't have been embarrassed but wouldn't have turned it round. This is what Jurgen Klopp saw in the players' eyes, this is what he's dealt with. A week ago, against Southampton, we threw away a lead, and our mentality at that point meant that we had no way of believing that we were able to resolve the issue. That mentality has changed in a week. That's how things start, with a change of mindset.

Asked afterwards if Liverpool were now capable of winning the league, Klopp simply aimed his most scornful attitude to the journalist and pointed out that he has been in the job for three weeks. If this is what he can achieve in three weeks, what can he do with the rest of the season? The Brendan Rodgers era seems like years ago already.

This is where it all starts.

FC Rubin 0 Liverpool 1

5 November 2015

THE NIGHT where it all went a little bit *Likely Lads*. Am I going to have to explain the *Likely Lads* reference? Probably. For the younger amongst us, it goes like this:

Two young lads, Bob and Terry, just starting their way in the world, going out drinking, going out on the pull. Growing up, basically. That's *The Likely Lads* as it was first shown in the mid-1960s. Black and white, innocent, young and, from our current perspective, somewhat slightly accidentally politically incorrect. Two series (before we became American and called them 'seasons'), most episodes now long lost in the BBC's careless purging of old tape footage, and then gone.

It resurfaced in the mid-1970s, with the greatest theme tune in the history of TV, as *Whatever Happened To The Likely Lads*, Terry, the perennial bad influence, returning from a seemingly accidental spell in the army, set to destabilise the relationship of the aspirational Bob and his fiancee Thelma. It's about the lost dreams of youth, what you settle for in life and the passage of time. The ideal would be to see an update set currently with the ageing James Bolam and Rodney Bewes revisiting their characters but all stories claim that the two hate each other, so no breath held on that one.

There's this one episode, though. This one, specific, football-related episode. Those of you who know this are already smiling.

Bob and Terry are avoiding the result of an England game. The game is played in the afternoon and, it being the 1970s and everything, not broadcast until *Match of the Day* later that evening. They avoid radio, they avoid friends, they avoid anything. They spend the episode running, refusing to listen. They mostly avoid their nemesis, the imperious Brian Glover, who is determined to spoil the surprise. They catch sight of a newspaper advert, 'England R…' is all they see. They speculate, 'Reign? Resilient? Ridiculous?' The punchline is that the game was rained off.

I've been *Likely Lads*'d twice now. The first time was in 2010. It was a family meal to commemorate the first anniversary of losing J's dad. Liverpool were playing United at exactly the time the meal had been booked for. J's family are all blue, with the exception of her elder brother, the red sheep of the family. He was okay with knowing the score, I was avoiding it, taping it at home, watching 'as live' later.

I did well. Got to full time. Got to the end of the meal. Made the mistake of going to the toilet before we left the restaurant. Came back out and J's mum looked at me with genuine sympathy and said, 'Ah, sorry love, that was bad luck.'

It happened again on Thursday night. A meal to commemorate the first anniversary of losing *my* father. His anniversary is actually Monday the ninth, but our Keith was in town on the Thursday, en route from a few days in Paris back to his home in the Isle of Man. A meal was arranged, fourteen of us at a long table. I wasn't *actively* avoiding the score, hadn't told anybody that I didn't want to know, I'd just taken the decision not to look at my phone, to avoid Twitter, to watch the match 'as live' when I got home. Kick-off at six, table booked for six, be home before nine, watch the game, be writing this on Friday morning.

I could see our Kev at the end of the table, could see him scrolling, looking. "One-nil" he said, looking up. "Ibe." Best-laid plans and all that. When we got home J decided that, being blue, she had no desire to sit and watch a Liverpool European narrow away victory. Reasonable enough. Friday morning before I got to it, 11am for reasons that will become clear in a short while.

It's an interesting experience watching a game that you already know the result but no details of. There's nothing riding on it, no angst, no fear of loss. You can look at the changes made to the squad (Allen, Ibe, Lovren all in) and analyse their performance in a calm, calculated manner. One thing is obvious though: Jurgen Klopp is taking the Europa League a lot more seriously than Brendan Rodgers was. This might not be particularly satisfying to the likes of Chirivella, Brannagan and Rossiter, who looked to be nailed on first choices for this competition, but it sits well with me. It's still the UEFA Cup, it's a competition that we have history with. We now have a European manager who quite fancies the idea of winning it, whose current ethos is 'I don't rest players who don't need a rest, I pick teams to win games and the most important game is the next one'. He might make changes but they won't be huge and they'll quite possibly allow players to make a statement. They certainly did in Russia.

There's a control to the game, a dominance that you might not expect. English teams don't win in Kazan (although, sometime in the last fortnight Kazan have decided that their name is now FC Rubin, which seems like Real Madrid suddenly deciding they're FC Real now, it's just odd), English teams don't draw here. Liverpool don't win on Russian soil. Until now. Now, we win on Russian soil. We win and we dominate. We don't look like an away team, we have absolute control and utter calm. The cutting edge still isn't there. Until it suddenly is, until the space opens up for Ibe in the middle of the park and he bursts and he slots and he's now a game-changer. It's the Ibe moment that we'd expected last season, the one that we'd hoped for, the one that shows that he can put end product to potential. There's every possibility that this is a defining game for Ibe. He's all pace and power and threat and all that joy in his game seems to have re-emerged. He's man of the match by some distance and the next morning's Twitter is filled with vines of Klopp moving towards him after the game and yelling 'Ibeeee' in pure joy. The player he'd criticised for not being prepared enough to enter the pitch as a substitute in his first game in charge seems reborn, the first obvious beneficiary of the Klopp era.

Another possible beneficiary, a very surprising one given his public image as being very much a 'Brendan Rodgers player', is Joe Allen. He's everywhere tonight, the fulcrum of the midfield, the Lucas for the evening, pulling strings, orchestrating, organising, covering the ground that you don't expect. The longer hair and beard combo that he's decided to sport this season seems to have convinced him that he's Andrea Pirlo. Long might he labour under this idea. There are many good things to say about Joe Allen and they aren't said often enough. Perhaps tonight could be the start of a change.

Oh yeah, and... that Stone Roses announcement that I was more interested in than the fate of Jose Mourinho? I'd hoped that a third Roses album was due to drop imminently (come on, we can do this stuff now, sit in a press conference and say, 'the album came out thirty seconds ago, start buying' and watch the world go into meltdown). What we actually got was an image on the website at 7pm announcing two gigs at the Etihad and a headlining of the *T in the Park* festival. No press conference, no statements, no sign of the lads and quite definitely, for now, at least, no new music.

Sod it. Friday morning, internet queuing, took a while but hit it in the end, two tickets sitting in the stands on the Friday, the first night of the two which swiftly became the second of four and probably more. Eighty quid a pop, not on until next June, the interest on that cash must be quite nice. Doesn't matter, it's something to look forward to. Always have something to look forward to. Some time after this book ends, I'll be off to see the Roses live again. Top one, sorted, etc.

Liverpool 1 Crystal Palace 2

8 November 2015

'TWENTY-EIGHT MILLION for you, you fucking donkey bastard?' We'll come back to this sentence in a bit.

Si's in town for the match so we meet up in The Sandon beforehand. "What do you reckon?" he asks. "Six-one," I decide, "I'm the world's most optimistic man." And then we talk about Michael Head's performance on Friday night at the Philharmonic Hall's new Music Room. Absolutely majestic, solo but accompanied by a choir, a gig where I realise how many interesting people I've met in the last year. A gig where I'm not standing alone in a room full of strangers but bumping into people. A gig where I end the night walking through Liverpool as Friday turns into Saturday, in the Caledonia pub with a live jazz quartet and then in search of St George's Hall's poppy display with an excellent photographer I met through Si, but has worked for the same company as I did and knows people that I know. All of us that didn't know each other finding out that we all know the same other people. Small world and all that.

We make tentative arrangements for the December 12 weekend and the just-announced gig that Mick's doing at The Florrie, the following day's West Brom game and possibly going out for breakfast on the Sunday morning, all depending on rehearsals and performances. It's all natural but it's also how life has changed in the last eighteen months, pinching myself at the 'I don't work in a record shop any more' moment yet again. There was a moment in the late-night Liverpool poppy-photographing expedition that I suddenly thought, 'oh yeah, I made two music videos as well, didn't I?'

And that's basically the best part of the day done with. The football just gets in the way from here on in.

Can we use the five thousand-mile journey home from Kazan as an excuse, then? God knows, we need something. It's not that we play badly per se. Not as a team, not as a whole. There are individual shockers going on but the majority of the team is gelling in performance and attitude and belief. The dynamism and aggression aren't what we've seen recently but that's not the problem. The problem is that we're victims of our own undoing yet again.

Palace start well but aren't overly threatening. Their lead comes from our defence making mistakes in the midfield area and our midfield making mistakes in the defence. Moreno doesn't deal with a ball in the middle of the park, it breaks, pings across the area and again, yet again, *yet* again, Emre Can clears as far as an opposition shirt. It's another assist that Can has provided an opponent with and it's emblematic of his whole afternoon. The German lad is shocking today. I like Can but in this game? Absolute liability. Anything that could go wrong today does so at the feet of handsome Emre.

Mignolet is on the same plane of thought as Can. He manages another excellent save to add to his collection for the season but demonstrates an absolute lack of thinking. There's a glorious Mamadou Sakho moment. He lands awkwardly from a contested header, clutches his knee, stretchers appear pitch-side, he walks off, sees Lovren ready himself, so the big Frenchman shakes his knee a bit and walks back on. Cue tumultuous applause, cue Simon Mignolet bizarrely deciding to play a short pass out to a lad who couldn't walk just seconds earlier, cue danger. Again, always again.

We believe, though. After the Chelsea turnaround, we believe that we can come back into this. We, players and crowd alike, believe that we can do this. For now, we believe this. That's going to change. The equaliser is inevitable and deserved. Clever hold-up by the once again excellent Ibe to play in the rampaging Clyne, a back heel from Lallana, Benteke in the wrong place (that will become a theme in the second half) and Coutinho curls it in. There's only one team in this game, only one team that will score from now on.

We push. All the way through the second half we push, but we're blunt. Benteke is enduring one of those torrid afternoons that strikers sometimes endure. Nothing is happening and he looks a very, very long way from anything resembling full fitness. He looks shot and the Sturridge and Ings injuries are looking costly. We've no cutting edge and only Origi on the bench to theoretically provide that. The crowd is becoming restless and that restlessness, that edge, is flowing down the stands to the pitch. There's a voice a few rows behind me that I've not heard before but can't stop hearing today, 'Second ball, Liverpool, second ball.' That's the basis of Klopp's entire game, you know, mate. He might have mentioned this concept to the lads. Not sure that you yelling every few seconds is giving them anything new.

There's a Benteke moment. The Belgian squares the ball in front of the Kop when every fibre of every body in the ground is shouting 'shoot' (don't think the shot's actually on if we're being honest) and that's when the guy behind me yells it. The first sentence of this chapter. *Twenty-eight million for you, you fucking donkey bastard?*

Apart from the fact that it's possibly the first time in the history of the English language that anybody has used the phrase 'you fucking donkey bastard' and ignoring the fact that Benteke cost thirty-two million, did you see the Chelsea goal? The United overhead kick? The chest-to-volley in pre-season? Have you noticed that the lad's scoring all these totally different goals? Have you noticed that he's basically scoring every other time that he walks on to the pitch?

This is our problem at the moment. This is our problem at home. We're impatient, we're negative, we're critical, we're doing everything but support. The lads on the pitch are less of the problem than we are and we need to sort it. The negativity is pervasive. And it gets worse by the minute.

There's only one team that looks like scoring, so it's the other team that finally does it. Eighty-one minutes in and Palace score. We fall back on our old ideal of failing to deal with corners and Palace get two chances to tuck it away. They take the second. Obviously, it's a Liverpool-supporting Scouse lad who scores it. Thanks fate.

And five blokes to the side of me get up and walk out. As do many more. The opposition has scored with eight minutes of normal time to go. Add on the added on bits and we're looking at about twelve minutes of football to go. Things can happen in twelve minutes. Istanbul happened in six minutes, Robert Lewandowski scored five in nine minutes not so long ago. Things can happen in twelve minutes. But people aren't going to believe that, they're just going to go.

Seriously? What can be so important that you're willing to give up twelve minutes of a game you've paid a lot of money for? Do you really think the traffic is going to be that bad? If you do, if you're not willing to put up with the hardship of getting home from the game then give your ticket to somebody that is. Give it to somebody who cares. It's not about how old you are, it's not about where you're from, it's about, as Ian Brown put it, 'where you're at'.

It's a disgrace. It's that easy, don't give excuses. Thousands of people leaving with ten minutes to go because the opposition have taken the lead? It's a disgrace. And it's one that the manager comments on. 'I saw people leaving after the goal and in that moment, I felt lonely.' If you want a dictionary definition of 'supporting', it's the polar opposite of that moment.

Klopp tempers his initial comments a little with the fact that it's the responsibility of the team to ensure that people don't want to leave early, that they make sure fans fear leaving early, fear the possibility of missing something incredible, but the onus is on us here. We need to embrace positivity, we need to project attitude. We need to sort ourselves out. And when I say 'we', I don't mean 'we,' I don't mean all of us. I don't know anybody who walked out early, do you? Have a word then, thanks.

The fallout continues, Sakho left the pitch a few minutes after he probably should have. It's not another ACL to add to Ings and Gomez, but it *is* ligamental damage. Eight weeks out by the looks of it. Could have been worse but now we're running out of centre-backs as well as forwards. The possibility of Thiago Ilori returning from his failure to see any game time in his loan spell at Villa and revisiting his stalled Liverpool career seems very real.

The unbeaten run is over. Jurgen Klopp has his first defeat and we have an entire fortnight of pointless international friendlies where Roy Hodgson can prepare his chosen squad for the inevitable crushing disappointment of an early Euros exit in the summer. Two weeks in which we can stew and worry and prepare the negativity that we'll greet the idea of playing City away with.

We seriously need to get a grip.

9 November 2015

I'M NOT going to write in depth on this but I can't *not* mention it. This is what's really important. Arranging to meet Si before the game on Sunday was an important thing. It took my mind off the time and the date.

A year ago today, as I write, by date, a year ago yesterday by the day of the week, at two minutes past two on Remembrance Sunday, my dad passed away. Arranging to meet at three meant that at two I was getting ready to go out. I didn't notice the time, didn't think about it too much and too specifically.

The minute's silence before the game could have been uncomfortable, but I thought of those that the silence was designed for. The rendition of *You'll Never Walk Alone* was glorious. Looking around the stadium that my dad knew for sixty years through victory and loss and change and tragedy and triumph, looking from *his* seat at the scarves and the colour and the standing and the singing of our song was joyous. It was for him. It was the song that we played to him in hospital and it was the song that we played at his funeral and, here and now, it was for every single good moment that we'd ever spent together. It was for every single good moment that he'd spent following these various lads, these thousands of various lads who have worn the Liver Bird on their chests and it was beautiful.

I miss my dad, I carry him with me, today and every day. RIP Dad, YNWA.

London and Paris

17 November 2015

THERE ARE things that you half expect to write about, Rodgers out, a new man in, injury crises, that kind of thing, and things that you never dream of putting here, of having to put here, of actually happening, but it's the latter that we're going to have to talk about.

It's almost impossible to *not* talk about Paris. It's one of those 'where were you when…' moments, like 9/11, 7/7, JFK, RFK. It's one of those moments when a previously obscure name, an unknown site, becomes globally known for the worst reason of all.

This is how it was for us, then:

International fortnight, no real football, J had booked a couple of days off work, a long weekend, a chance to get away, have a break. Tickets were bought to see Nicole Kidman in the West End on the Saturday night, a hotel near Covent Garden booked for Friday to Monday, a chance taken to see London as something other than a business venue.

The Friday had been a fine day, a decent train journey, first class, cheap if you book in advance. Why wouldn't you do it? A taxi ride to avoid the 'suitcases on the Tube' moment and then a wander down to Waterloo for a viewing of the new Bond film *Spectre* on the biggest Imax screen in the country. Booked from the train, the wonders of technology, sat in the front row so not entirely ideal, but beggars/choosers etc. We hit Waterloo early after our first realisation that everything in Central London is closer to everything else than you realise, found a lovely little Polish bar with art on the walls, ate bread, olives, and soup, drank red wine and killed time.

The film was okay. Not even vaguely in the same league as Skyfall had been, a little too Roger Moore-ish in a world which no longer requires Roger Moore Bond films. Not as clever as it thought. A good Bond at the heart of an average film. We walked back across a windswept Waterloo via the South Bank, hit the hotel bar for wine and bar snacks as the second half of the England/Spain game developed.

England were their usual selves, nothing happening, flattering to deceive, pointless. There had been complaints from the squad that they felt they hadn't received the credit that they should for their post-World Cup form but no acknowledgement that they hadn't really played anybody of any note, and that they would struggle once they did. Against Spain, they struggled. At nil-nil, I asked J if she wanted England to win. She replied that of course she did. I didn't, I wanted a Spain victory. Why? Because it'll be funny. That's my England stance, watching them lose is funny. Doesn't affect me at all, can't be bothered with them and their delusions of grandeur. All England have existed for in my lifetime (apart from winning their only trophy before I'd turned three) is injuring Liverpool players.

Sod them. I sat and analysed the complete lack of shape that the team possessed, queried the tactics and square peg/ round hole ideology. I also took great delight in the fact that Raheem Sterling's inability to play the correct ball through for the left-back overlapping on the flank led to both Sterling's dispossession and the hole in the defence that was exploited to provide the Spanish right-back with the chance to convert in a world-class manner. The beauty of the Cazorla goal was simply icing. 'There you go, that's what the Euros are going to look like.'

The analysis padded its way towards 10pm, with Lee Dixon and Ian Wright endlessly pontificating. A couple on the couch opposite us started to make their presence known, with the girl swearing loudly and frequently. 'Take your missus up mate, she's bladdered,' I muttered, in a version of my actual words, which has been substantially cleaned up for these pages, and J started to consult Twitter.

Reports of violent incidents across Paris, multiple sites. Then this vine from the France vs Germany game. J hasn't looked at it before showing me. 'They reckon you can hear an explosion on this,' she says and we watch it together. We watch the moment that Patrice Evra thinks about playing a short pass back to his central defender and then there's this *noise* and we look at each other and this is serious, absolutely serious, and Evra just plays the ball back in a manner that says 'this doesn't matter, something just changed' and he's right.

We've no idea whether the game went on. As I write, on Tuesday, 17 November, I've still no idea whether the game carried on or not. I've seen no mention of it anywhere. We leave the bar and we sit up until about one, watching the world get worse. Again. It's like we've had to watch this news too many times already, but it keeps coming and it's way beyond comprehension. The attack on the Stade De France is shocking but, let's be honest, not totally unexpected. The fact that a football ground in Europe hasn't been targeted by suicide bombers before now is amazing.

Are any of us really searched when we attend a league game? Doesn't happen, does it? One man with a suicide vest could cause carnage. It looks very much as though this was the intention at Stade De France. It looks as though that attack was actually foiled. Things could have been far worse than they were. It's a horrible thought.

It's the attack on the Bataclan that really hits me. It's a venue that you only really know if you're a fan of bands of a certain size, a venue that you would see in NME announcements of your favourite semi-obscure indie band's European jaunts. That the target is this venue, that the target is a show by Eagles Of Death Metal, who the majority of the world is pretty unfamiliar with, is evidence that it could be anywhere, could be any of us, that everything is now random and the ideology that believes itself at war with us, the ideology that in no way represents the religion that it purports to be *of*, isn't making a political point, isn't selecting its targets with any easily defined reason. This is slaughter for the sake of slaughter, indiscriminate and random.

We fall asleep to the sound of Sky rolling the news onwards and with the very real worry that here we are in the middle of a busy tourist section of a capital city, that anything is possible now, that a theatre containing a performance by a Hollywood 'A-lister' has to represent a potential target and that we're a long way from our sons.

London doesn't feel tense the next morning, doesn't feel threatened, doesn't feel wary. There's no increased police presence that we can see, there are no bag checks at the theatre. Everything feels normal and normality feels like the best answer to the events in Paris. Normality feels like the best way to honour the victims. Not living our lives would be a betrayal of theirs.

Saturday is Portobello Road and a homely pub in Bayswater. It's Carnaby Street and Seven Dials and Charing Cross Road and the hope that the book shop at 84A from the Anthony Hopkins and Anne Bancroft film is still there. It's not. Saturday is finding our way around a city that we've been dismissive of in the past and falling in love with it in the way that we've fallen in love with Paris and Rome and Amsterdam. Saturday is about a memorable night at the theatre and a fine meal and watching the world walk by. Saturday is about normality and always should be.

That's how it was for us then, terrifying and too close, a reminder to think of your loved ones and embrace your life because it's too precious not to.

And, as we returned to thinking about football, thinking about the Reds and their restart and their chances in the league, knowing that we were starting off again with a visit to the home of the team that looked most likely to simply walk the league, I decided to write a preview of the game for *The Anfield Wrap*.

At least, it started off as a preview. Somewhere in the writing it became a critique of those that leave early, a criticism of negativity and a call to arms.

Frankly excellent title courtesy of Gareth Roberts.

The Calm Before We Storm It

I'M CALM. I've had two weeks off, had all the international stuff, had time to empty my mind post-Palace, post the latest Palace debacle. I've had time to let the fury dissolve, I've had time away. I've had that moment of panic, the one that most of us probably had, the moment where we realised that terror is now aimed at the twin loves of many of us, football and music, and that things are even less the same than they were previously. I'm calm enough to think about it rationally, though, calm enough to realise that you can't avoid talking about Paris in the context of everything else that we do, calm enough to realise that everything might seem fragile but that we need to carry on with all the fragile stuff because carrying on with the ordinary is important. Carrying on with the ordinary is vital. Of all the unimportant things, football is the most important, and all that.

I've listened to the post-Palace early exit debates, read the comment pieces. I've listened to people take differing sides on the disappointment dash, understanding (if not condoning) or condemning the 'it's eighty-two minutes, we've conceded, I'm off' attitude.

Me personally? I thought it was disgusting. Thought it showed a lack of belief, lack of trust in the ability of the players and management to turn things round. Showed that, a week after we came back from an early setback to dismantle Chelsea, we still didn't believe that we could do at home the very thing that we had already done away. Home versus away, that's going to be the crux. In a minute or two. I've listened to the argument that you can be so disappointed by something that the only natural reaction is to get up and go. And I kind of get it but... no. Just no. Don't do it.

Don't leave early. Don't leave anything early. It's that attitude that means that I've sat through the entirety of Forrest sodding Gump, so it definitely has its pitfalls. Guy Ritchie's 'Rock'n'Rolla', though? Walked out on that. There are limits.

Does that mean I've never left a game before the end? No. It doesn't. I've done it a couple of times. In the eighties, a Cup replay against United. First game was at Goodison, replay at Maine Road. Kind of remember them scoring late on to kill the game off and we thought 'we're getting a kicking here', so we did one. Got back to the train, lay on the floor in the dark as the bricks were thrown. Think leaving early was justified on that one.

The game at Old Trafford where Sami was sent off after about twelve seconds? I was in the directors' box, long story, don't ask, with the understanding that I was keeping fairly quiet whatever happened. First goal, quietly upset. Second goal, muttering. Third goal, on my feet, pure, loud, Bootle invective. Fourth goal? Already on the escalator. Wembley, FA Cup Final against Chelsea, expensive ticket in among Chelsea fans, long story, don't ask, final whistle goes, our lads look devastated, I think, 'sod yer, should have tried harder' and I'm gone. I'm in a bitter mood and I'm taking it out on our lot underachieving and I'm off. Whistle's blown like but I'm still thinking of this as early. There are Chelsea fans leaving with me, leaving before me. Because cup presentations are boring, aren't they? And there's hardly any transport in London. Really don't get that one.

And, as an aside, the family who were walking in front of me after our Palace game? Looked like tourists, looked like they were on a nice family day out, mum and dad consoling their young son, who was in floods of tears, they stayed to the end. If you're in tears and you're still there, you win. Are you well enough to walk? Stay till the end. Other opinions are available.

So. The calmness and all that. I'd intended to start with the terrible admission that I'd never done an away league game. Then I remembered the United loss so we'll caveat that to 'I've never done an away league game anywhere other than a directors' box'. Come on though, working every Saturday from 1980 through to 2014? I've got a bloody good excuse. Need to get to one, though, looks a good day out, that. Looks, from the outside, like the lads who spend all that cash do it with a reason. Looks like they do it so they can go and have a good time, enjoy themselves, enjoy the game, get behind the lads in red. I don't know but I don't think that the lad a few rows behind me who was screaming 'twenty-eight million for you, you fucking donkey bastard!' at Benteke was yelling the same thing as Christian waltzed through the Chelsea box. I don't think that the constant muttering of 'that Sturridge lad doesn't want to play' is happening at United or at Villa or Spurs.

I don't know all this, I'm making an assumption, but I think the negativity of 40,000 who scream at every mistake isn't happening in the 3,000 who have had a drive and a laugh and maybe a bevy on the way and aren't getting out ten minutes early to get a bus because they're in Norwich, and those ten minutes don't mean anything anyway. I don't know this but I believe it. I believe the away lads are there for the right reason. I believe they're doing the whole supporting thing right. I believe there's less whingeing and more singing. I believe there's less criticism and more basic, honest to god, genuine support. Tell me I'm wrong if you like, I'm fine with being wrong, but I believe in the lads who are doing the aways. I believe that they're having more fun than the rest of us.

And that's why I'm calm. That's why I'm calm about City. I fully believe that it's easier for the lads in the shirts if they're away, if the only people claiming that they're 'fucking donkey bastards' are the opposition fans, because they expect it from them and they don't care about them. City fans claiming Sturridge is a lightweight who can't be bothered? Arsed about that. Southampton fans ridiculing Lallana for keeping possession? Arsed. Bluenoses maintaining against all evidence that Sakho is clumsy? Again, arsed. They can deal with that, can deal with scorn and ridicule. From the others. Shouldn't have to get it from us. Have I mentioned this before? Sure we're going over old ground here.

Two weeks ago, I was concerned. I was worried. I thought that this would be the game where the whole selling Sterling saga would come back to bite us, could see him growing game by game, watched that hat-trick the other week and thought, 'he's ready'. I read Aidy Ward's comments about whether Raheem would *celebrate if he scored against us and thought, 'the world thinks this is a done deal'. And then, on Friday night, in a hotel bar in London, before everything happened, I watched Raheem Sterling play for England and I saw a catalogue of wrong choices and poor passes and culpability for Spain's first goal by not having the awareness to provide for the overlapping left-back and I thought, 'still potential, still not the finished article, I'll have Clyne against him, I'm having that.' Nice cross for Rooney's goal, like. Other than that though...*

The City that started the season? I'd have been scared of them. The City that continued? Not so much. The City that played Newcastle? Not at all. That City we can take. A City where we hope that Aguero doesn't win his battle for fitness? A Liverpool with a Daniel Sturridge who seems to be fit and raring to go? Even if it's from the bench? A Liverpool with Sturridge and Benteke and Coutinho and Firmino on the same pitch at the same time running at the pale blue defence? I'm having that Liverpool.

A Liverpool playing away from home with unity and positivity behind them in the stands? I'm having that Liverpool. I'm having that Liverpool in a big way. That's the Liverpool that took one look at a fourth-minute Chelsea goal and went 'it doesn't matter' and made sure it didn't because they believed and they had the backing of those who believed and, before it was even spoken, they had the manager's credo of 'we'll make sure that nobody can leave early because anything could happen' in their hearts.

The international break was the best thing that could happen to our season. The fact that we return away from home, return with a major test, play the league leaders with a nine-point gap that can be changed to only six, that we've had the chance to work on mindset and attitude on the inside of the club? That, right there, is an opportunity. Win this one and Jurgen and the boys can return to Anfield with a chance of sorting out our *mentality,* our *attitude,* our *belief. We're starting again, we're doing this, we're beating City.*

I believe this. I'm calm.

What can I say? Obviously I'd totally forgotten that City were scoring goals for fun at one point, although their last few games had been slightly more arid. I'd forgotten that Kevin De Bruyne was looking worth every penny of his huge transfer fee. And then *this* happened.

Manchester City 1 Liverpool 4

21 November 2015

IT'S THE third goal. Obviously it's everything but the third goal *is* everything. The third goal is emblematic of everything we are this cold November teatime and everything that we could possibly be becoming.

The third goal is everything because the third goal goes like this:

Raheem Sterling, the wonderfully anonymous Raheem Sterling, has the ball on the right of our box. City are beginning to look as though they might be thinking about exerting some pressure. Sterling moves the ball out to Kolarov, who slides a pass into the area. The imperious Martin Skrtel passes the ball towards the edge of the box. Adam Lallana reacts with more urgency than Sterling and pokes the ball in the direction of James Milner. Milner is faster than the onrushing City shirt, pokes a sliding toe towards the loose(ish) ball. Firmino, being held from behind by Mangala, strokes it back to Milner and Milner sprints.

It's *vital* to remember that, at this point, both Milner and Firmino are playing in the right-back position. Milner hits the midpoint of City's half, plays a ball infield. Emre Can has a slight touch, possibly a slight mis-control, and the ball falls to Coutinho.

Young Phil shoots, as is his wont these days, and Joe Hart parries away. Shot saved, problem dealt with. Except we're not doing 'problem dealt with' today. Moreno picks the ball up, has two choices, Coutinho or Can. He picks Coutinho, Coutinho moves it to Can. Can takes the ball away from goal, plays the most audacious back heel you've ever seen back to Coutinho, who now has the freedom of the penalty area. He draws Hart and passes, gently, delicately, beautifully to Firmino, who is onside by roughly the width of the ball that he is now tapping into an empty net.

We're thirty-three minutes into a game at the home of the team that is supposed to run away with the Premier League this season and we're three-nil up. Of these three, Roberto Firmino has scored one and made the other two. Arrivals are being announced here.

It wasn't supposed to be like this. Nobody saw this coming. I was bullish but prepared to be foolish (if we'd lost, I'd have simply deleted the previous chapter), but being this bullish would have been ridiculous. Klopp announces afterwards that, at half-time, the players were surprised to be leading in such a convincing manner. This is the mentality that he needs to/ intends to rectify: you have this convincing lead because *this* is what you're capable of, you are capable of doing *this* to the league leaders.

We have travelled to the Etihad and we have set down a marker. *This* is what we can do. *This* is what we are, what we might be becoming going forward, and the 'going forward' is everything here.

Firmino could have a hat-trick. We could be five goals up at half-time. Seven goals wouldn't have flattered us today. The 'one' in the scoreline flatters City. It's our mistake and it briefly brings the idea that City might be able to recover sufficient composure and threat to turn this game around in the second half. Teams have been beaten from convincingly one-sided three-goal leads before. We know this, we did this.

City actually threaten us in the second half. It was unavoidable. They have quality and, once Pellegrini makes the changes in shape and personnel that he should have made after twenty minutes, they start to look something like the City we expected, but it's too little, too late. The game has been won with determination and pressing and breaking and speed and passion and skill. It's been won by wanting it more and by surprising the opposition. It's a tactical war between two managers and the one in red has just shown his worth to all around him.

The debate prior to the game revolves around the availability and fitness of Daniel Sturridge, around the viability of fielding him in a two-pronged attack alongside Christian Benteke, the assumption being that the Belgian will lead the line.

Both are on the bench. In their place, we have a three-pronged attack of Firmino, Coutinho and the once again utterly tireless Adam Lallana. Lallana is looking like an ideal Klopp player, the three up front looks like an ideal Klopp formation. It's certainly a formation that has completely confounded the opposition's manager and players. The three are supported by the endless availability of Emre Can and James Milner, all forward motion and pressing and moving and flicking and bringing in others. There's flexibility and adaptability all over the field, we're playing a '4-1-we're coming to get you' and it's gorgeous.

City, for their part, and from the start, have no formation at all. They're a bunch of individuals hoping to weather the oncoming storm and probably the wrong individuals at that. They have nothing. They're lost, dazed. They have absolutely no idea what's happening to them.

As Coutinho dispossesses Sagna to thread a ball which Firmino, racing across the box in the most gloriously counter-intuitive manner, plays back into the path of the hapless Mangala for the French defender to give us the lead, they don't know what's happening to them.

As Lallana tips a header from the halfway line for Firmino, all pace and power and desire and determination and the vision for the pass to Coutinho, which nobody else in the ground can see for the beautiful second goal, they don't know what's happening to them.

As we score that perfect third, they don't know what's happening to them.

As Lallana hunts down a City throw-in to allow Ibe to rampage and set up Benteke for a chance denied by Joe Hart and the Belgian's own lack of substitute zip, they don't know what's happening to them.

But we do. We know, *now* we know, looking back at the highlights, we know, we can see it coming. Benteke hasn't long to wait to make an impact. A Lallana corner, a nod down from big Chris and there's Martin Skrtel redefining the word 'thunderbolt' with the sort of volley that centre-halves dream of.

Now, City know what's happened. We've gone to their place and we've dismantled them. We've set down a marker, we've made an announcement. And we've done it without four of our presumed first eleven: no Sakho, so Lovren steps up to the plate and shows that maybe he *can* do it. No Henderson, so Milner puts in a captain's performance. No Sturridge, not needed, kept on the bench. Benteke only on for ten minutes and he has an assist to his name. We're in the wonderful position where, at three-one up, our manager decides to see out the game by putting on another striker and we get the fourth.

It's special, it's sublime. That first half against Arsenal at Anfield in the 2013/14 season? Possibly even better than that. Unexpected and beautiful and right. There's nothing in it that shocks. It feels like it had to happen. Chelsea then City, it had to happen.

21 November 2015. Mark it: the day Liverpool began again. It all starts here, it all starts with this. It all starts with that third goal.

23 November 2015

The Boys of '65

THERE'S A photo that I've shared on Facebook a few times over the last year. It's a photo that I mentioned a few chapters back when referring to the fact that I'd realised my age mid-match, a photo of three lads who've gone to Wembley to watch Liverpool bring home the FA Cup, the treasured, cherished, anticipated, never-yet-won FA Cup.

They're dressed in overcoats. Other photos from the day show them in shirts and sweaters. The overcoat photo is in black and white, the others are in colour. The colour is very, very predominantly red. The colour photos are in Liverpool, the black and white in London. There's probably a meaning somewhere in that.

They're in Trafalgar Square, feeding pigeons, which have come to rest on their arms. My dad's on the right, the other two men in the photo are my uncle Len and uncle Jimmy. Len is married to my mum's sister, Jimmy is my dad's brother. Two years younger than him. I've noticed now, for the first time despite looking at it many times, that my dad has his hand resting lightly on Jimmy's shoulder. I shared the photo last year when dad passed away. Jimmy loved that photo, his sons had it printed and framed. It's a photo of family and friendship and fandom and it's everything that the three of them were in the middle of the 1960s.

Lenny passed away in 1997 and was much missed by my dad, by all of us but so much by my dad. Jimmy was present last year throughout my dad's illness. I've grown to know him more

153

and know him better now than I ever did before. The older you get, the more you realise that your parents, your uncles, you aunties are just like you. None of us ever grow up. It doesn't matter if you're a man in your late seventies, you're still the same lad you were when you went to London with your mates for the match. I realised in the last year, in visits and chats, that Jimmy was just a genuine, lovely man. There's nothing better in life than that, is there?

Jimmy passed away at four this morning. A year and two weeks after my dad, his brother. It had been expected but it still came as a shock. He held his love of Liverpool all the way.

Good night Jim, sleep well mate.

YNWA.

Liverpool 2 FC Bordeaux 1

26 November 2015

REBIRTHS, REVIVAL, reformations, the things that bring tough decisions. Jurgen Klopp's revitalised mighty Reds are at home tonight against FC Bordeaux (sure we should be getting the phrase 'Girondins de' in there somewhere), with a win guaranteeing qualification for the Europa League knockout stages.

And that's all well and good but I bought a ticket to see legendary Scouse nineties R&B (proper R&B, not the Rihanna nonsense) mavericks, The Stairs, ages ago. Add to the fact that this, their first gig after a twenty-year separation, might be a complete one-off, the fact that it's the last time that I'll attend a show at the stunningly wonderful Kazimier before it's converted to yet more student accommodation for the city centre and you might see the quandary here.

I drop tweets asking if anyone has the stage times. I consider the idea of giving my gig ticket away, but I really want to see these. I don't consider the idea of missing out on Jurgen's mighty Reds. Post-City, that seems like a really bad idea. Anything could happen tonight. It could be glorious. And exactly the same description applies to The Stairs gig. A tweet back: they're on stage at half-nine. Which seriously doesn't work. They'll have been on stage for half an hour before the match actually ends. Add time for walking to car, add further time for driving into town, parking up, walking to the Kaz. I'm not seeing this, am I? I opt for the stupid decision: I'll do both. Even if I only see the last ten minutes of the set. This is the way my mind works sometimes, utter lack of common sense.

The bad news breaks as I'm parking up and heading to the ground. Football-related bad news. Sturridge-related bad news. Bench on Saturday, unused, expected to take some part tonight, sent for a scan instead, reported a problem with his foot after training. This is the point where I drop the endless optimism that I'm aiming for and concede that we're possibly never going to see the best of this lad again. He's looking more and more like a player whose career will crawl towards a premature, underwhelming end on a treatment table, a Jamie Redknapp for the twenty-first century. I really hope I'm wrong on this one, but I'm starting to doubt it.

Of those who were there, it's probably the Christian Benteke show. It's an odd night for the big lad. He doesn't really play particularly well but he has flashes. He seems ponderous but he has bursts. He misses easy chances but pulls off the incredible. He's frustrating at times but he wins the penalty, the very, very soft penalty resulting from the Belgian being held in exactly the manner that we never receive penalties for. It brings our equaliser and then, with genuinely the last kick of the first half and no time to restart, he scores a goal of such genuine class and power that the only sane response is 'what the **** was that?'

It's a take from a Clyne cross, with all the space in the world for the ball to fall and the Belgian to turn and hammer a shot with no apparent back-lift but all the power that you'd wish, and score what turns out to be the winning goal.

He also puts the ball in the back of the net once on either side of that wonder strike. One ruled offside after he nets from a lovely Jordon Ibe through ball, another after the referee bizarrely decides that he's fouled a Bordeaux player in the build-up.

The ref. Yes, the ref. Let's do the ref, shall we? It's okay to say it as we've won. There's no possibility of anybody claiming sour grapes when you've won. It was possibly the single worst refereeing performance that I've ever seen. Clueless in every way imaginable. Bordeaux players fall over? They receive free kicks. A Bordeaux player jumps for a ball, lands on James Milner? He receives a free kick. The ref is spectacularly wrong in almost everything that he does.

Ironically, the one decision that he manages to get right doesn't help us at all, but that's okay because Simon Mignolet isn't helping us at all with this one, either.

Mignolet receives the ball, looks to play it forward. Nothing on, no movement that pleases him. Looks again. And again and again. For a full twenty seconds, which is slightly longer than the six which are allowed. Presumably nobody thought to acquaint Si with this specific rule. Indirect free kick. A touch to the left and it's in the top-right corner. And that's how we go behind, by shooting ourselves in the foot. Again.

It's the kind of free kick that you know should be given but very rarely see, although most teams'goalkeepers don't embrace the bizarre as willingly as Simon seems to. January beckons and there aren't many who would be shocked at the sight of a new goalkeeper on the shopping list.

Two-one up at half-time, the game's pretty much put to bed. All that remains is a combination of slightly missed chances and bizarre decisions from the officials. It's not the glory of City away, it's a six- or seven-out-of-ten home European game full of six- or seven-out-of-ten performances and nice cameos from Joe Allen and Kolo Toure, showing a strength to the squad that we sometimes forget. It ensures that we progress to the knock-out stages, where we will inevitably meet Dortmund at some point. In a big stadium in Switzerland with a shiny trophy sitting on the touchline would be nice. Job done, six- or seven-out-of-ten will do.

The Stairs, though? They're inventing new numbers to describe The Stairs' set. I nearly give up during the walk to the car, nearly give up in the traffic in Scotland Road, nearly give up at the lights across London Road. Ask at the door 'have I missed them yet?', to be told 'there's a bit left'.

I get half an hour and it's incendiary. It's massive and powerful and psychedelic and bluesy and it has to happen again and again and again and you can't quite figure out why the world doesn't know these four lads. Apparently, the ten songs that I missed by refusing to leave the match before the final whistle were just as stunning. Principles, got to have principles.

26 November. Decent night, all told.

Liverpool 1 Swansea 0

29 November 2015

FRIDAY MORNING. Jurgen Klopp gives his pre-Swansea press conference and he drops a bomb. Daniel needs to learn the difference between 'real pain' and 'just pain' apparently. On Thursday night, he knew very little about the injury. By Friday, he knows enough to decide it's not actually an injury and that Sturridge should sort himself out. The fact that the forward appears on the bench on Sunday afternoon is quite surprising and possibly indicative of Klopp's attitude sinking in a little.

The fact that he's accompanied by Jordan Henderson is equally shocking. All indications were that the captain was still a few weeks away from making his Klopp-era debut. By the end of the game, we've experienced cameos from both, although neither make any great impact.

It's a nothing game. It's a game where we're not particularly bad, not particularly good. There are a lot of players who look as though they're not really at the races, although the fact that they're playing in what basically amounts to a hurricane might hold some influence here. Firmino looks 'leggy'. He looked leggy against Bordeaux. The expectation was that he would start on the bench today, with Joe Allen – withdrawn early against Bordeaux – taking a midfield berth. Lallana's in midfield. Sometimes. Sometimes he's not. Things move round. Firmino and Ibe, excellent again, are behind Benteke but too far behind Benteke. The lad's too isolated.

It looks, to me at least, at the moment, as though Benteke will be a season-long conundrum. He doesn't have the movement that you would expect from a Klopp player. He certainly doesn't have the mobility and flexibility that we saw in the Firmino/Coutinho/Lallana interplay at City, but there are moments, there are flashes. You can see him hanging on the shoulder of a defender, flexed, tensed, ready to move, on his toes, waiting, gesturing for the right ball. The right ball doesn't come. Communication might resolve this. We might be looking at the building of understanding and patterns in a squad which is still learning about itself.

If we are, then we might be in a very, very hopeful place right now. As underwhelming as the Swansea win was, it was a win. More specifically it was all of the following:

A win on a Sunday after a European game on a Thursday night.

Our third win on the bounce.

Our third win in eight days.

Jurgen Klopp's first home league win.

All of these are obviously very good things. All of these are the things that you hope the game will be when you set out, when you walk under the new stand with the wind howling through its architecture, when you take your seat with the cold biting at your face. You might hope for record scores, you might hope for drama and flair, you might think, as I did, after we finally score with another fairly kind penalty (look, if you jump with your arms out then you're going to concede penalties) that we'll go on and net two or three more, but ultimately all you want is the win.

There's a worry in the way that we once again revert to panic immediately after taking the lead. There's a worry in the number of corners that we concede to Swansea in the closing minutes, even if there's calm in the aftermath, when you realise that the visitors didn't manage a single shot on goal, but above all there's satisfaction in the grinding out of a necessary win.

And it was a weekend for grinding out a necessary win. The kick-off was preceded by a minute's applause for Gerry Byrne, who had passed away on the Saturday, a man so committed to the cause that having Bob Paisley diagnose Byrne's collarbone as broken in the second minute of the 1965 FA Cup Final drew the response 'don't tell anyone' and saw him complete the game. Ensuring the win seems to be in his spirit.

More prosaically, for once, every result that we needed to 'go for us' went for us and we capitalised on the situation, which we never do.

Everton dropped two points at Bournemouth in the time added on for the pitch invasion that met them netting the apparent winner after dropping their initial two-goal lead. Unlike every other Red on the planet, I'm taking no pleasure in that just in case my wife reads this. City won, but that's okay. We've had them. United and Spurs cancelled each other out quite beautifully in a stultifyingly dull game. Arsenal surrendered their lead to Norwich and saw more influential injuries hit them as Sanchez limped from the field clutching his hamstring. West Ham drew, Southampton lost.

Suddenly, we're in the dizzying heights of sixth but only two points off fourth and, crucially, only six points behind the leaders. Most importantly, we've played everybody that you'd consider problematic away from home. Everybody around us now has to visit us. Might be a decent time to start making our home form as impressive as our recent away performances. Grinding out a win in the teeth of a storm seems like a start.

Southampton 1 Liverpool 6

Capital One Cup Quarter-Final
2 December 2015

I HADN'T even sat down when it happened. Not sat down at St Mary's, watching at home on Sky. I was in the kitchen, pouring wine, a civilised drink for an evening's viewing. The roar went up, clearly the roar of substantially more than the three thousand travelling fans.

"You. Are. Fucking. Kidding."

No, they weren't. Or, possibly, Emre Can and Alberto Moreno were. Can makes this bizarre leap that he thinks might be an interception in our right-back position, the Southampton man steps round him, makes Can look foolish in the extreme, and slings a cross in. Mane loses Moreno with the ease that forwards in the box tend to lose Moreno and heads home. Forty seconds in and it looks as though we're going out of this competition, as though Jurgen is getting a second loss against his record. That's how I felt. I doubted. Look at the chapter heading if you've forgotten. I was wrong, I was very, very wrong.

I'd been busy. Things to do, much of it revolving around watching the process of Parliament as David Cameron dragged us towards a war which will last until our children are old enough to worry about their own grandchildren's futures and will play out everywhere but the lands that he's decided he needs to impose air strikes on. I'd seen the team, but not the bench. Knew Randall was playing but not that Clyne was having the night off. Finding that out worried me, particularly since Randall was being found out with every Southampton attack, targeted at every opportunity and once again found wanting. Initially. Found wanting initially. It's the 'initially' that's important. Tip for opposition teams — if you see Randall on the pitch try and get past him in the first twenty shaky minutes. After that, he's immaculate.

Which is a perfect summation of Liverpool's evening: shaky for twenty, immaculate thereafter.

Southampton's first goal looks as though it will be followed by more of the same. We look lost, shaken, at odds with ourselves, clueless, lacking in creativity, lacking in resolve. And then we don't any more. Then we're in the game. It's as though a switch is flicked and suddenly everybody understands what they're there for.

It starts with Sturridge. First start under Klopp, totally unexpected, all the supposedly smart money was on a cameo from the bench. He gets an hour but his important work is done in the space of four minutes. A pass brimming with beautiful intent from Joe Allen elicits a heavy touch from Sturridge, taking him wider than anticipated, and a yell of 'dog of a first touch' from a still-disbelieving me, then he shuffles, shuffles again and shoots. The angle's ridiculous, the finish gorgeous.

The second is better. Emre atones for his bizarre first-minute challenge with a drag back through his own legs to lose his marker, a quick dart and perfect lob. Sturridge meets it with his first touch. Through Stekelenburg's legs, hopefully with a cry of 'megs', and nestling nicely in the net. The Daniel Sturridge show has done its job and we're comfortable.

We're more comfortable after the third. Last minute of the half, a Lallana corner looks overhit before Alberto Moreno seeks his own salvation with a shot that appears to be a glorious goal until replays show that a distinctly onside Divock Origi has touched the ball on its way past his position a foot from the line.

As first goals for your team go, it's slightly mundane. His second goal, though? That's something, that's the player that we thought we were spending ten million on. Ibe hits the field on the hour mark. You know this, you haven't forgotten this. The substitute for the Sturridge show, an hour being enough for the night, point proven. Ibe slots a perfect ball to the edge of the area, Origi hits it first time and it's basically world class. Genuinely. If it happened in an international we'd be talking about it for weeks. If Wayne Rooney scored it, we'd never hear the end of it, if Anthony Martial scored it, Sky would declare at that moment and never broadcast football again. Honest to God, that good. You haven't forgotten this.

The fifth is more Moreno atonement, a cross to Ibe, a chest, a slam. Looking immaculate. Can't use the word immaculate often enough, it's all that works. The sixth is Brad Smith and Divock Origi. Anybody have money on that combination? I didn't even know Smith was on the bench, wasn't sure he was still at the club. Turns out that he *wasn't* still at the club, he'd been let go and then negotiated a new deal. Call this one a rebirth. Last time we saw him, Brendan Rodgers was sacrificing his promise and potential at Stamford Bridge. Rodgers' seeming decision to play the lad out of position in order to prove a point about limited resources looked to have destroyed Smith's chances of a Liverpool career. This sublime cross providing Divock Origi with the completion of a perfect hat-trick might be the start of something else. It's certainly a chance.

There had been ten minutes after half-time when Southampton changed their shape and looked as though they might threaten to pull a second goal back. Our fourth, though? Our fourth ended that idea. We eased past the tattered, demoralised Saints, our six changes, our 'weakened' team, decimating the strongest side that they could field. We took that initial setback and we responded, we responded magnificently. We played football, scored goals. Players were given opportunities and they took them. It's all you can ask for.

You can't understate what we did here, we went to a tough opponent, made changes, rotated, played a new formation, 4-4-2 diamond and let's be honest here, I didn't spot that. I thought we were going with a flexible 4-3-3 but the boss says it's a diamond so I'm not going to argue, and we made the whole thing look comfortable.

The evening was about surprises: personnel, formation, performance, quality, confidence. The evening was about the clinical: seven shots on target, six of those in the back of the net. The evening was about intent. This, again and again and again, is what we can do.

Newcastle 2 Liverpool 0

6 December 2015

WHERE WE all come to earth with a bump.

It had been such a good weekend up until that point. Friday night, had been out drinking with old mates. Intended to have a few beers, arrived at the bar to find that we were ordering the best bottle of red on the menu. Gloriously messy from there on. Saturday had been an incredible set from Ian Prowse's Amsterdam, with their Christmas homecoming gig becoming a two-hour force of nature that passed in the blink of an eye. Saturday had been getting home near midnight and catching up on the excellent Dr Who season finale accompanied by a nice glass of white or three, making for a fine end to the day. Sunday was relaxing and then we kicked off.

Jurgen summed it up best himself in the post-match press conference: What went wrong? Everything. The beginning, the middle, the end. And, speaking on Alberto Moreno's thoroughly wrongly disallowed wonder finish: the linesman thought that you were not allowed to create world-class goals if you play this shit.

He's up for some world-class swearing at the moment is Jurgen. Showing a marvellous grasp of Anglo-Saxon with his very, very accurate summation of our performance as being 'shit' following hard on the heels of his 'I can't forget about this fucking loss to Crystal Palace' comment. If Palace concerned him, then God knows what this one's going to do to his mind.

Liverpool were abject. As devoid of ideas, as desperately poor as the worst moments of the end of Brendan Rodgers' reign, possibly actually worse, every bad habit back with a bang. No creativity, no urgency, no invention, a stark reminder that these were the players who looked so poor before Klopp's arrival.

And yet, and yet...

Panic set in the moment the game ended, the fanbase divided itself again. Those who had ridiculed those of us who had started talking about title charges found vindication in the loss, found some kind of satisfaction in watching their own team concede two goals to a Newcastle side that had struggled for identity all season. There was talk of us not wanting it, talk of complacency. The truth is that the team worked as hard as it had in far more successful games, the defence solid, the midfield pressing. When Newcastle had the ball, we lunged at them in pairs. Unfortunately, they did exactly the same to us and were more effective in doing so.

The truth is that the Newcastle display had nothing to do with complacency and was far more concerned with players simply not imposing themselves on the game. Add to this the fact that, for the first time, Jurgen simply got his game plan pretty damn wrong.

The 4-4-2 diamond that had proven so spectacular at Southampton disappeared, to be replaced by the far less attractive 4-2-3-1 'Christmas tree' shape in a forlorn nod to the imminent festive season. Lucas and Allen held. Which is quite probably one holding midfielder more than was strictly necessary in the situation. Ibe, wonderful when he came on against the Saints, ran from both right and left, Firmino took the centre and completely failed to link up with Benteke, who had a bafflingly static game, and James Milner was so anonymous that I've just had to consult the website to discover the identity of the eleventh man.

Milner, as ever, works hard but chose today to offer little positive contribution again. Ibe ran, looked for options, found none, ran again, looked again, ran and repeat until frustration.

Not with the lad – the lad was one bright spark in a dismal afternoon – but with the lack of options offered in front of him.

Nothing worked. We gifted Newcastle a first with a deflected cross looping off Martin Skrtel's knee, gave them a second with a counter when we were pushing everything forward and introduced Sturridge, Lallana and Origi too late to provide the cutting edge we needed. We saw a perfectly good – no let's be honest, an incredible – Alberto Moreno goal chalked offside by yet more fallible officiating, but were in no position to complain as we didn't really deserve that moment of class (see Jurgen's comments earlier about 'being shit').

A bad day, a bad loss. They happen. To everyone. The distressing aspect of this is that the entire world seemed to write off Liverpool's season before the final whistle. We'd built an inflated sense of our abilities, built a myth about our potential and now we were exposed.

One way of looking at it all. Another way is that we lost a game that we shouldn't have, we're nine points away from the top when we could have remained six, we're six points behind City when we could have been three. We failed to take advantage of the teams around us dropping points and, instead, dropped points of our own, bringing the screams of 'same old Liverpool, build us up just to let us down', which are always so joyous to hear.

This loss could be important, could be vital, if we treat it as the learning experience that it needs to be.

Perhaps the rotation of the entire front three isn't as necessary as it seemed. Perhaps a midfield containing Lucas, Allen and Milner isn't as mobile or incisive as we need it to be. Certainly the absence of both the suspended Can and a Jordan Henderson who is clearly being treated with serious kid gloves wiped all urgency from that part of the pitch. Perhaps, at the moment, Firmino is only effective when partnered with Coutinho. Perhaps, and I think this is a big one, Firmino and Benteke can't play together.

Which brings us back to the Benteke conundrum. Far and away the worst player on the pitch and I genuinely have no idea whether it was his fault, the fault of the players around him for failing to provide the appropriate service or the formation. I do know that when the ball drops to him two feet from an open goal, he should place it gently in the net rather than scoop it over the bar. There's very little excuse for not taking that kind of chance.

The joy of writing this episodically is that there's every chance I'll be proven wrong with another world-class strike from the lad by the weekend. I have no intention of revisiting this opinion if that happens, but as we stand you can only think that Christian Benteke is rapidly becoming fourth-choice striker at the club. Sturridge is obviously number one, with Ings and Origi both far better suited to the system and style that Klopp wants to play than the lad we paid the big money for.

Work to do, then, but not the outright disaster that many want to portray it as. We move on from this. It'd be nice if people would make the effort to believe that. Shame it ruined a perfectly good weekend, though.

And after? What happened after? Well, Everton drew with Crystal Palace on the Monday night, which meant that Palace went up to sixth and we dropped to eighth, now six points from the top four. Ground lost but not too much and Everton stayed below us. Small mercies, and all that.

And then Daniel Sturridge's hamstring went. I say 'then' as apparently it happened during his cameo at Newcastle. I'm currently in the mood to blame Benteke based on the idea that if he'd been any better on the night then we wouldn't have had to risk Sturridge. Does that seem unfair? Not that bothered.

FC Sion 0 Liverpool 0

10 December 2015

NOTHING HAPPENED. Nothing at all. We went to Switzerland, hit Sion at roughly the same time that Geneva went into full-on terror alert, armed guards at the UN and everything, apparently (although the reports vanished as quickly as they appeared), came away with a draw, won the group that we had already qualified from. And nothing happened.

Fielded a strong team. Stronger than we needed to, given the fact that the only people who seemed less interested in the match than us were the home team. And nothing happened.

Brad Smith played well. Firmino didn't. The former's performance adds promise, the latter's doesn't really signal anything. Still not sure if the Manchester City version of Firmino is the real one or not so I'm going to assume that it is, if that's all the same with everybody else. Optimism and all that.

Henderson made his first start under Klopp, Coutinho came back from injury. Neither did a great deal because nothing happened. We played ninety minutes, plus added time that nobody on the planet wanted, on a frozen pitch (left-hand side actually covered in ice) and nothing happened.

The stats show twelve attempts on goal. Six per side. Don't remember a single one. Fell asleep on the couch. Twice. In the first half. Possibly the worst game of football I've ever seen. Utterly pointless.

In the knock-out stage, don't need to play another Europa fixture until next year, it was only ninety minutes out of my life that I won't get back. Still. Nothing happened.

Liverpool 2 WBA 2

13 December 2015

CONTEXT. CONTEXT is everything. So, here's some context:

Friday. Friday was the Bunnymen. Two nights at the Academy in town. First night booked was Saturday but it was announced about a week before they played Sefton Park in August and I wasn't in a 'buying tickets for the gig after next' mood, so I missed out. By the time I felt like shelling out, Saturday was sold out. Luckily they added a Friday. Hate missing The Bunnymen, think it's only happened twice since 1981. And they were immense. As always. Still one of the best live bands on the planet, even if they rarely play more than ninety minutes, even if they rarely surprise you with the set list. It's usually pretty obvious, usually touches all the bases for the classics and the hits, although they seem to have decided *The Back Of Love* isn't for them any more. Gutted to find out that they played *Heads Will Roll* on Saturday night, though. *Ocean Rain* as well. We didn't get *Ocean Rain* on Friday but *Heads Will Roll*? Haven't seen them do that in decades. Sods.

Saturday? Saturday was Michael Head at the Florrie in The Dingle. South Liverpool. Pretty sure my dad lived in the road the Florrie sits on when he was a kid and as it used to be a school he might have even gone there. No idea, wish I'd known.

Mick was, again as always, impeccable. Damn fine night out with good mates. Even if Shack's *Comedy* appeared on the setlist but didn't actually make it to the night, as someone decided to call for the as yet unreleased *Queen Of All Saints*, wonderful but *Comedy* is something else altogether.

All of which set Sunday up for an afternoon of drinking at *The Anfield Wrap* pre-match bevvie and Jurgen Klopp's first encounter with the beautiful game as practised by Tony Pulis.

That's my context. Shall we go with Liverpool's?

We're not playing well at home, we didn't play well at Newcastle, we've just put in the most non-existent performance of all time in Switzerland and then had to fly back, entailing time needed to recover from both game and travel, before playing on Sunday. And we're playing a Tony Pulis side, which always means packed defences, big lads alternating between falling over and kicking our lads and endless, endless, endless, time-wasting.

And our home fans aren't exactly burning with the fervour of blind loyalty at the moment. Or even the gentle murmur of content and hope. We're a touch poisonous at times. I might have mentioned this.

Jurgen's in the papers on the Saturday saying that we might see the best atmosphere in ten years at today's game. Seems unlikely when we go in. Gets less likely as we progress toward throwing away a lead, and then something happens.

And it's the 'something happens' bit that makes Jurgen Klopp do what he does, what he did. The thing that he did that divided us just a touch. Right, let's do the 'something happens' bit, then. The first twenty are great. We have purpose, we have passion, we're playing our way through the typical Pulis 'dogs of war' midfield. We look threatening, we look like we're going to do this. This time, it looks like we're going to do this.

We score first and it's lovely. It's a Coutinho lobbed cross for Lallana (yes, Lallana, rising above a pretty damn big defender) to head down into the path of the arriving Jordan Henderson. Yes, a midfielder arriving into the box and sweeping the ball into the net. Hasn't happened a lot recently.

And our heads don't fall off. We go ahead and our heads don't fall off. We look for a second, we press for a second. And then there's a corner and there's Simon Mignolet flapping at the ball as it passes by him and there's a drop in the box and there's confusion and an equaliser and James Milner is on the floor with his head in his hands and nobody knows if he's injured or in despair.

And the team stand and trudge, genuinely *trudge*, back to the centre circle as though the idea of kicking off is the worst thing in the world. Shoulders are down, heads are down. Heads have gone, heads have fallen off, fallen right off.

It gets grim. There's the second West Brom goal just before half-time and it's offside but only offside because there are three West Brom players clearly, blatantly, offside when the free kick floats in. None of our lads appeal for it, though. Their heads aren't in the space where you appeal for things. Nobody's entirely sure who gives the offside. The ref doesn't seem to give it and the linesman definitely doesn't give it. Until both of them do after protracted discussion. Pulis is livid.

The second half is poor. The second goal is poor. The second goal is another corner. The second goal is another poorly defended corner. It comes in, Olsson flicks it and it's in. Mignolet's less culpable on this one, but still...

The lad's a great shot stopper but against a Pulis team you won't have to deal with shots, you'll have to deal with crosses and punts and he can't. He just can't. And the crowd is poisonous again. At least, around me the crowd is poisonous again. Insults are raining.

There's a tackle. There's a loose tackle on Lovren and the lad who, let's be honest, looks like he might be pretty hard, is rolling and screaming. From where I am, it looks like a leg-breaker. The substitution is inspired, not Toure, who remains on the bench, but Origi. Reshuffle time, Can in defence and we're going for it. Ibe to one side, Origi to the other, the perplexing Benteke in the centre.

An aside here: Benteke starts well, a couple of things *nearly* happen for him but there are blocks and interceptions and after that it's long balls to his head and no invention. He might have something that will work for us, but we're not letting him show it.

There's an impetus, an impetus that's aided by the eight minutes of extra time provided by the Lovren injury and suddenly the push is an onslaught and the crowd are (mostly) completely behind the team. One or two voices of dissent, but otherwise…

The Origi equaliser is fortuitous in its conclusion, the ball skewing wickedly from a defender's back, but immaculate in the fact that he tried, that he rode a tackle he could easily have gone down for and got a shot in. It's the wanting it, it's all about the wanting it. And we want a third. All of us, those on the pitch, those in the stands, we want a third. And the manager most of all. He's whipping the crowd up, he's waving wildly, he's cupping his ears. He's arguing with Pulis, which is always nice. There's not enough time, though. The third doesn't come, the final whistle does and we're standing and leaving and it's all 'two points dropped but a point rescued' and applauding, half-turned towards the pitch, as we file to the narrow exits and then it happens.

Klopp's on the pitch and he's pulling together everybody in red and he's dragging them to the Kop and they're starting to grasp each other's hands and lift.

And this is the moment that social media decides to ridicule, this is the moment that every opposition fan, and specifically the other half of this city, rains disdain on. This is the bit they don't get.

I get it. I think I get it. Right away. It's not a celebration. It's *not* a celebration. Celebrating a two-all draw, a two-all escape, against a mid-table team would be ridiculous. It's not necessarily a thank-you. There's a thank-you in there but it's not just a thank-you. The fans didn't pull the team through, the team didn't pull the fans through. Something clicked, something happened. The linking, raising, saluting? It's an acknowledgement. It's an acknowledgement that we're all in this together. It's acknowledging the fact that the fans stayed, that they didn't desert in droves as they did when Palace took their lead. They stayed and they got behind their team and their team responded. And that's what happens. That's what happens when everything moves as one. This is how you *create* a turning point, this is how you change your season. You get people on your side. Jurgen's done this with the team, now he's done this with the fans. Everybody loved him already. This took the next step. This is the moment that everybody was *with him*. It's a masterful moment of management and other teams' supporters are seriously not going to get this.

There's no reason for us to care. Let others scoff. He's our manager and small moments like this are where he makes a long-term difference.

A complete contrast to Thursday: something happened here.

Watford 3 Liverpool 0

20 December 2015

TWO WORDS, two numbers, adding up to bloody desperate reading. This is the up and down bit, isn't it? This is the middle of the plot, this is the main character being tested, this is his belief being questioned, this is the challenge. Appropriately, since I saw *Star Wars: The Force Awakens* between the end of the last chapter and the start of this one (quite magnificent, thank you, does everything that you want a *Star Wars* film to do), this is the *Empire Strikes Back* moment, everybody fractured, some gathered for support, others vanished and looking for solutions to insoluble problems, seemingly nothing but despair ahead.

Still, *Empire* turned out fairly well as it shifted into *Jedi*. Maybe this will. Without all the sodding teddy bears, obviously. Looking rough at the moment, though. All this time that we've been lamenting the lack of opportunity that Klopp has had to work with the squad, we've been pinning our hopes on the idea that 'when we hit the easier run, when we have a week between games, that's when it will all kick in'. That was a week between games. So, what happened? The worst Liverpool performance of the season. By a very long way. One down after three minutes. Adam Bogdan has his chance to prove right those who claim he can't be any worse than Simon Mignolet and he decides that the best way to do that is by showing he's actually less secure on corners than the sidelined Belgian. Yes, Ake kicks the ball from our ginger reserve keeper's hands, but only after he's fumbled an easy catch, only after he's dropped the most inviting ball a lurking Watford lad could wish for.

The second's not his fault. The second's Skrtel's fault. It's a ball lobbed over the top. It's not even a particularly long ball. It's a ball that Skrtel should deal with. He's neck and neck with their lad, but he's not strong enough, he's brushed aside too easily, always on the back foot, never at the races. Two down. Before half-time. At Watford. Our 4-3-3 which prospered against City is found out in the most disastrous manner by a Watford team who embrace the most old-fashioned of 4-4-2s. We're out-fought, out-thought, out-played. There are ten minutes at the start of the second half when some Jordan Henderson-inspired mobility looks as though it might drag us back into a game that we didn't deserve to be in. But that fizzles.

Origi's on for an injured Skrtel, which not only gives us the bizarre sight of Lucas as a centre-back, a positional change which means he has a terrible game in both midfield and defence, but also the terrifying concept that our only currently fully fit centre-back is Kolo Toure, who the manager doesn't want to put on the field.

Origi at least *looks* as though he might trouble the hosts. But that fizzles. Benteke and Ibe emerge in the seventieth minute, which probably tells us all we need to know about the manager's opinion of our current number nine. He might deny morning rumours that the Belgian is on his way to Chelsea in the January window, but surely the only discrepancy here could be destination and timing? The 'out' side of the claims looks pretty accurate. He adds very little. Again. Possibly poetic as he is the direct replacement for Firmino, who also added nothing to the game other than a whole new definition for the word 'anonymous'. Nobody emerges with credit. We're second best in every area. To Watford. Nothing against Watford, they're a decent team, playing well and on a good run. But. Watford. They're Watford. We're second best to Watford. Our pressing game appears to have disappeared. Watford have it. And they're better at it than us. United and Everton drop points on the Saturday, we fans laugh and look to capitalise. We stop laughing very quickly.

Three-nil away from home to a team that we should be expected to handle with relative ease. A third goal which is nothing more than a formality. We don't turn up, we don't want it enough, we don't demonstrate ability or passion. It's pitiful. And suddenly, the week between games is the last thing that we need. A week to work on this shambles before we return to Anfield to host the league leaders Leicester.

Seriously weird season.

Liverpool 1 Leicester 0

26 December 2015

SO, AS Christmas passes by and we do the festive programme thing, where do we stand with this 'seriously weird season'? Mourinho's gone, courtesy of a defeat by Claudio Ranieri, himself the first in a long line of Chelski sackings since Roman bought his little toy and now in charge of the lads who are visiting us today. Hiddink's in at Chelsea. Again. Maybe this is the Chelsea way now, recycling old managers for a second crack. Jose's fall was almost Shakespearian, a character brought down by his own inherent flaws, in this case his absolute arrogance and the fact that he always gets found out in his third season. Doesn't do legacies, Jose. Hiddink's a worry, though. Mourinho in charge until the end of the season and we were looking at relegation. Guus might get the lads to mid-table.

The other worry in this situation is that Jose is clearly going to walk into Old Trafford and do his usual two-year job, rescuing the United boys from the current LVG comedy show. Definitely preferred the status quo on this one.

Us, though? Where are we? The team that failed to show up at Watford and Newcastle and against West Brom vanished today. Hopefully a turning point, again, a sea change. A permanent one this time with a bit of luck.

We're more inventive today. More traditional as well. Traditional seems a decent thing against a side as traditional as Leicester. They do 4-4-2 so we do 4-4-2. At times. At other times we do other things. We're pretty much bare bones. Sturridge is 'having a pre-season' apparently. After the game, he'll tweet about the great three points and say that he's 'ready to go'. Klopp will say he isn't. Jurgen's not being tempted. Jurgen doesn't want to be talking about Daniel Sturridge in ten years' time, he wants to sort out the issues now, wants him in the most intensive training of his career but doesn't want to risk him in matches.

He's had a conversation with Benteke. A 'man conversation', it would seem. Christian 'knows what he needs to do'. Which appears to be 'sit on the bench'. We start with Origi up top, Firmino closest to him and it looks as though it might work. He's threatening, he's moving, he's doing the pace and the power. Until he does his hamstring and, supposedly 'knowing what he needs to do' big Chris enters the fray.

We get both versions of our expensive Belgian: we get the one that puts the ball in the back of the net from a delightful Firmino ball – honest to god, 'Firmino', 'delightful' and 'ball' all in the same sentence, not quite the 'City' Firmino but the best he's been since then. Perhaps we should give the lad time to settle? Look at Ozil: all the snap judgements last year had it that he was lazy and uninterested. Amazing what a year can do isn't it? Quality has a tendency to reappear. Maybe adaptation to the Premier League is an actual thing?

The instinctive Benteke wins us the game, the Benteke that has time to think about things fails to double his tally in the last seconds as Kasper Schmeichel takes the 'goalie goes up for the corner' route and we break. Four of our lads in the Leicester half when the ball comes forward from the left-back position and only one of the opposition's defenders. Which I'm pretty sure constitutes offside, but what the hell. We charge, the goal's inevitable. Until Benteke clips it straight at the defender's feet. Cue seconds of panic as the entire ground can see a Leicester equaliser loom.

Doesn't happen. Obviously. It seems odd to be celebrating a one-goal victory over Leicester, but that's what we're doing and we're pretty damn justified in doing it. We've been strong, resolute, we've created, shown purpose, shown determination. Jurgen says that we were too complicated in our approach to

Watford. We simplified things for this one. Simplification works, might be worth trying more often. A few more goals might be nice as well.

Can't take this away from us, though — first team all season to stop Leicester from scoring. Actually a fairly major thing. It's odd. They've rocked up at Anfield and we've looked at them and, in the flesh, unedited for TV, they're genuinely nothing special, but we're the first team to stop them scoring. We've stopped Vardy and Mahrez, who have both been devastating. Stopped them to the point that they're both pulled and replaced with big lads so that they can lump it forward and play percentages. Lovren and Sakho (our only fit central defenders if you ignore Kolo, who's clearly not getting a game) have dealt with everything at the back, Hendo and Can have looked like a real partnership whether in the middle of a four or sitting behind a three and Chris (now our only fit striker if you ignore Dan's claims for the moment, as Jurgen is clearly doing) scored one but could have had a hat-trick.

They look like small victories, sound like small victories. It's down to us to make sure they're not. Time to make all the small victories count.

Sunderland 0 Liverpool 1

30 December 2015

West Ham United 2 Liverpool 0

2 January 2016

FULL DISCLOSURE. I'm fond of full disclosure. I could pretend that I'd written a chapter on the Sunderland game on New Year's Eve – which was my intention, giving a little shine to a performance that could be best described as perfunctory but containing a little hope and some positives — and then followed with a more depressing piece on the West Ham game this morning (January 3, if you're wondering, waiting for the moment when I'm needed to run wife and son to Goodison for a game versus Spurs that might see Everton move ahead of us into the giddy heights of mid-table), but the depression from the latter would seep into the former and infect it with the dread of the coming year.

I think it's probably apt, perhaps vital, to talk about the two games together with the former managing to both hide and signal the woes of the latter. I'm fairly certain that there's a symbolism in the two acting as a piece, so let's see if we can dig for that symbolism together, shall we?

This is how the old year ended:

There had been an *Anfield Wrap* recording in the afternoon, a quiz, a moment that I'd been dreading, knowing that my limited memory of basically anything was to be exposed to the world. I somehow managed to finish second of five despite being very clear that I'd consider anything other than last place a major success. A fortuitous run on remembering the shape of Jamie Redknapp's injury-strewn Anfield career and the ability to describe Troy Deeney as 'the Watford lad who thinks he's got bigger balls than he has' on the day that he decided to call out Liverpool's *inabilities*, in one of those 'describe the word on the paper to your partner' rounds made me look more informed than I actually am.

Drinks followed. Watching the game on TV with drinks followed. The Hope and Anchor, on the corner of Maryland Street, which I'm fairly certain held part of the former students' union, which I gigged at in 1985. Then another recording, where we talked about immediate reactions to the game that we had just endured.

We came out looking like we were ready for a fight, ready to battle for the right to play football, always a good thing against a Sunderland side, always a necessity against an Allardyce team. We looked like we were ready for the fight. We just didn't look like we knew exactly how to conduct it. There was energy, there was determination. All that was lacking was application. And shape. And system. And some kind of connection between the lads who are supposed to stop the goals going in at one end and the lads who are supposed to put them in the net at the other.

There's an excuse: we're down to the last men standing and seeing Henderson leave the pitch with a recurrence of the heel issue that the papers claim is untreatable and kept him from Klopp's initial teams didn't help. The injury situation would have been difficult if we were in mid-October. In the depths of the 'who figures out when we play these games?' festive season, it's bordering on the ludicrous. Sat in the pub watching this kind of 'non-game', I asked the obvious question: 'Can you remember any other season like this one for injuries?' The answer came quickly: 'The Boersma season.' The season that Souness brought his mate in to do the training and hamstrings snapped all over the shop. It could be that Klopp's famous double sessions are taking their toll, could be that these lads just weren't fit enough, that the casualties are a necessary by-product of improving them for next season. It could be that we're seeing the true shape of the rebuild process and that this true shape might involve accepting that the hopes of a few weeks ago are going to have to be tempered.

We have one fit striker and he doesn't seem to have anything in common with any of the players behind him. We're playing a 4-2-3-1 but the '2' only seems to work if it's Henderson and Can. With those two, we have a drive from midfield, we have forward thrust. With Lucas in place of either, we lose momentum. The '2' doesn't link with the '3' in front of them — in the case of Sunderland, we're talking Firmino, Coutinho and Lallana — and those three don't seem to link together at all despite the hope that the City performance gave. Firmino is becoming an almost Benteke-level puzzle. He seems to be capable of either the sublime or the ridiculous but nothing in between the two. Against Sunderland, he's capable of a beautiful shot which is tipped on to the post by the keeper. Ten minutes earlier, he's also capable of playing the ball on to his own knee and then into touch. The idea that he only plays well when linked with his compatriot Coutinho also appears to be a myth. The two aren't linking here and Philippe has reverted to his early-season stance of 'I don't trust anybody else so I'll take shots from anywhere'.

Extenuating stuff again: the fact that there's a big lad up front who's alternating between not moving and moving in the wrong direction can't be helping the focus of any of our several number tens. I'm rapidly losing patience with Benteke. Don't see how it's possible for him to ever fit any pattern of what we'd consider to be Liverpool play, but there's this one thing that he can do pretty well at times – he puts the ball in the back of the net. He has a decent second half against Sunderland, possibly not the half that you'd want to see him have in the position that he's supposed to be playing, but decent nevertheless. He's scored within twenty-three seconds of the second half starting and he carries out some fine work as he drifts wide and picks up the ball, as he drops deep and picks up the ball. He looks natural in his desire to link up play. Unfortunately, there's nobody to link with. The lad needs a partner. Unfortunately, all the prospective partners are injured. We have a broken squad. A Firmino might be the answer up front with him, but he's carrying his own frustrations, some of which are *his* desire to drop deep and wide for the ball. Dropping deep and wide is a big thing for us at the moment, direct and fast isn't. Direct and fast needs to be.

We get the other side of Benteke again as we aim for the final whistle, one on one with the keeper for the second game running, hits straight at the keeper for the second game running. Frustrating but probably man of the match. Complain about him, give him man of the match, truly odd situation.

Sideshow moment – Klopp falls out with Allardyce over a truly horrendous foul on Sakho, tells 'Big Sam' to 'fucking sit down'. Which is great. Klopp has had touchline disputes with three opposition managers now: Allardyce, Pulis and Pardew. If you'd polled Liverpool supporters over who we'd like our manager to not get along with, it would have been those three. In that order.

So, talking about it on the podcast, kind of came to the conclusion that it was frustrating but we ground it out. That there are clearly issues here but that one-nil wins will do to disguise them.

Then we head to West Ham and the disguises don't work any longer.

There's one change to the team: Ibe in for Lallana. Presumably the idea is that we get forward with pace and get the ball in to Benteke. That idea's supported by the fact that we're playing Moreno forward as often as possible. Nobody appears to have told Benteke about this: he's dropping deep. Not wide, just deep. He's as static as they come. West Ham have Andy Carroll up front and he's looking far more mobile than our current number nine. The two most expensive players in Liverpool history both on the pitch at the same time, neither very good and only one looking likely to score. Which he obviously does, West Ham's second, a deep cross from their right, into the box, Clyne out-jumped by a bigger lad. It's a carbon copy of their first goal, which would indicate that we don't learn. Anything. Ever.

We could score. We *could* score. Can hits the bar, there's a Benteke header, there's a Firmino header, there's a Lucas header cleared from the line, there's a Joe Allen header. A few headers that, isn't it? We could score. We don't and we don't deserve to. We're second best all over the place, we're disconnected again, our back four doesn't know where our midfield is, our midfield two don't know where they're supposed to be or where each other is and definitely haven't figured out where the three behind Benteke are. The three behind Benteke aren't connecting and have no idea what the big Belgian lad is doing because he clearly has no idea what he's doing. If you're Andy Carroll, you're looking at the current number nine and going: 'And they reckoned *I* didn't fit?'

No wonder he celebrates his goal so enthusiastically. West Ham? Decent showing, solid, the kind of team that we struggle to break down, like two-thirds of the league then. Broke well, took their chances and could easily have scored a few more while we were just wrong on every conceivable level.

Klopp is asked later if he's disappointed. It's not a day for disappointment, he points out, it's a day for anger. It's literally the only moment of the day that carries any hope with it, our manager is furious. Good. I *want* our manager to be furious with that. Hodgson would have called it a hard place to come, Rodgers would have talked about character, Klopp is fuming. It's the right answer.

He claims that he only said three words to the players: one can only hope that it was something resembling 'that was shite' or 'fucking sort it'.

Unacceptable start to 2016. Happy New Year.

Stoke City 0 Liverpool 1

5 January 2016
Capital One Cup Semi-Final first leg

ALL YOU can ask for is a reaction. We wanted a reaction, Jurgen wanted a reaction, a reaction to the shambles of Saturday. Two days doesn't seem a great deal of time to work on solutions but something definitely clicked here.

The mood of the Twitter-verse to the game can probably be summed up by the sheer number of retweets and follows I managed to pick up after quarter of an hour with the simple message 'Jesus Christ, must have been a hell of a bollocking after West Ham'.

There's change. The formation's changed, the personnel's changed, slightly but crucially, and I think we've figured out who the manager holds most responsible for the lack of cutting edge at the weekend. He's asked by Sky why he's put Benteke on the bench, he tells them that he hasn't put Benteke on the bench, he's put Lallana in the team and he's counted up his players and there were eleven. They don't ask anything else. It's an almost Dalglish-esque piece of wrong-footing the media and yet another reason to love him.

He's gone for mobility and intelligence, he's gone for threading and delicacy, he's removed the temptation to lob high balls to a big man by not having that big man. We're kind of 4-1-4-1 to start, Firmino leading the attack but floating and changing with both Lallana and, initially, Coutinho, Lucas sitting protecting the centre-backs. It's nice experience for the moment when he becomes a centre-back himself. Takes about half an hour of the game before that happens. It happens as the second hamstring of the evening pops.

Coutinho's hammy goes first. A stretched pass into the box seems to account for that one. It's a shame as he'd looked livelier than of late and the introduction of his replacement, Ibe, in Phil's nominally left wing-ish position, blunts our threat for about ten minutes, the result of Ibe having to hit the pitch without a warm-up and in an unusual position. He settles, though, settles himself with a goal.

And if you're going to talk the goal, then you're going to have to talk about Joe Allen. Allen's immense tonight, his Pirlo-esque beard pushing him to perform at an appropriate level, the fact that he's sitting in an orthodox midfield position alongside Emre Can in a combination which *just works* probably crucial.

There's a Twitter argument about the goal, provoked by the commentators' bizarre misreading of the situation. They read it this way:

Lallana darts down the wing, pushes a ball into the area, Allen attempts a shot but skews it wide in an almost comedic manner, Ibe mis-controls and then recovers.

That's how *they* read it. The way it actually happens is this:

Allen looks up at Lallana's run, makes his own run into the box alongside Ibe, checks Ibe's position, motions that he wants him to run *there,* pointing out exactly where he's going, receives Lallana's pass and moves it on to Ibe in one perfectly executed flick across his body. Ibe takes the pace out of the ball with his left foot and hammers it home with his right. It's a beautifully worked goal, wonderful in its execution and all the product of Joe Allen's impeccable and intuitive reading and dictation of the play.

Allen is immense. Lovren equally so until he leaves the field with the second popped hamstring of the evening. We're left with Kolo Toure as our only fit *genuine* centre-back. Luckily Kolo is immense. Seeing a pattern here yet? One of those nights where we see strength in the face of adversity, defiance in the face of all the odds. Kolo obviously ends the evening clutching at his own hamstring after all subs have been used. Which leaves us with no fit centre-backs. At all. Unless Aston Villa will let us have Tiago Ilori back, of course. And the fact that they've refused to use him even once in their relegation battle would indicate that they will but that he might not be the answer we're looking for.

We've got Lucas, though. Lucas at centre-back. The papers will tell you that we ended the match with Lucas and Kolo at centre back. We didn't. We actually ended the night with a centre-back pairing of Lucas and Can once Emre had pushed the stricken Kolo forward into a position where he wouldn't be exposed.

The crucial thing, though, is this:

We ended the night with a one-nil win and an advantage to take into the home leg in three weeks' time and all this needs to be considered in light of the current state of Stoke. Stoke are a football team now, a proper football team, they're no longer the fading relic of the Pulis years. Mark Hughes has turned them into a team that knows what the grass is there for and has built exciting performances on the back of recruiting Shaqiri, Bojan and Affelay, even if nobody is entirely sure how those three ended up in the Potteries.

It could well be that this fact actually cost Hughes tonight, the fact that he refused to be Stoke, that he stuck by his new principles and didn't just hurl long balls into the box has possibly worked against him. By the time he reverts to the old 'plan A' and introduces the 'gifted' Jonathan Walters into the mix, it's too late. We have our foothold, we're ahead and we're keeping ourselves ahead with a lovely mix of resilience and invention.

We're everything that we weren't against West Ham, Watford, Newcastle. We look like the Liverpool that turned up for City and Chelsea. We've got our reaction, now all we need to do is repeat it against Arsenal and United with basically no fit players left to pull on a red shirt.

Should be fun.

Exeter City 2 Liverpool 2

FA Cup Third Round
8 January 2016

I'M WRITING this on the morning of the following Monday. Could have written it on Saturday morning but I had this theatre thing to go to (hey, I'm now invited to speak at stuff, that's cool), so didn't. Could have written it on Sunday but felt that perhaps a spot of 'formulating it' while I replayed *The Last Of Us* on PS4 would work well. Which basically just meant playing… you get it. I had an intro in my head, though. And it went like this:

I'd been seeing this girl. This is obviously a long time ago as me and J have been together for thirty years this summer. We're talking '83 going into '84 for the 'seeing this girl' bit. I say, 'seeing' but that might be overstating the case somewhat. We'd been out twice in the space between a mate's Boxing Day party and New Years' Eve '83, when she stood me up at midnight. Fairly sure I'd been dumped at that point, that point where I'd been alone as the bells were chiming the new year in, but I'd rung her to find out. Think she claimed it was a misunderstanding, so we arranged to see each other again. On Friday, 3 January 1984. Which is the night that Liverpool played Newcastle in the FA Cup third round at Anfield. The night that Kevin Keegan came back to play at Anfield for (what I remember as) the last time. I tried to change the date to the Saturday. She said she was busy. I thought that this was worth the effort, this one-week-old 'relationship', so I said 'okay, Friday'. And during the first half of the televised game, knowing that I would be leaving the house at half time, she rang me and said:

AND I'M sure that she has good reasons for the conversation that follows. No idea what they are/were, but probably exceptionally valid

"Do you mind if I don't see you?"

"Do you mean tonight or ever?"

She said: 'Ever.' So I said: 'Cool' and I got to the pub before the second half and drank heavily. I know the evening in The Black Bull (where I'd meet my wife two years and six months later) ended with a pint of snakebite containing a badly hidden rum and black. I then went round to the house of the mate whose party it had been and he told me that he kind of knew that the evening had been about to happen (she was a mate of his sister) and we drank most of a bottle of brandy. Strangely, I had no hangover the next morning.

And the point that I was going to make with all that pre-amble was that this Friday's game against Exeter was only marginally more enjoyable than that previous Friday night FA Cup game had been, and that the good bits were all to do with the company in the pub.

And then I got up this morning and found out that David Bowie had died.

I found out through Facebook. A friend had replied to a post of mine: I'd said that Blackstar (now, ridiculously, a mere three days old) was a triumph, my friend said she'd bought it on my recommendation and today found out he'd died. Said that another voice from her youth had gone. I assumed that, since the language echoed a conversation from Saturday about the death of '70s DJ Ed 'Stewpot' Stewart, that she'd conflated the two and was mistaken. She wasn't.

The morning was about tributes and reading what others had written about him and writing something myself. I wrote that there didn't '*seem a great deal of point doing anything today.*

But that's missing the point, isn't it? In his last eighteen months Bowie made Blackstar, he gave us one last work. So, whatever you do: write, make music, paint, sculpt, whatever, do it. Create.'

And then I sat and did nothing. Because there was no point doing anything. Got a text asking me if I could do *The Anfield Wrap* at four, said yes because it might stop me crying for a bit so I'm heading there. Which will probably mean a break in the chapter in about five minutes. You won't notice it, though, the thought will be as seamless as any I ever manage.

I watched the game on Friday night with a few of the lads from *The Anfield Wrap* in the splendid Bier public house off Bold Street. We'd recorded a show in the afternoon. There had been drinks. We watched the match in a pub. With more drinks. And then recorded our thoughts. With more drinks.

And here's the gap…

And I'm back. Discussed the match, discussed what it meant going forward and how Klopp is best able to deal with the situation that he finds himself in.

The rumoured team started floating around on Thursday. And it seemed skeletal. Interesting, intriguing, but skeletal. But you know how rumours are, you're never sure that they'll be anything more than gossip, hearsay and speculation. This, as has been the case for much of the last couple of years, was more than gossip, hearsay, etc. It was pretty damn close.

Bogdan. Smith. Randall. Ilori — back from Aston Villa round about lunchtime. Enrique. *Enrique?* At *centre-back?* Might be a laugh. I said so on Twitter. Could be a laugh, could surprise us, could be great. Brannagan. Teixeira. Kent. Kevin Stewart — that's the one who had me going 'who?' most. Jerome Sinclair, contract debate put to one side for the night, and Benteke. As captain. Big chance for Chris here, show what he can do, play himself back into favour. Sheyi Ojo on the bench. Got back from Wolves, picked up his boots, went to the game by the looks of it.

Spent the first twenty minutes gazing at the TV above us going 'Who's that? Where's he playing? Hold on, is Enrique

"It's a beautiful thing, ready to support the roof that will appear sometime before next summer…." *August, the skeletal frame of the new main stand* (Getty)

"The Everton result wasn't the cause, it was just the game before it would happen…" *October, the end of the Brendan Rodgers era* (Getty)

"We knew. We wanted Klopp, simple as that…"…and the start of the Klopp era (Getty)

"A shuffle, a small gap, a curl into the top corner. Very Coutinho." 31 October 2015, Chelsea 1 Liverpool 3 (Getty)

"It's the third goal...the third goal is everything." 21 November 2015, Manchester City 1 Liverpool 4 (Getty)

"It doesn't matter if you're a man in your late seventies, you're still the same lad you were when you went to London with your mates for the match." 23 November 2015. The boys of '65. Len Williams, Jimmy Salmon, Bob Salmon (author)

"Origi hits it first time and it's basically world class." 2 December 2015, Southampton 1 Liverpool 6 (Getty)

"Mayhem, majesty, everybody piled on everybody else, broken glasses." 23 January 2016, Norwich City 4 Liverpool 5 (Getty)

"Never let them tell you that you have no power." *6 February 2016.*
#walkouton77 (Getty)

"A good day out with a slightly bleak interruption at the centre of it."
28 February 2016. Wembley. A draw. Those *penalties* (Getty)

"When we talk about the fact that nobody does European nights like we do European nights and nobody does comebacks like we do comebacks, this, this, THIS is what we'll be talking about." *14 April 2016, Liverpool 4 Borussia Dortmund 3* (John Johnson)

"This isn't the end but hopefully it means that the souls and spirits of the 96 who we can finally say without contradiction were unlawfully killed at Hillsborough can rest a little easier now." *26 April 2016. Liverpool, St George's Hall* (John Johnson)

"So we end the home section of the season with another chapter of the Benteke conundrum." 11 May 2016, Liverpool 1 Chelsea 1. The last day of the old main stand (Getty)

"This is my dad's seat, this is the seat that his back leant on to watch the glory. I keep the memories. The memories are everything." (author)

"When he scores his goal, it's right and appropriate and deserved." 18 May 2016. Daniel Sturridge when everything was still possible (Getty)

'There She Goes, Three Little Birds, The Poor Scouser Tommy.' 'How are they supposed to cope with all this?' 18 May 2016, Liverpool 1 Sevilla 3. Not how this was supposed to end (Getty)

actually playing left-back?' and trying to join the dots. Once the dots were joined, the verdict went like this:

Their first goal is a far-too-easy ball played in. Our equaliser is a nice finish by Sinclair. Their second is the most comical piece of goalkeeping anybody will have ever seen from a corner and could well signal the end of any Anfield career that Adam Bogdan might have dreamt of having. He puts an arm up but it's the wrong arm and it kind of flaps in the wind as the ball drops into the net direct from the Exeter corner. Our equaliser, thank God for our second equaliser, is about a loose ball in the box and the quick instincts of Brad Smith.

Some of the lads came out of it okay. Ojo looked good when he came on, Smith and Randall look like they can cope with experienced centre-backs next to them. *Not* Enrique, whose positioning was as haphazard as ever. Ilori was okay, didn't do much wrong but didn't exactly put an imprint on the game. Brannagan was similar, tidy but unspectacular. Kent was out wide and that's about it. Teixeira looked sharp in the first half, looked as though he wanted it, looked like he was ready to grab the chance he'd been given. Sinclair scored. Benteke did very, very little. Actually became more terrifying as the first half went on but managed to involve himself more in the second. Conundrum.

Overall? Still in the FA Cup, bringing Exeter back to Anfield, where rumour has it we'll play the kids again. If we do, they won't have the problem of half of them never having met each other before, might even benefit from a week of working together. Could yet turn out okay. Just don't let Enrique and Benteke play alongside them.

Liverpool 3 Arsenal 3

13 January 2016

THERE ARE nights when I almost envy the neutral. They get to enjoy the spectacle, the thrills, the ups and downs without the anxiety which accompanies passion. They get the beauty and nothing but the beauty.

And there's always a beauty to midweek winter night-time games. Generally, it's a feeling that you get with European encounters. It's the home leg of the group stages of the Champions League, the first taste of the knockout stages, a march to glory. You can get it, to an extent, with domestic cup replays. But midweek league games? They're generally not the big ones. Arsenal, though? Arsenal's a big one. Arsenal on a wet Wednesday night, walking across a sodden Stanley Park with the lights of the ground illuminating the rapidly filling skeleton of the new main stand, bag of chips from the Goodison fish bar in hand (my superstitious regime for the last few years) and George, blasting out Bowie's *Starman* at 'crossing the park' volume levels? This is beauty, this is anticipation. This is the start of yet another run of games that could define the season. Every run of games seems to define the season these days but this sequence, five games in nineteen days, United to follow on the heels of the Gunners this Sunday and then cup games a-go-go, seems particularly, specifically, defining. A chance to set out stalls.

And I'm confident. The team was announced before I left the house and it was strong. No Benteke, which I felt was probably a good thing. It looked all 4-3-3 and false nine and stuff. It's not. It's the most traditional 4-4-2 of all time and it's magnificent.

Arsenal have no idea what's hit them. We're everywhere, we have speed and we have desire and we have skill and we're hunting in packs. They're swamped in the middle and threatened up front where Klopp's decision that Firmino and Lallana are now a forward partnership looks inspired. The visitors are controlled, dominated, subjugated by the perma-movement of Can and Henderson as a central duo who look more and more like a genuine, honest-to-god partnership every time we manage to put them on a field together. James Milner's back and he's obviously missed the whole footy thing because he's everywhere and he's linking everything.

We're a little less convincing at the back and that becomes quite crucial, quite quickly, but let's do the nice stuff first, shall we? Firmino has his best game for the club. His first goal is a thing of wonder. He picks up on Cech parrying well from a Can shot and slots the ball beautifully between a pair of gaping Arsenal legs. He's whirling away, ripping his shirt off as he goes, hurling it somewhere in the direction of the Anfield Road end. The obvious, inevitable booking almost proves costly minutes later as he decides it's time for a robust tackle. He avoids censure, he carries on, he influences, he moves and his second goal is a thing of utter, imperious beauty. A Milner slide, a look up and a powerful curl into the top right-hand corner.

We're twenty minutes in, we've scored twice and we should be thinking about repeating the joy of the 2013/14 blitz. One issue, though:

Simon Mignolet picks the day that the notion of a new five-year contract complete with pay rise is floated (cue major Twitter fume) to have a very, very *Simon Mignolet* game. We don't have the lead that we deserve. Our one-nil lead lasts four minutes before Aaron Ramsey exposes the fact that, no matter who we field in our four, the lads at the back can't handle sharp movement in the box. There are at least three players culpable in the goal but Mignolet's beaten at his near post, which is kind of basic. I'd spent lunchtime on a podcast defending our 'keeper, comparing his erratic nature to Grobbelaar. Claiming that he'd come good. Wish I hadn't bothered.

He does it again on the other side of Firmino's second goal. A corner. Again. Always a corner. Not dealt with, across his body and into the net. The goal's credited to Giroud, although nobody's entirely sure how much the Arsenal lad knows about it or how much contact he makes. It's not Bogdan-esque — luckily for Si as the ginger lad from Oldham has disappeared completely in favour of Danny Ward, recalled from good work in his Aberdeen loan — but it's getting there. Arsenal haven't been in the game at all so far but they're in it now. We've let them into it. You would think that Mignolet must surely realise his culpability when his vice-captain is standing in the box berating him after both goals in front of forty-thousand people.

Mignolet isn't to blame for Giroud's second goal, ten minutes into the second half. Kolo gets turned easily but Giroud's a quality player. And this is what large swathes of the crowd forget in the period that we now spend behind in the game: Arsenal are good, Arsenal are sitting in first place as they arrive, Arsenal could well win the league. There were always going to be times that they would be on top, but the key is how you react to those times.

The team, and the majority of the support, respond well. They keep going, they keep pushing, they keep creating. We're behind in a game where we should be home and hosed, but we keep going. There's only one team playing football, only one team threatening. We don't look like we could pull a point back here, we look like we could win.

We don't. Obviously. You know that, even if only from the chapter heading. Joe Allen's on for a tiring Emre Can and the equally tiring Adam Lallana is replaced by...

Hold on. This is either the maddest substitution of all time or the most inspired. We've signed Steven Caulker on loan from Southampton, where he's not getting a game. Or is it actually from QPR, who had loaned him to Southampton?

How are you supposed to keep up with this stuff? Twitter is obviously furious. 'Can't get a game for them? Why are we bringing him in? Should be doing better than this, there's no money, is there? The Americans are stitching up Klopp, aren't they?'

Well, he's a centre-back whose hamstrings are currently intact and he's here until the end of the season. If it doesn't work, then it doesn't work. If it gives the lad a chance to kick-start his career, then we've made a good move. It's a win/win, isn't it?

Bringing him on as centre-forward, though? Seems deranged until you realise that he's more mobile than Benteke, that he's taking up better positions. We've got two big lads up front and suddenly Arsenal have something to deal with.

In fairness to our expensive Belgian conundrum, it's his header that supplies Joe Allen with his equalising volley. A Joe Allen volley. It's the beard working its magic again.

We're level with seconds left to play and Caulker has become a centre-back again. It's one of those draws that feels like a victory in its nature, but simultaneously leaves you rueing the defending that cost us a night of glory and two essential points.

We slip to ninth in the league, four points off fifth, three behind United – which could, on this form, be rectified on Sunday afternoon – five points from the top four, but we've just had one of those magical nights. We've had a night for the neutral, we've had a night of spectacle and at times, the times when we were leading, when we really needed that push, wonderful atmosphere. We keep showing that we can go head to head with the biggest teams in the league and be more than their match.

The Arsenal fans? The ones dreaming of winning the league? Watching that equaliser go in, limiting the extent of their dreams momentarily? They must be shattered. I'd sympathise but... it doesn't even start to take the edge off Michael Thomas's goal in '89.

Ignore the table. We're building.

Liverpool 0 Manchester United 1

17 January 2016

AND THIS is what the season's doing to us, isn't it? Lifting us up just to hurl us down again, though you could happily argue that Liverpool have been doing that for decades now. A United team that is clearly there for the taking, really, really *there for the bloody taking* rocks up at Anfield on a Sunday lunchtime and we outplay them for the entire game across the entire length of the pitch, apart from the bit that contains the things which have the nets hanging on them. You know them? The *important* things, the things that count.

We're blunt. We're creative and we're fast and we're moving and we're pressing and there are lots of moments, but none of those moments tie together into the thing that counts. United have one shot on target, United have a goal, United have three points. That's all that matters in the end really, isn't it? It doesn't matter how many times Lucas can chip the ball forward for Lallana to run on to. Doesn't matter that Lallana can see his header saved but react well enough, quickly enough, to retain possession and set up another attack. Doesn't matter how beautiful Firmino's half-volleyed raking cross field pass is when it falls to James Milner and he blasts over. Doesn't matter that the ball falls to Henderson with space and time if he chips it into De Gea's arms, that Emre Can can pull off a delightful shuffle to make space for his shot if De Gea can pull off an equally delightful double save in response. Doesn't matter that Lucas can spend the afternoon out-jumping Fellaini, who is about three feet taller than him, or that Kolo Toure can spend the afternoon shackling Rooney, who is about twenty years younger than him. Doesn't matter. None of it matters.

All that matters is that United put the ball into the net and we didn't. All that matters is that United have De Gea at the back, and it's almost impossible to beat De Gea, and Rooney at the front while we have Mignolet at the back. Mignolet, who has a new five-year contract now fully signed and photo opp'd, who is at the very least partially responsible for the goal in that he has *no bloody idea* where the ball is after Fellaini's header hits the bar. He doesn't see the ball drop to Rooney, he's looking for it in the net. He doesn't recover in time, he gets his arms up but he gets them up too late and too low. We've conceded from *another* sodding corner. And you knew it was going to happen. United knew it was going to happen. Liverpool knew it was going to happen. And so it happened. Again. And again and again and again.

If we win, though? If we win, people are talking about a strong Liverpool performance with attacking verve, flair, determination, organisation. Wins give you that perspective. Wins show you that you've played well. Losses tell you that it doesn't matter how well you played, you were terrible. Shite. Shite was the word that echoed round the back of the Anfield Road on the approach to the walk across the park.

"They didn't want it." That's what the guy in front of me was saying. They didn't want it. I didn't even have time to process the thought, didn't have chance to process the query 'Why *wouldn't* they want it?' before he followed up with ' and *he* didn't want it either — playing United at home with no forward?'

Didn't take long that, did it? Anti-Klopp complaints. Brilliant. Let's question the desire of the manager that we had all wanted for his immense desire to win, whose entire joy in football comes from beating the teams that he's not expected to. 'Didn't want it enough?' Have you actually watched him on the touchline? Show me someone who wants it more.

The simple truth is that we didn't win this game because we don't currently possess a striker that we can trust to put the ball in the back of the net. Benteke? The Benteke conundrum is that he's a 'one-in-two' player, but you don't actually *believe* that he's a 'one-in-two' player. He comes on, he links up nicely but he looks like a lad who needs a partner. Firmino looks like he needs a partner. Milner does, Lallana does. We have all these technicians but we have no focal point, no focal point that isn't currently injured anyway.

Sturridge, Ings, Origi? All currently unavailable. Any one of those three changes this game. They're the lad that's on the end of the raking pass, they're there when Firmino bursts between two defenders and needs somebody sharp to pass to, somebody effective, somebody who will put the ball in the net because that's his job. They're not there, so we don't score, so we don't win. United have a great goalie and a lad up front who has scored more goals for one team than any other player in the Premier League era, who is the all-time leading scorer for his country and will be the leading scorer for his club. Rooney puts the ball in the net because that's what he does.

That's the difference. That's the only difference. We're better everywhere, we're far better than United *everywhere*. Except where it counts.

I'll make the building argument again, shall I? We're building. And we clearly need to do it from the front.

Before and after United

A blast from the (recent) past

BRENDAN'S BACK and he's doing the media thing. It's well timed, he's on Sky's *Goals On Sunday* prior to our 2.05pm kick-off. The traditional 2.05pm Sunday kick-off. He follows up with a slot on the *Monday Night Football* show alongside Jamie Carragher, sliding virtual counters around a virtual pitch, explaining tactics and methodology.

And he's fine. He looks well, which he quite definitely didn't when he left the club, he speaks well, speaks in the past tense about Liverpool in the same way he spoke about us when he was here. Great club to have the opportunity to manage, privileged to have that opportunity, all that kind of thing. Sound like platitudes, but I don't doubt for a second that he fully means them.

There are clearly non-disclosure agreements in place – the severance pay cheque isn't hitting the account otherwise – and he'll want another job so he doesn't want to be the guy who slags others off. He's obviously not going to say anything overly contentious but what we get is this:

Brendan didn't have final say on transfers. Kind of confirms something that we already guessed but after all the talk that he received final say when he signed the new contract, it's surprising to hear him say it. There were lists that he could choose from. There's no indication he was able to place names on those lists.

He hadn't wanted Balotelli. He'd planned his play around Alexis Sanchez replacing Suarez. He didn't get that. Ricky

Lambert ends up shouldering more responsibility than was ever intended for a fourth-choice substitute option.

The owners thought that, in Balotelli, they were getting a £50m player for £16m and that Brendan was the man to develop him. Which kind of ignores pretty much every single second of Mario's career to date.

He thought that we had Dele Alli. He'd done his bit, the deal didn't go through. He doesn't point fingers, he doesn't criticise but there's an implicit point here. We missed out on a kid who could prove to be a major talent and it was clearly *somebody's* fault. We'll probably never know who. But we'll guess.

None of it is revolutionary, none of it seems to be intended as a point-scoring exercise. It's simply stating the position that he was in and his thoughts on why we didn't follow up second place with a charge on the title.

That's Sunday. Monday sees him talking tactics with Carra and his big telly. He talks about 'getting more lines' on the pitch, about the places he'd seen ideas implemented in the past and his reason for recalling and adapting those ideas. He's clear and precise and calm. He doesn't come across as particularly passionate but, as was argued in a *TAW* podcast that we recorded the following Wednesday, that could simply be a case of how you behave in a TV studio as opposed to a dressing room. God knows, I understand the panic that settles the moment that you realise that you're live on radio to an audience of a certain size. On TV to millions? I might come across as less witty than I normally am. Which is a terrible thought.

Across two sets of TV appearances, our ex-manager comes across as a man who, despite some of his own poor player choices, fell at the last hurdle largely through a set of circumstances beyond his control.

I almost wrote the word 'failed' but I think that's unfair. We seem to have written Brendan slightly out of history at the moment. His replacement by Jurgen was so swift, so certain and so right that we stopped thinking about Brendan before he was out of the door. Ultimately, he took us to the brink of the title and he gave us the most fun we'd had in years. Wish him luck.

The Anfield Wrap

20 January 2016
Pre-Exeter

ONE OF those pieces that you write knowing you have a short
window where what you're about to say will have any relevance
(which probably makes putting it here a little odd as it's about
seven months out of date at the very, very least), but it feels
like the right thing to write, so you do. This is how I felt before
the Exeter game.

*You know what? I'm quite prepared to go out of the FA Cup tonight.
Start the fume lads.*

*I'm happy to sacrifice the whole thing. That's how I feel right
now. Which is odd because it goes against everything that I believe
in, both as a Liverpudlian and as a human being. I think that if
you're in something then you should want to be the best at it. When
I was in bands I wanted to be as big as The Beatles. Anything else
would be ludicrous.*

*If you're Liverpool Football Club, then you should want to win
everything. It's what we do, it's what we exist for. At the moment,
though? Trying to win everything is beyond us, it's hurting us.*

*It shouldn't. The squad that started the season should have been
enough to see us challenge on multiple fronts. I was one of those who
was shouting that we could win the league. Shouting it all over the
place I was. Under Brendan. Once Jurgen came in, I upped that
claim to 'we're going to win everything'. Grand National, Boat Race,
Eurovision, the lot. Right now I'd just like to see us win another game.*

I'm dreaming of a nice comfy two-nil. Something boring and routine where we play okay-ish and put the ball in the back of the net a couple of times from about a yard out in a Dirk Kuyt style.

If we're going to do that, then we could probably do with some players being fit, which probably means not playing them quite so often. The injuries and the sheer number of games over Christmas have killed us.

We're on our knees and we need to get back up. There are things that need to happen now and one of those things is that we need to start using that awful word 'prioritisation'. We need to finish as high as we can in the league. It's the bread and butter and all that and it gives you a decent mindset to go into the next season with, gives you a base to work from. You want Jurgen to win the league next season, don't you? Right, then we need to finish top six. We need the European football which will attract European footballers, we need to be something that people will believe in. Nobody goes from outside the top six to coming anywhere near winning the league. Ever. Except us, obviously.

Want a trophy? Cool. Let's start with the League Cup. We're in a good place for that, let's be strong in that. And let's be strong in the UEFA as well. These are things that we currently have more chance in. And yes, the UEFA could get very tricky after Augsburg but it's about being seen to challenge in Europe, it's a Klopp thing to win.

Does the FA Cup matter, then? Of course it bloody matters, it's the FA Cup. One of the many, many reasons to hate the Mancs is that season where Fergie decided that if they were going to have a week in the sun for the world club thing, then they couldn't possibly compete in the FA Cup as well. I don't do picking and choosing. And I'm not suggesting 'actively' sacrificing it, I'm just saying it's not necessarily a bad risk to take.

I wasn't saying this a fortnight ago, after the kids had scraped their way back into the Exeter game. I was very vocal about the fact that I wanted to see a stronger team for the replay. I wanted to ensure that we progressed. I'd got over the idea that playing Enrique at centre-back would be a laugh. I'm over all that now. I'm happy with the fact that it's the same lads again. I'm okay with the idea of Enrique wandering around trying to figure out where he is and whether it's where he's supposed to be. I don't think it'll be a laugh, the Enrique thing. I think it'll be hideous and worrying, but I'm okay with it.

I think the lads are probably good enough to do it at home. I think Exeter had their chance, I don't think they get a second one, think we'll give them a nice payday and send them back down south. And if I'm wrong? Then we're out. And I'm okay with that, I'm prepared for that.

I'm prepared to go out of the FA Cup because there'll be weekends without football, there'll be blocks of days where Jurgen can think about the next game and the next game will stop being 'the day after tomorrow' for a short while.

There will be lads who get a bit of a rest, we won't be pushing Jordan past the limits that his heel will take, we won't be killing Moreno and Clyne by making them do every second of every game, we won't be running out of centre-backs and we won't have Adam running around so much, doing so much linking that he can take a bit of time in training to practice shooting and maybe we can even have time to see if we can blend Bobby F and big Chris into some kind of partnership.

You can dream, can't you?

I love the FA Cup. Apart from the whole semi-final being at Wembley thing. And the Villa game last year, obviously. But I'm prepared to go out of the FA Cup. Just this season. Just to give us time to get the squad into shape so it can win games in the league. I'll let up on the whole 'nobody cares if you finished fourth or finished sixth or eighth, they only care if you won stuff' and I'll let one go. Just to give Jurgen a day off at some point. Just so we can see him smile again because he had ten minutes to teach the lads how to defend corners.

And if we win? Cool. Be happy as Larry with that one. Play the kids next time, though. There you go, that's what you call a turn round, from 'play a stronger team in the replay' to 'play the kids next time, play the kids at home versus West Ham'.

Okay. Might have gone a bit far with that last one. And in the run-up to the West Ham game, I'll be the first at the barricades demanding a first-choice team on the pitch but as it stands, at this very moment, that's how I feel because I'm quite prepared to go out of the FA Cup.

Right. Who wants to start the fight, then?

And hardly anybody did. Doesn't really matter because what happens next is this:

Liverpool 3 Exeter City 0

FA Cup Third Round Replay
20 January 2016

THE THING about playing lower-league teams in cup competitions – and sometimes you forget that when people talk about 'League Two opponents' what they actually mean is the old Fourth Division – is that you can't win. I mean, obviously you can win, we won. I saw us win a nice comfy three-nil, so one goal better than I'd hoped. I saw us win a nice routine game without ever being really troubled. We won. End of.

Morally, though? Morally you can't win because if you do then you'll be told that you were supposed to win anyway. And if you point out that you've just fielded a team full of kids then you'll be told that your 'kids' should be talented enough to win. If you struggle against them, you're castigated. If you ease past them, you're disregarded. And the 'it was those lads' cup final' argument almost never washes.

The kids, though, the kids did great. Ninety minutes of control with no particular threat from the opposition and a fair bit of the stuff from us. There *were* a couple of tweaks, bringing a bit of experience to bear on the situation. Allen and Ibe come in and both are splendid. Ibe is probing the defence all night, Allen nets his second goal in a week and adds the epithet 'free-scoring' to his name.

I was on an *Anfield Wrap* Tuesday Review after the initial Exeter game, the show where tactics are talked and everything is delved into in a serious manner with some depth. Which obviously begs the question 'what are you doing there, Salmon?' I'm there, though, and I put forward the idea that, if we were to play the same side, or virtually the same side, then there was every chance that they would have had a couple of weeks of training together, that they would know each other, that they would have knitted.

It looks, unusually, as though I might have been right on that one. The team that seemed like it had just met in the first leg — because it had — was cohesive and organised. The shape was strong, the movement fluid. There were impressive performances in every area.

Smith and Randall continued their strong showings in the full-back positions, Ilori appeared composed and assertive, comparisons to Dominic Matteo were made by a few, which might not sound like the greatest of praise but would indicate that he's able to do a job in the squad. Brannagan was assured and steady in the first half, gaining more zip in the second and displaying excellent passing all night. Kevin Stewart, still so new to me that I keep forgetting his name, was a surprise package, sitting in the holding position. He was everything that he needed to be, carrying the ball forward, breaking up play, passing well, always where he should be, recovering his own mistakes when needed. It'd be nice to see if he can do a similar job against harder opposition.

Which is true of all of the lads out there last night. Teixeira was endlessly inventive, flicks and tricks and feints and jinks and a well-taken goal to seal the evening, but the question remains 'can he repeat this in the Premiership?'

Ojo appears as a substitute again and, again, is a revelation. He might have, as Jurgen maintains afterwards, a lot to learn but he has the tools to learn with. There's a natural energy and aptitude to his appearance here, eighteen years old but strong and fast with vision. His first Liverpool goal improves with every viewing.

Our captain for the night? Bizarrely and wonderfully, it's Jose Enrique. And he does nothing wrong. He seems to have decided that he's going to be Jan Molby for the evening, move as little as possible and spray the ball round. He's fine. I'm pleased for him. It might be a goodbye. If so, it's a good one.

There are two side stories to the win which might prove to have a long-term impact on the team:

Jon Flanagan returns. His second half substitute entry is perfectly stage managed by Klopp. He's had his half-time warm-up, the teams have had five minutes and he's introduced into play in order to receive a justly deserved ovation. Twenty months out and he's back. And instantly taking charge, talking to the back four, organising. We've been missing a leader. Perhaps it's not beyond the bounds of imagination that Flanno could help in that department. Nice to have a Scouser in the first team reckoning, though.

Then there's the Benteke conundrum again. There appear to be two of him tonight. One of him is involved in two goals, playing a wonderful one-two through the Exeter box with Brad Smith to lead to Joe Allen's opener and threading a delightful diagonal to Teixeira for the third, defending well at set pieces and linking up play for the midfield to run on to.

The other Benteke appears to completely lack positional sense. He makes the wrong runs or doesn't run at all. He's stationary on the penalty spot when he needs to drop back or push forward, he's on the edge of the area when he needs to be on the penalty spot. He's Andy Carroll-ing it all over the place. He's no threat at all. He's the Benteke who is clear with the 'keeper to beat and runs the ball out of play on the touchline. But he's got an assist and he's involved in the creation of the opener and he's forced an excellent save from their 'keeper and he's rampaged across the park absolutely untouchable. All while supposedly being useless. He's redefining the word dichotomy.

Three-nil. Job done. Exeter sent home. Six thousand Exeter fans with a long journey back. Six thousand from an average attendance of three thousand eight hundred? Pretty impressive. Maybe they'll all turn up at their place from now on where they can sing anti-Steven Gerrard songs and chants about 'we pay your benefits' to their little hearts' contents.

Love the FA Cup.

Norwich City 4 Liverpool 5

23 January 2016

A CHAPTER heading that doesn't come close to encapsulating the madness of the game, although quite possibly brings every manic second flooding back to those who saw it. A game which managed to show every version of Liverpool that we've ever imagined to lurk within the red shirts at exactly the same time. Casual then capable then wretched then devastating. And back again. And back again.

I'm writing this on Monday morning. Thought about writing it on Saturday afternoon, immediately after the match while the madness was still fresh. Shoot from the hip, write from the heart, get 'all the feels', as the young people seem to say. Thought 'No, I'll watch the highlights on *Match Of The Day*, I'll watch the game again. Try and figure it all out.' Knew that I was recording *The Anfield Wrap's* Tuesday review this afternoon, thought it might be worthwhile sounding like I knew what I was talking about, thought that if I was analysing the match then I should try and sound analytical.

Do you want to try analysing that? I've watched the whole thing again. Every single second. I've tried to figure out how we are so ordinary and then so in charge and then so bloody appalling and then back in it and then on top and then pegged back and then winning. I've tried to take the emotion out of the game and look at formations and look at how Norwich exploit ours and how we manage to retaliate, and I've tried to figure out who was the catalyst for the comeback. It's virtually impossible. It's too much. In most analysis, you think about formation and pressing and two or three incidents that change the game. Here, there's nine of the buggers. It's ninety-five minutes of madness topped by the greatest celebration of all time.

The idea that a week off gives players chance to rest and prepare is blown out of the water by the first fifteen tame, tepid, minutes. We're slow and Norwich aren't and they're willing to push and we've forgotten how to press. We look like we're in for a long day, another unnecessary defeat. And then we're not. There's a lovely pass from Milner, who'll go on to be possibly the worst player on the pitch – and God knows there's competition on that front – and Firmino bounces a lazy flick in off the keeper. Lazy in a good way, languid, confident, assured. There are replays and the replays show that it was going in anyway. Or that it wasn't. Or that it was, depending on which replay you're replaying. It's the against-the-run-of-play thing that you hope for.

Suddenly, we're rampant. There's a break from Milner which begs for him to simply chip the keeper. He doesn't. There's a well thought-out free kick which involves a pass across the line to Moreno for him to blast home in the way that Daniel Agger used to do. He doesn't. It's suddenly clear. A clinical Liverpool, the 2013/14 Liverpool, would be three up by now. This isn't the 13/14 Liverpool. It's all about quality and we're missing it. We're missing the thought processes that make the best players the best players. We're missing the intuition. We're missing the Liverpool that was pushed and pulled forwards by Suarez, Gerrard, Sturridge, Coutinho and Sterling. Two are still here but injured, one seemingly semi-permanently. You pay the big money for the mindset, you pay the big money for the instant decision-making. Sometimes you pay less and get lucky, a Sturridge, a Coutinho. Mostly, though, you get what you pay for. We're not the 2013/14 team. Two years is one hell of a long time.

Then Norwich have a shot on target. And score. This is how it works at the moment: you play Liverpool, you shoot, you score. A corner. Again. Poorly defended. Again. The ball drops, awkwardly admittedly, and Sakho doesn't deal with it. Mbokani's back-heel is pretty damn magnificent, but he shouldn't have the chance to execute it.

The next goal is the most inevitable goal in the history of football. Steven Naismith has signed for Norwich from Everton. He scored against us on his debut for them over the park. He was always going to haunt us today. The run he makes to receive a pass beyond our defence is intelligent because Naismith's an intelligent player. He's a workhorse, a good pro and a seemingly genuinely decent bloke. He deserves his goal. Our defence deserves nothing. Can, Lucas, Moreno and Mignolet – all culpable in this one. The truly annoying thing is that the move that cuts our defence open has been used three times in the game already. Norwich know that there is space to exploit in the triangle of fresh air between Sakho, Moreno and Can and they're going to exploit it. Repeatedly.

Two-one down at half time with worse to come. The penalty is madness. Moreno brings down Naismith in the area, gets away with it so decides that he should do it a second time for effect. And then stands there with his hands raised in a 'Who? Me?' pose. We're three-one down and there's no coming back.

Then things change. And I honestly have no idea why. I've watched it again. And again. And again. The Jordan Henderson goal that drags us back into the game seems to have more to do with Norwich losing concentration than it does with us changing anything. A cross from the right, a Firmino flick, a fine Hendo finish and he's in the net, retrieving the ball and darting to the centre circle, screaming at his team-mates. Something's changed. Hopefully forever but who knows?

The equaliser is gorgeous. Firmino flicks it in the centre of the park, Milner picks it up, lobs it beautifully to Lallana for Adam's second touch since replacing Ibe and the man who doesn't do assists and goals hits it first time to provide an assist for Firmino, who started the move with that flick. It's sumptuous, it's Liverpool.

The moment that we move ahead for the first time in an hour is the result of a Norwich calamity. The most beautifully misguided back pass and Milner is moving clear again. And let's be honest, everybody — *everybody* — expected him to goon it again. Another conundrum, James Milner. For me, he's been the worst (no, let's make that the most frustrating) player on the pitch, yet somehow he's still *on* the pitch. He's been too slow, he's added nothing to the game, he's shown no real spark of creativity but he's made one, scored one and been involved in another. Ibe being subbed before Milner? Clearly protecting the full-backs. Seems to have worked. All we have to do is see out this four-three lead that we've gained for ten minutes or so.

It's a dead-ball delivery again, isn't it? From the Norwich half. A seventy-yard free kick, caused by Benteke, the world's most expensive plan B, unnecessarily straying off side. The punt forward falls in front of our back line and isn't dealt with. We have three centre-backs on the pitch now, Caulker's on and playing at the back, which must be nice for him, none of the three deal with it. Sebastian Bassong unleashes a pile driver. Sebastian Bassong. For the love of God.

Jurgen had been questioning the five minutes of added time before Bassong equalised. Now he's furious. Until Lallana does *that*. Can, competing with Milner for the award of most ineffective man in the team, curls a lovely ball into the area. It pinballs, it bounces, Caulker has two bites at it, it drops to Lallana. The shirt's coming off before the ball's in the net, he's whirling away. Jurgen's racing towards him, *screaming* for the hug. You know what follows. Mayhem, majesty, everybody piled on everybody else, broken glasses. You're in August (or later), whatever's happened between now and whatever *now* that you're in, this is folklore. This is a moment.

That's me trying to make sense from madness, trying to rationalise the irrational. This was the day we proved that, even when we've given up, we find a way not to give up. This is the kind of day which gives birth to legends. This is the kind of day that you build on. Build on it.

Liverpool 0 Stoke City 1

2nd leg, Capital One Cup semi final
Liverpool win 6-5 on penalties
26 January 2016

SLIGHT MISCALCULATION by the police at the end, I thought. Letting the Stoke fans out of The Anfield Road End, at the same time as the home fans were trying to funnel themselves through the channel under the main stand, so that they could sing *We Are Stoke*, *We Are Stoke* repeatedly as we crossed paths could have been an issue. The flashing lights that sped past us as we exited the park and rounded the corner of the cemetery would indicate that, somewhere down the road, it had been.

We'd been okay. No issues. Apart from the little fat bloke who was unhappy that Kev and I had left our own ground in our own city and headed for the entry to Stanley Park discussing how offside Stoke's only shot on target and the only goal of the evening had been.

'What the fuck are you fucking complaining about?' he screamed, barely looking at us. 'You fucking won, didn't you?'

'We're talking about a linesman getting a big call wrong again,' I replied.

'Yeah and what about all the fucking yellow cards you should have had tonight?'

We could have gone with the 'Jesus, were you watching your lot fall over and roll round every time anybody breathed too hard in the road behind the Kop' argument. Or the 'for a big lad, that Arnautovic doesn't half need to lie down a lot' point of view. Instead, Kev went with the simple 'Yeah, whatever.'

Little fat man wasn't happy with this tactic.

'Whatever? Whatever? Don't you fucking whatever me.'

Which was articulate and well argued and as far as he got before his own fans turned on him with 'What kind of language is that to use in front of kids? There's a six-year-old girl here. Talk like that in front of your own kids, not in front of ours.'

We left them to it and walked on through the mud and the dark and the rain and talked about the blatant handball in the area that we didn't get and Milner being bundled to the floor then moved to the obvious question.

Kev: 'Are you driving down?'

Me: 'Yeah.'

Kev: 'Thought you would.'

Me: 'Shall we park in the same place?'

Kev: 'Might as well.'

We've got the route now. Two semis and two finals under Kenny. Three good days out, one not quite as enjoyable, ruined by probably enjoying the Everton semi too much, the Chelsea final seemed a bit of an anti-climax. One disastrous semi under Brendan last season that we'll try not to think about. We know our route, though. Wembley. Again.

Which is obviously the best thing about the night. The celebrations at the end. The Mignolet penalty saves. Both wonderful but it felt bad booing Crouchy for his. I mean, it worked but it's Crouchy, even if he's currently sporting the worst beard in the history of mankind. Makes him look like Catweazle. Or the lad from Stereo MCs. Joe Allen, though, Joe Allen's got a lovely beard. Might have mentioned this previously. Pirlo-esque. And, again, Joe Allen enters the fray, bolsters the midfield and scores the beautiful, decisive penalty.

Other than that? We were pretty awful but they had nothing. We managed one shot on target. In the ninety-seventh minute. They managed their sole shot on target in stoppage time at the end of the first half. Blatantly offside, definitely mentioned that one. I'd argued that Hughes employed the wrong tactics in the first leg. He went full-on Pulis here. Got all the dark arts back out. Goalie to Crouch to knock down for Walters. That's your tactic. Other than that, fall over a lot lads, see if the ref's daft enough to go for it. He was.

Ultimately, it doesn't matter. No matter what TalkSport's presenters might claim on the way home, Stoke *weren't* the better team for three of the four halves. We were and we won. And we're going to Wembley. End of.

Except for this. This happened earlier. I'd mistimed leaving the house, thrown off by the quarter-to-eight kick-off again. Hit the park just in time to walk into the game in the midst of a thousand or so Stoke supporters. I'm wearing no colours so they don't know, but I'm there as they start singing en masse "Sign on, sign on, with hope in your hearts and you'll never get a job' which they've obviously made up themselves, there and then, so spontaneous is it in its wit and political awareness. I hear a Scouse voice behind me ask one: 'So, are you Tories then?' The Stoke reply is 'Christ, no.'

Sorry mate, the second you sing that, you're a Tory. 'You'll never get a job?' Because the Potteries are a paradise on earth, aren't they?

We round the corner, one astute individual points at the new stand and enquires in song 'What the fuck, what the fuck, what the fucking hell is that?'

That, my friend, is the building where we'll keep our European Cup. The one we have forever for doing that five times thing. Hopefully, in a month, we'll have another cup to sit with it, the cup that we've won more often than any other club.

The 'sign on' chants, the 'this is a library' song, the 'who are yer' shouts: you know what these things are, don't you? They're a sign of a small-club mentality, a set of supporters who know that they don't win things and live in the full belief that it will never happen. Lose that mentality, embrace the fact that your manager wants to play football, allow him not to have to revert to Pulisian principles and you might actually start to be something.

In the meantime, we have another date with the southern branch of Anfield. We know the way.

Liverpool 0 West Ham United 0

FA Cup Fourth Round
30 January 2016

"I'm forever blowing bubbles, pretty bubbles in the air, they fly so high, they reach the sky then like my dreams they fade and die."

I'M NOT meaning to have another pop at opposition fans after the whole Stoke thing. Okay, I am and I will in a second, but first: serious question, serious psychological point. I get that 'I'm forever blowing bubbles' is one of the great traditional football songs. I've done the research, it's got a forty-year start on *YNWA*. The Hammers' lads have been singing it since the 1920s. All to do with them having a player nicknamed 'Bubbles' because he looked like a lad in a soap advert, apparently. Seriously, don't ask me.

But it's not hopeful, is it? 'Like my dreams, they fade and die?' You've got a club anthem about your dreams being destroyed? All your talk of winning the World Cup for England and your anthem embraces the inevitability of loss and despair? You've accepted failure from the off, not exactly inspirational, is it? Puzzled me for years.

They sing other songs as well:

'Sign on, sign on with a pen in your hand and you'll never get a job.' Like the 'pen' line lads, well worked. Most away fans don't think of changing the 'with hope in your heart' bit. Clearly an inventive bunch.

In response to *Stand Up for the 96,* the West 'aaaam (read that in a cockernee accent) go with 'Sit down if you're unemployed.'

Lads, you're from the East End. You're not Chelsea. You come from a place that was as devastated and left behind by Thatcherism as we were. You're the same as us, you have the same chance of employment or unemployment as we do. The difference between us? We don't give up, we don't accept the inevitability of defeat. We have hope in our hearts. That's the point, it's in the song. Want to know why we don't have anti-West Ham songs? It's because you don't bother us, you're not important, we don't worry, we don't care.

Rant over then, back to the football. FA Cup fourth round. Can do this one quickly because we'll be doing it again in just over a week:

They make five changes, we make ten. Mignolet's the only one who keeps his place and that's only because Bogdan has undergone some kind of Stalinist purge. He's written from history. One flapped arm at Exeter and he's an ex-person.

The rest is a mix of the kids, the fringes and the returning.

Clyne and Lovren come back. Allen's in as captain so we stick him on the left wing. Smith's in, Caulker's a centre-back for an entire game. Brannagan and Stewart take the middle, Ibe's got the wing, Teixeira sits behind Benteke.

And we're good. Against a supposedly stronger West Ham team, we're good. We hunt in packs, we close down, we harry and hassle and we break convincingly. We don't score, but you can't have everything, can you?

They impress. The kids impress. Stewart and Brannagan improve each time you see them, Lovren and Caulker (I know, not even vaguely kids) are solid, we're good going forwards, we're good going backwards. Two games on the run now where we haven't conceded from a set piece. Against sides who like set pieces. A revolutionary new approach.

Benteke remains an issue. He's a mixture of the passable and the ridiculous. Decent hold-up play, nice linking, but poor decision-making when it comes to shooting chances. He could have a goal and an assist if he keeps his head, but his head's gone. Maybe if we could take him out for a while, take the heat off him, let him make bit-part appearances while he rebuilds his clearly shattered confidence, but there's nobody else, is there? It's that simple. So we have another match where we make most of the running and don't score, another match where the presence of Ings or Origi, never mind Daniel Sturridge, would probably bring a win. A cup game with no winner means another cup game. Still, I said I wanted a shadow side for this. I got a shadow side and they did well and they'll get another chance to do well at Upton Park some time next week and then perhaps on to Blackburn. Perhaps we'll even have time to sign a shadow striker to play with them.

Leicester City 2 Liverpool 0

2 February 2016

THE THINGS you go through to watch a match. Not any real hardship, if we're honest, not an 'our kid taking a week to go across Greece and down through Turkey on the way to Istanbul' kind of thing. Simply chasing down a semi-decent stream to watch the game on iPad with a couple of glasses of wine. Perils of modern life, eh? It used to be that, if you weren't there in person, you'd spend the evening glued to the radio and then catch highlights on *Match Of The Day*. If it was on.

Fifteen minutes into the game, I finally get a stream. Small, blurry figures run round a field about two inches deep. Can't tell who's who, can't decipher the subtleties of formation. The commentary is in French. Then that stream falls over and I find somebody showing ESPN Brasil with a commentary in Portuguese. I'm not even sure it is Portuguese. I'm not even sure Portuguese is a real language. It sounds like bits of French, Italian, German, Dutch and Russian slammed together. I might be watching an imaginary TV station.

What you can see on this imaginary TV station is this: we're running round a lot, don't look any worse than Leicester, which is a terrible sentence to have to write in any season, but we don't look like scoring. They look like scoring, though. It's Vardy and Mahrez again and it's not like they're a particularly well-kept secret anymore. Everyone knows what they do. We let them do it. And then we have no reply because we have no strikers that aren't broken.

If we'd kept Leicester out, then there was always a chance that we might nick one. We didn't and we didn't. Brought the first team back in after a rest, needn't have bothered. It's just not there at the moment. Confidence and skill and energy and passion, none of it is present.

We end the night eighth in the league, eleven points off fourth place, sixteen off the top. Might as well admit it now, we're *not* going to win the league. I was wrong on that one. Top four looks virtually impossible, top six difficult. The season looks like it's about cups now. We've just hit February.

To add to this burden, the club decided to preface the disappointment of the performance with the exact details of next season's ticket pricing structure, an initiative which had been the subject of plentiful social media speculation the previous day. The speculation had been close but actually didn't go far enough. The fume was massive and looked like it was only just starting.

Liverpool 2 Sunderland 2

6 February 2016

THE FOOTBALL doesn't matter. I mean, obviously the football *matters*, the football always matters. If it didn't, then we wouldn't have done what we did today.

The football's a sideshow today, very little more than that. From the moment that you take your seat at Anfield today, your eye is on the scoreboard and waiting for the clock to tick over into the seventy-seventh minute.

The number 'seventy-seven' is designed to have multiple meanings here, historically notable for being the year of the glory that was Rome and currently notable for representing the most expensive non-hospitality ticket at Anfield next season. It serves as a symbolic time within a game for a visible gesture.

It's only four days since the Leicester game, four days since the announcement of the 2016/17 price structure and the inevitable furore which followed. In those four days 'Spion Kop 106' (the lads who sort the flags for each game) and the Spirit of Shankly organisation, both having been fruitlessly involved in discussions with the club on ticket prices, have organised the first of what might be many protests. We 'WalkOutOn77' as the very successful Twitter hashtag has it.

I'm on *The Anfield Wrap*'s 'Radio City Talk' show on Thursday afternoon and I admit on air that I'm torn. I admit that I don't know what I intend to do on Saturday. I know the walk-out is the right thing to do, but there's those eleven lads in red shirts on the pitch. Walking out feels wrong but right. Walking out feels drastic but necessary.

I'll be honest, in the darkest days of the horrendous Hicks and Gillett, when SoS first came into being with the express intention of forcing the owners to sell the club to somebody even vaguely appropriate, I didn't get it. I didn't join, I didn't demonstrate, I accepted the situation and did nothing to change it. I thought change was impossible, so I made no attempt to be involved. It was only after the sale that I realised how wrong I was.

It was only through reading Brian Reade's magnificent *An Epic Swindle* account of the time under the two warring cowboys that I realised how much work had gone on behind the marches and the outcry, how much influence the e-mail campaign to the club's corporate sponsors had brought to bear on the Royal Bank of Scotland forcing the sale. All this in the time before social media carried its current weight and when there were significantly fewer corporate partners.

By Friday morning, I knew what I was doing. I asked my fifteen-year-old Evertonian son what he would do in our place. He wanted to know why it was even a question.

If we're lucky, and it looks as though we might be, you're looking at this sometime post-August and the subject of my February writing is folklore due to what it achieved in the face of supposed cynicism and doubt. If we're lucky, this happened once and the once was enough. I might not need to raise the subject again.

Do the football bit at this point. We'd been positive, had a very offensive line-up, seemed to be playing some variant of 2-2-everybody else but couldn't score, lacking firepower again. Firmino sat as the only striker of any kind in the eleven, although we had Benteke and the Sturridge that we were told definitely wouldn't be involved both on the bench. I'm sure that I'm not the only one who thought that Dan's hasty reintroduction to match day duties had more to do with the prospect of keeping us in our seats than it did with actually playing him. I'm also sure that I'm not the only one who thought that Jurgen Klopp's emergency appendectomy was the most conveniently timed disaster in the history of man.

Perhaps Jurgen's internal organs coming out in sympathy while the club escaped their manager, possibly publicly, supporting the fans.

Firmino was enough. Scores one, makes one and by seventy minutes we're as comfortable as the 82 per cent possession we registered in the first half would indicate.

You know what comes next. The clock ticks forward, the singing starts. 'Enough is Enough, Enough is Enough, you greedy bastards, Enough is Enough' followed swiftly by a wondrous *You'll Never Walk Alone* sung at the players, sung at ourselves, sung at each other, the main stand applauding the Kop, pockets already on their feet. 'We are the famous, the famous Kopites' followed again by 'Enough is Enough', conducted by the figure of death patrolling the front of the Kop, his robes a reflection of the black flags that had replaced the usual banners before kick-off. And major credit here to the 'Spion Kop 1906' lads.

The only flag retained from the usual display of colour was the recent addition for young Owen McVeigh, who passed away before Christmas. Everything went, this stayed. A beautiful touch. All those songs melted into high-pitched whistles to signal the exit and ten thousand people stood and left. That's ten thousand minimum. Other estimates say fifteen. Magnificent.

The thing that impressed me most was the sheer number that departed from the current (and very much the heart of the issue) main stand. Those of us who nobody expected to show this solidarity, those who most thought would just accept the situation, those who, like me, didn't act in the H&G era. There seemed to be an expectation that the walk-out would be a couple of hundred militants on the Kop, maybe a lone individual here and there, possibly a thousand at most.

The plans were criticised, derided, branded as ineffectual and argued over on Twitter. The arguments carried on as the team decided to clock off for the day and revert to the seemingly ingrained default setting of 'sheer inability to defend'. We were told that the blame for eleven highly trained athletes allowing a two-goal lead to dissipate into a draw that Sunderland had done nothing to merit lay at the feet of those who had walked. That we had broken their concentration, that they were only human (I'll have that they're that, I've argued it myself about the criticism that they receive) and they were bound to be affected.

And *that*, I'm having none of that. Is anybody seriously telling me that at no point in the team talk were the words 'look, the fans might walk out on seventy-seven minutes, just crack on and do your job' used? I don't believe it. I've watched the last thirteen minutes. Twice. My walking out doesn't make Simon Mignolet arrange a shambolic attempt at a wall for Adam Johnson's free kick, it doesn't make Lallana switch off until the ball flies past him and it doesn't make our utterly disastrous keeper flap the ball into the net. It doesn't make Sakho not stick close enough to Defoe and allow him to turn and equalise.

And if it does? If it does? Then we're just showing the club the importance of a strong fanbase, of the fabled twelfth man that they're willing to exploit in every possible manner, and of what happens when they're not there. Of what can happen when they've replaced the lads with the flags with the lads carrying club bags. It's not pretty, is it?

Looks like it's registered as well. There's a glorious photo of Ian Ayre as he looks at the vanishing Kop from his directors' box vantage point. His expression is that of a man who's just realised how badly wrong this has all gone. It's the expression of a man who can see his job vanishing with the fans.

The news breaks on Sunday night, courtesy of Tony Barrett at The Times, that FSG entered emergency board meetings immediately after the match and are considering reviewing the 2016/17 pricing. 'Considering reviewing' can easily equate to 'thinking about thinking', but it can also equate to the start of something. A bunch of lads who go the match looked at what was being done to us all, decided that they weren't ready to accept it and organised something. In four days, they organised something. And thousands of us agreed with them, and thousands of us reacted, and we might have achieved something.

Never let them tell you that you have no power. Never believe it.

West Ham United 2 Liverpool 1

FA Cup Fourth Round Replay
9 February 2016

I KNOW. You're sitting there thinking, 'go on then, you were quite happy to be knocked out of the cup, weren't you? Go with the kids, take the chance and all that.' You might have been waiting, thinking 'wait till the West Ham replay, mate, let's see how you feel then. I've seen how it all works out, you're not going to be happy.'

The perils of writing this as it happens. I knew that you'd get this kind of inconsistency from me. It sits nicely alongside the 'Benteke looks a poor buy/Benteke looks as though he might be the answer/if Benteke's the answer, then it's a stupid question' flip flopping, alongside the 'Emre Can looks to be a Rolls Royce of a player/Emre Can's doing my head in/Emre Can's looking disciplined now' mood shifts. Performances change, situations change, my opinion changes with them. Like the wind.

How do I feel? Gutted, absolutely gutted. We were majestic. Ten changes again, rumours say that there were going to be eleven, but Danny Ward had a cold so Mignolet started. Wonder how that would have turned out? If Ward had started, would he have loaded all his weight on to his right leg when facing the free kick in the last second of extra time, so he had no chance of getting to the ball as it headed across goal? Or would Ward not have made the saves Mignolet made in normal time? Damned if I can figure out whether Si's the hero or villain on this one. Pretty certain he contributes to us going out of the FA Cup, but think he might have also kept us in it.

Same goes for Lucas. His hands are on Valencia's back but the West Ham lad makes the most of it. Are we really calling that a foul nowadays? Quite probably just a case of yet another ref making up for the fact that he missed the blatant penalty that Ilori had given away earlier. We were talking Lucas, though. Lucas Leiva is a centre-back now. Not just pressed into service for emergency, actually starting there. We have a centre- back pairing of Lucas and Ilori and in front of them we have a central midfield pairing of Stewart and Chirivella, and there's no way this should work. Smith and Flanno as full-backs, Ibe, Teixeira and the beautifully returning, intelligently free kick-taking Philippe Coutinho (come on, rolling it under that wall was impertinent genius of the highest order) all sitting behind Benteke. Coutinho reinventing the art of passing, Coutinho making Benteke's movement look sharp for the first time since… well, since the lad was at Villa probably. All of this with the threat of Origi and Sturridge on the bench.

We make ten changes and we look strong, we look sharp, we're moving, we're pressing, we're intelligent and it's the most fun we've had watching Liverpool in bloody ages. We are imperious. And we don't deserve to be behind at half-time and we don't deserve to lose. We're facing a strong West Ham team with our kids and their mates and we're the better team. And there's this point round about the hour when the boss (back from his appendectomy very quickly) decides that Phil and Joao have done enough and he throws on Dan and Divock. Suddenly, from a standpoint of having no forwards at all, there's three of them on the pitch. Origi's fast and tricky but Sturridge is immense, his feet are incredible, his movement's beautiful, he looks as though he hasn't been away. Keep him fit and he's world class. We know this, maybe this time…

Sturridge makes Benteke look better. Christian drops and picks the ball up, moves it on, suddenly has options to link to. There's a difference. There'd been a difference in the first half as well. The big lad is only denied a hat-trick by Randolph having the night of his life in the Hammers' goal. There's a moment when the TV cameras catch Chris and Dan debating a free kick and Christian's actually smiling – first time we've seen him do that. Maybe football's more fun to play if you're enjoying doing it? Maybe that's the key to him playing well? That he's going to enjoy what he's doing?

And, no, I can't defend his failure to convert that volley that drops nicely to him in the second half or the fact that he doesn't hit the six-yard box in the first half when the cutbacks are happening, and that one on one he fails to bury once again. But I'm *not* going to blame him for us not being in the next round of the FA Cup. I'm not going to blame him for the heartbreak of that last second free kick. I'm not going to blame anybody for anything from last night, they were too good. All of them. They all deserved the chance to face the long-faded might of Blackburn in the next round and show, once again, how much fun playing football can be, how much fun watching a Liverpool that does this can be.

Deserved better. Sometimes that happens. Gutted.

(Oh, and the West Ham fans? Steven Gerrard songs then 'Sign On' songs and a lad down the front waving wads of money at the travelling fans. Stay classy, lads. In your new, government-built, government-sponsored, public money paid-for stadium that your Tory baroness chief exec was lucky enough to successfully bid for. For a constituency that returns Labour MPs, you're proving to be Tory as hell.)

The Climbdown

10 February 2016

I'M AT the theatre when it happens. Good play. *I Know All The Secrets In My World*, a virtually wordless piece by England's leading African theatre company, a father and son rebuild their relationship after the sudden death of a wife and mother. I'd expected family secrets, heated conversations, a heavily dialogue-driven piece. What I got was a stylised representation of grief, emotionally charged and well choreographed to a dark soundscape. Give it a try if it's still around, you might like it. It's about reconciliation and reconciliation's always a good thing.

Which is obviously the way that I've decided to drag myself into writing about this. Reconciliation. This is reconciliation. Or a start, at least.

I leave the theatre and Twitter's gone mad. I've only been in there an hour and the world's changed. FSG have climbed down. There's a price freeze on tickets. For two years. I've got all this on the phone and I'm walking through town and I need more detail. I need to be home. I'm slightly gutted that I missed all this and I'm excited about the fact that we achieved something, that we achieved something massive.

The iPad's not charged and the plug is further away from the table than I'd like so I'm eating microwaved Chicken Katsu and pushing the table towards the charging cable. I'm contorted and I'm furiously scrolling backward through Twitter to the actual announcement point. I want to feel the shock again.

An apology, that's the first thing, the announcement starts with an apology. There's something of a defensiveness to it in terms of the three really high-profile guys at FSG feeling that they've been misunderstood, but there's an apology. That's a start. That's good. Then there's the price freeze. No £77 matchday tickets. Highest ticket stays at £59. No season tickets poking their heads over the 'grand' mark, staying as are, lowest priced going down by twenty-five quid.

All good, then the biggies hit, the ones that aren't in the headlines, the real surprises that take the whole thing to a level that I don't think anybody expected immediately.

Categorisation stops. All matches now cost the same. And yes, somebody hit immediately with 'doesn't that mean that they can charge more for the cheaper games now?' and it might but at the moment, who knows? Let's hope that it actually means that they're not putting *anything* up. We can dig into the details later. And do we really think that they'll use this climbdown to hide a little bit of a stitch-up job? It'd be the single most stupid thing that they'd done since, well, the middle of last week.

The £9 tickets which were being offered for a handful of games and added up to about eighteen hundred tickets across the season in matches that nobody would actually be asking to see? There are now ten thousand of them and they cover the entire season. Every single game.

This is what they've done. And credit to them for it. FSG have looked at the situation that they've caused, the response that they created and they've managed it. In terms of business management, it's masterful, it's decisive and it's creative. It's also notable that their Liverpool-based CEO, last seen on video last Friday, which was clearly 'mufti' day given that he'd turned up for work in a t-shirt and V-neck sweater combo, telling us that we were wrong and we could like it or lump it as there were always people who *would* buy those seats at those prices if we didn't, is completely absent from all this.

Fifteen thousand of us stood up and walked. There were those in the ground who thought it was foolish and that's okay. I get that doubt, I've been part of that doubt. This time, I wasn't. I'm glad that I wasn't. I'm proud that I was a small part of this. We did this. The Tories next then, eh lads?

Aston Villa 0 Liverpool 6

14 February 2016

THIS IS how it works. I know I've probably started other bits like that, but sometimes that's what you need. Sometimes it's about transparency. Most matches I'll sit back and think about the whole thing, decide how I felt about it, watch the game again, highlights at least. Work it all out. But when you go to Villa and put six past them, then it seems right to write in the middle of the buzz. Which might mean that you don't over-analyse, don't review, perhaps even get things in the wrong order because there are so many of the things to talk about. You'll spot that bit. You'll probably spot the bits that pop in from a Monday morning edit and have a bit of recall rather than being full of the rush of Sunday afternoon. It all adds up to the same thing, though.

It's not even difficult. We don't have to be devastating, we just have to be decisive. Aston Villa were sitting at the bottom of the table before kick-off today for a very good reason: they're terrible. There must be nearly five minutes in the first half where they look as though they might threaten to break into the game, but that vanishes pretty quickly as they seem to realise the depths of their own hopeless nature and surrender to it.

I'm sure there's every possibility that a team this utterly abject saw the team sheet go up, clocked the fact that we were able to play our first-choice front three for the first time ever and knew that they should have spent Sunday at home doing the ironing. Sturridge, Coutinho and Firmino combining and showing, without breaking sweat, that they might well be the answer.

There's a fluidity across the front line that we've lacked all season. There's movement, invention, flair. Sturridge is on the right then in the centre, then the left. Firmino's dropping, poking, prodding, battling for the ball, winning things back and never giving up. It's the never giving up that wins the free kick that gives us the second goal. Coutinho's happy just to dictate the entirety of the play and let Milner, then Can, then Henderson, burst past him as they see fit. He's happy to regard Moreno as the overlapping winger that he's clearly decided that he truly is. We're high again and mobile again and full of purpose again.

It's amazing what having forwards who know where the goal is can do for you, isn't it?

Yesterday, Everton had 34 attempts on goal, more than any other team this season, and lost one-nil. You look up in the second half and we've had ten attempts, eight on target and six of them are goals. We've won six-nil away from home and we haven't had to excel to do it. We just look like a commanding, capable, clinical Liverpool side. That's a hell of a thing to be. We look like Liverpool. I like it when we look like Liverpool. Hopefully we'll do it more often from now on.

Want a defining moment? Okay, I'm watching at home, I'm desperate for the loo, it's three-nil and Sturridge is going off. Now's a good time, substitutions are always a good time. Divock Origi is waiting to come on. I hear the televised roar from upstairs and something in my soul knows who it is. I'm downstairs and it's four and Origi's the fourth, the fourth of six scorers. That's defining, that's decisive.

Let's see if we can do the six, shall we? It's half an hour after the game, I've re-watched nothing, I can hear City playing Spurs in the other room. So, without re-watching or reviewing:

Sturridge. Fifteen minutes to get his first away league goal in, oooh ages. Stands between two defenders who don't seem to realise he's on the pitch and heads between them from a gorgeous Coutinho cross.

Milner. A free kick, won by Firmino hassling a poor lad who just wants to let the ball go out so he can have a quiet afternoon. A ball in, Sakho tries to jump for it, but it just sails straight in.

Can. A cutback, a blast. What he should be doing more of.

Origi. After twenty seconds on the pitch? All pace and power and precision.

Kolo. Another unmarked header. As though the lads at the back felt that they'd tried too hard for Dan's and wanted to look really lax.

Clyne. He has a go at it and the keeper saves, as he already has earlier and quite spectacularly, Origi has a go, it's smothered and then Clyne decides he should put it away anyway. So he does.

And that's the bit, isn't it? The bit where I get the goals the wrong way round. It's Clyne *then* Kolo. That's what happens when you're doing stuff from memory and your memory's gone all giddy.

We start with all three of the big guns. We end with none of them. We end with Stewart and Origi and then Benteke on the pitch. We bring Benteke on at the point that you think 'the only way this could get worse for Villa is if Benteke scores'. We bring on Benteke on a day that is genuinely a day for shooting fish in a barrel and he still doesn't score. Might be a message in that one, Chris. If it can't happen today, then it's never happening. Still, can't have everything, can you?

Back up to eighth but only three points off fifth, nine off fourth, but you never know, do you? We can do today without looking like we're straining. We can do commanding, comfortable, confident. It's almost as though not being able to put out the team that you want to put out could be seen as limiting and being able to put out that team can suddenly remove those limits.

Augsburg next then Augsburg again then City at Wembley and we've started to look like the sort of team that scores six goals from six guys away from home. Onwards.

Augsburg 0 Liverpool 0

Europa League Last 32
18 February 2016

THE FIRST Augsburg game isn't what we think it's going to be. All the buoyancy from the Villa game disappears very quickly. All of a sudden, we don't look like the kind of team that scores six goals away from home. We look like the kind of team that doesn't score away from home, the kind of team that runs out of ideas fairly quickly.

It's a consistency issue. Klopp's pretty open about that in his quietly fuming after-match interviews. Not 100 per cent happy, he says, and it's clearly something of an understatement. There's no way that he didn't spend the days between the Villa win and the Augsburg game telling the players 'this is what you're capable of, do this again, build up a good lead and you've got next Thursday off to sit at home and think about Wembley while the kids play the second leg'. There seemed no obvious reason why we should struggle with this one. Augsburg weren't the most formidable of opponents. They're probably the team we'd have chosen if offered, and they lost their only real goal threat very early in the first half. They weren't going to win. But then, neither were we. A bright start becomes a settling for what we've got, becomes a goalless draw becomes, very probably, the same lads playing again on Thursday and then *again again* on Sunday.

We're in a strange position at the moment. The team that started against Villa and was unchanged for this game (a first for Jurgen, being able to name an unchanged side) feels like it's probably 'the' first-choice eleven at the moment. But probably only until the end of the season. There will be changes. We know two of them already in the shape of Matip and Gurjic. Deals are done for those two lads and you'd imagine they're destined for the first eleven. Jurgen's talking about wingers, so you'd think there are one or two other players who can consider their place to be under threat. These lads, the ones out here tonight, aren't necessarily building for the future. Some of them, not all of them.

We can't argue that these specific lads need European football this season in order to prepare them for next season, as they might not be here for it, but the club needs it, the fans need it. We need to see success. The FA Cup is gone, the top four looks likely to be out of reach, the League Cup concludes on Sunday. If we go no further in the UEFA, then what's the rest of the season really about? We need a strong team in the second leg. We need to ensure that there's more to play for.

We also need a strong side out on Sunday. For very, very obvious reasons. A cup is a cup is a cup. And cups breed cups, winning breeds winning. The 2001 treble started with the League Cup, it had to. It's the first thing you can win in any season. It teaches you how to win things and the single most important thing this side, or however much of this side that will be together next season, can be taught is how to win things. Winning the League Cup gives you a chance of winning the UEFA Cup because *you know how to win*.

A comfortable win against Augsburg would have given more preparation time for the final against City, would have given the confidence of knowing there was one less thing to worry about, of knowing that one more job had been done. Now we have to go strong in both games. Augsburg away? An opportunity missed. Let's hope it's the last.

Liverpool 1 Augsburg 0

Europa League Last 32 Second Leg
25 February 2016

DEAR UEFA/FIFA/THE Telly/Whoever,

6pm kick-offs? They're horrendous things, absolutely horrendous. You do realise that people are basically still in work while you're kicking off, don't you? That it's actually pretty difficult for the home fans to get to the ground in time for kick-off? That's why people are still taking their seats after quarter of an hour. That's why people, quite a few people, managed to miss the only goal of the evening. It might even be why the goal itself, a James Milner penalty which gently squirmed its way under the goalie's body, seems such an anti-climax, almost dreamlike. 6pm kick-offs mess with your body clock, make everything seem like it's in the wrong place at the wrong time. Which might be why I was in bed by half-ten, with my body convinced it was midnight. But that's my problem. Let's talk about the football, shall we?

They had an eye on Sunday. You could see it in the way the pressing stopped in the second half, in the way they kind of accepted that the penalty was going to be as good as it got. You could see it in the way they realised that Augsburg's goalie's decision that he was going to have a worldie was probably going to carry on into the second half, so they might as well stop testing him. After all, what's the point in working your arse off to get a shot in if the lad's just going to do *that* again and again and again. He's on fire, clawing efforts out, stopping them from creeping in at the post, dragging them from under the bar, catching everything that crosses his path, basically doing what keepers do. Buy him. Buy him now. Or when the transfer window opens. Probably more realistic doing that.

Not that our own keeper's that bad tonight. He has a lovely moment when his entire defence has let him down and he has to charge out of the area to tackle a lad. Bit mad, bit more of that please, Si.

We're nervy, though. We're nervy all over the place. Good in the first half, playing football in the first half, sprinting into pressing in the first half, shooting, flicking, combining, working, looking smart. Hendo and Emre are running the midfield, the lads up front are everywhere and Milner's filling in every crack that he can find. Lucas is centre-back when there are other centre-backs actually available to us and, other than one woefully under-hit back pass which nearly kills our European dreams, he's great, he reads everything, he stops pretty much everything. We're looking good, we're looking like we'll score four or five. And then we don't. The second half comes and we're not as potent, not as threatening. We're not pressing, Augsburg are. They're threatening a break at any moment. We are, and I might have mentioned this, nervy. It might be the 'looking forward to Sunday with a full team out and not wanting to get injured' factor. It might be the 'they only had to score one and stop us scoring at the start of the night to go through and now we've scored that doesn't change a single thing' factor. It might be the 'if we go out here and then lose on Sunday, the season's basically over' factor. But something makes us nervy, subdued, loose, ineffective. It's a forty-five minutes that feels like clinging on, like an Augsburg goal is coming. It's an inviting of pressure and a conceding of set-plays. It feels like the inevitable is looming.

And loom it might, it doesn't arrive. The obvious Augsburg equaliser doesn't happen. We don't impress but we survive. The job's done, the only comment that you can hear as the ground empties is: 'We'll have to play better than that on Sunday.'

We'll have to play better than that on Sunday.

AND I finish writing all that at two minutes to noon on the Friday morning. Just in time for the Europa League draw, which provides us with the wonderful spectacle of 'some bloke' (President of something? No idea, I don't know who's in charge of anything any longer. I know that Sky is covering the election of Blatter's successor at FIFA and I know that it doesn't really matter because, let's be honest, we don't trust any of them, do we? Head of UEFA, though? Platini's gone and I don't know who got the job, so we'll carry on calling him 'some bloke') asking Alexander Frei questions in English, which Frei then answers in German. That's fair enough, it's his first tongue, but questions in English and answers in German are basically weird. And very bad television for both nationalities.

Frei proceeds to pull the ballot balls from the bowl, open each and laugh as he finds a piece of paper in each. There's supposed to be a piece of paper in each, Alex, that's what they're there for.

We hit the halfway point and I turn to J and say "I make that eight balls left and three of them are English. You can see what's coming, can't you?"

Frei's odd, nervous laughter becomes more pronounced as he opens a certain ball. More pronounced still as he reads out the words 'Liverpool FC', almost hysterical (okay, slight exaggeration) as he pulls the next from its comrades. The camera's tight in on his hands, you can see the M and the U. "United, we've got United."

In a fortnight's time, we have the Mancs at Anfield in a European knockout game. A week later, we go to their place. It must be the shortest away trip that we've ever made. Bring it on.

Liverpool 1 Manchester City 1

Capital One Cup Final
28 February 2016
(And then there were those penalties)

WE WERE in the team hotel. I know how that sounds, it's not like that. Most years, we wouldn't have been but then, most years, nor would the team. Jurgen had changed accommodation in order to not stay in a hotel that had seen only losses for his teams. For our part, we were there because our Keith needed to pick up a ticket.

We'd intended to go to The Green Man. We'd been pretty damn pleased that it had been in our pub allocation this year after going missing for the last few visits, when we'd basically ended up drinking warm supermarket lager outside a Wembley branch of Kwik Fit. It felt like tradition was returning. It felt right. It basically sat alongside the idea of parking in front of the same flats for the fifth consecutive Wembley visit in the 'this is what we do' file. This is what we do. We go to Wembley. We're Liverpool and we go to Wembley.

Only one problem with all that at the moment. The last actual victory in those five visits is beginning to feel like a long time ago. The Everton semi-final in the year that Kenny took us to Wembley three times in ten weeks and still lost his job at the end of it all. We came out of that spell with a Carling(?)/ Capital One(?)Worthington(?)/Rumbelows(?)/ Milk(?)/sod it *League* Cup win against Cardiff and a loss against Chelsea in the FA Cup that nearly, nearly, nearly became a glorious comeback. Follow that with Brendan's woeful capitulation against Villa last year and Wembley seems in danger of turning into a good day out with a bleak interruption at the centre of it.

And today's a good day out with a slightly bleak interruption at the centre of it. Not 'changing formation five thousand times and not showing up against Villa with all the atmosphere left in the alehouse' bleak, but still disappointing, dispiriting, a missed chance.

We're in the Hilton because Keith had no ticket. Our cousin's husband knew a lad who knew a lad, though, and suddenly Keith's sorted with a Club Wembley seat. Which is obviously great and why we're in the Hilton rather than The Green Man.

It's clearly a fine hotel but somewhat lacking in atmosphere when compared with the pubs, as demonstrated quite beautifully by the tweet that shows our pub of choice to be filled with pyro in a gif that could be inside, could be outside as it's nothing but pink smoke and singing. It looks great, looks like it's bouncing, like it's the most fun you could ever have. To balance this, we have really good toilets and the knowledge that the team themselves are in the building.

You'd think that the hotel the team have chosen to stay in would be on lockdown of some kind. You'd think that you'd need a Hilton keycard of some kind to get in. Perhaps be carrying ID or reek of money at the very least. You wouldn't expect them to be letting just any knobhead wander in and out quite freely, but they are. I know because I am that knobhead.

We're in a room upstairs watching the United game on big screens. We know the Liverpool team bus is outside, know it has to leave eventually, although, in fairness, the lads could quite easily walk to the ground, boots in hand, go the full Billy Liddell. Might take a while, like, but there's loads of balls knocking around outside. They could join in a quick three and in on the way. We know there's a buzz building outside, we can feel it. Peter's lad has gone down to see the team. Pete decides he'll follow him, our Kev says he'll go as well. I'm not going, I'm adopting the attitude that I'm fifty-two, I'm way too old for that kind of thing. I'm adopting that attitude for nearly a minute before I think 'Might as well, mightn't I?'

I hit the bottom of the escalator and the security lad takes one look at my £5 plastic bottle of Budweiser and says: 'You can't have that down here, mate.' 'Fair enough,' I say and do the sensible thing, walk back up the escalator, stick the cold, damp, bottle of Bud in my arse pocket and come back down unnoticed. These security lads are looking after our team, you know.

We're at the back of the throng, Peter's standing on a stool as though it were 1976 and he were too short to see properly in the Kop. 'How old are you?' I ask. 'Fifty-five but don't tell me mum.' Honest to god, no idea how we got this old. Last time I looked, we were all in our twenties and we were winning things.

Cameras are out and we're filming closed elevator doors which open with a bing so that we're now filming lads in suits walking out, round a corner and out of the hotel. We're standing ten yards from the team. *The team.* I'm fifty-two years old and I'm filming the team and I'm having the time of my life and I don't care. Benteke's huge, Klopp is grinning like nobody you've ever seen in your life. There's singing and everything's great and everything's hopeful. I'd been calm and measured all morning, all sort of 'well, it's a game of football, it'll be fine', but now I'm excited and it's a proper cup final with teams wearing suits and getting a bus to the match through throngs of fans, It's everything that we're here for and it's too long since we last did it and you know, just *know*, that we're good enough. We can do this.

We didn't. You know that. It's not like you've forgotten, is it? And you know how it happened, so we don't need to do a blow-by-blow account. What we *can* do, though, is figure out what we learnt from the whole thing:

Jurgen Klopp took us to a final with a team that wasn't his and he had that team stand toe to toe and trade blow for blow with the most expensively assembled team in the country, had them take that opposition team to the good old penalty lottery.

Someone has to win that lottery, someone has to lose it. We lost it, it happens. We know how all those other lads felt now, the ones that we beat and celebrated in front of.

Obviously the nature of those penalties is somewhat disappointing. If you're one-nil up after the first pair are complete, then you've a bit of a right to think that you might be on for a win. Think we kind of assumed that going to pens would kind of take care of the result. It doesn't, though, does it? It didn't. And I'm not going to get into the 'Why didn't Sturridge take one? Why didn't Henderson take one?' argument in the same way that I didn't enter into it with the random lad who grabbed me outside the ground saying 'Have you seen Jordan Henderson? He was supposed to be here today but I haven't seen him anywhere.'

Sturridge couldn't walk after about eighty minutes and Henderson was probably our most influential player in extra time. He was certainly the focal point for all the intent, all the energy. He was the lad trying to drag us over the line. If neither of those were up to the task of taking one of the first five penalties, whether physically or mentally, then I'm not taking issue with them.

I'd love to say it was a weird final but it wasn't. It was a typical final. Nobody wanted to lose. A cagey first half followed by a busier second, followed by a mix of the manic and the mundane as both sides try to win in extra time without losing. The busyness comes because we need to up everything after we give City a lead, need to start playing.

And that's a thing that we learn. We learn that we can't trust our left-back and our goalie. We know this already but today assures us of the fact. The weird dichotomy of Mignolet is that he's entirely to blame for the City goal, but he also keeps us in the game with four very good saves. The problem is that there are too many occasions where you need to qualify Mignolet mistakes with '...but he also...' type comments. You can blame him at two points on this one, though, and Moreno at one but it's a kind of continuous one. Between them, the two hapless lads make a mistake sandwich.

Mignolet kicks long, to the touchline. Which is always a mistake. His long kicks are a mistake, his short kicks are a mistake, his kicks are… you get the message. Milner and Clyne challenge for the header but Sterling wins it. Sterling. *Bloody* Sterling. At least he still can't shoot. We could have shipped three before we'd got a single shot in if Sterling could shoot. Thank Christ he's not the player that he and his agent think he is.

Aguero ends up with the ball, which is bad enough in itself. That Moreno has lost him already, then decides that he should chase him and loses Fernandinho's run so that he can replace one mistake with another, just adds to the issue. That the City lad then puts the ball between Mignolet's legs and off his elbow into the net is insult and injury combined. Klopp's patience with the left-back lasts longer than ours does. He waits until the lad's been found out of position too many times and has almost given away a penalty before pulling him and sticking Lallana on to allow James Milner, a right-footed midfielder rather than anything resembling a left-back, to put in a more tactically aware shift in Moreno's stead.

We look better once Lallana's on the pitch. We look urgent, we deserve the equaliser. We've had the majority of the ball, we've bossed the first half. City have changed tactics for basically the first time ever because they don't want a repeat of that mauling at their place. They're willing to let us play football and see if we can break them down. And for the workrate that we put in, for the fact that we don't stop going and for the fact that we've made them fear us, we deserve the equaliser.

Or you could look at it this way: for the fact that we don't have a shot on target until the eighty-third minute and City could have put five past us, we don't actually deserve anything. It's not even fine margins, it's wide divisions but both clearly conflicting arguments are correct. It's that kind of match.

And in the extra half hour, it's the kind of match that could be decided by tiredness. Origi's on for the anonymous Firmino, Sturridge has no option but to do the full two hours as the loss of Sakho to a collision with Emre, which brought back unwanted Spackman/Gillespie comparisons, has severely dented our substitution gameplan. We've survived against Sergio Aguero with a centre-back pairing of Lucas and Kolo. Anyone have any money riding on that? No, thought not. Anything could happen in this last half-hour but it doesn't. And then there's the pens. Which I'm not talking about. Other than to say, Lucas's isn't that bad, Lallana's is pretty good, Caballero does well to get to both. Coutinho, though? Phil, it's a free kick, lad. Without a wall. Treat it like a free kick. Or, just twat it. Whichever. Don't mind which one of those you choose, the little stutter, though? The hesitation? No. Don't. Ever again. Ta.

There's a near four-hour drive home, fuelled by coffee, chocolate and Lucozade. There's not as much conversation on the way back as there was on the way down. There never is after a loss. There's not a cup to take home. Could do with a couple of big games on the horizon in order to bounce back, say…City at home in the league and then two games versus United in Europe?

Yep. That'll do us. Season's not over yet, there's still work to do.

Liverpool 3 Manchester City 0

2 March 2016

THE WORK starts here. A loss tonight, combined with Tuesday night's league programme results, would have seen us stranded in eleventh place and way off the pace. Below Everton, below United, below Chelsea, whose season has obviously been appalling, below *everyone*. Marooned, desolate, destroyed, out of reach of anything much, league season probably all but over in the first week of March. A City win would have put them back into contention for a late title shot.

There was also the small matter of Sunday's defeat adding context to the game. Everything to play for then. And we played for everything. *Everything.*

The 'parking further away from the ground now because some bluenose traffic warden ticketed us' combined with the 'your chips will take a couple of minutes' combined with the 'it's bloody freezing walking across Stanley Park and it feels like that big stand's miles away' meant that I missed the kick-off. Again. Missed the first minute. Missed Flanno go through Raheem Sterling and ensure that there was a bit of physical pain to add to the psychological suffering that was unleashed from the stands every time he looked at the ball. He might have survived Wembley unscathed, he might have picked up a cup that he actually had no influence on, but we were closer to him tonight and we outnumbered the City fans who had managed to not sell out their end despite living twenty-eight miles away, and we were going to let him know that we weren't overly enamoured with him. Forty-five minutes he lasted. Forty-nine million of your hard earned oil pounds for a lad that you have to pull at half-time because you're two-nil down and he's not looking likely to influence events? Priceless, as they say in the ad breaks.

We're immaculate tonight. We're pretty much perfect in every single department. There's no Sturridge, that's obvious, the lad was out on his feet through extra time on Sunday. There's no Sakho – that little head-to-head with Emre was always going to see him ruled out – and Lucas has a muscle issue which isn't entirely shocking given the colossal nature of his Wembley efforts. Coutinho doesn't leave the bench. Coutinho doesn't need to leave the bench.

Pellegrini complains later that his players were tired because they'd played for two hours at the weekend and had played three games in eight days, conveniently forgetting that Liverpool had played three in six and the middle of those three games was against Pellegrini's own side. As 'ignoring Liverpool altogether' statements go, it's as random as Raheem's post semi-final claim that, 'this was the reason he joined City, to play in finals', totally missing the fact that he was playing against his previous employers in that final.

If there was tiredness in our legs, we swept it away with waves of determination. If there was tiredness in City's ranks, it was placed there by endless waves of red, pushing them back, breaking over them, repeatedly breaking over them.

Three matches against City this season. Three matches against, as I've already pointed out without actually checking the veracity of the claim, the most expensively assembled squad in the Premier League and we've won two, drawn one, scored eight and only conceded two. We've lost a penalty shoot-out to the team that quite fancied the idea of winning a quadruple this year, to the team that thinks it has a genuine chance of winning the Champions League before their new manager arrives. As we stand at the end of Wednesday night, it looks very likely that Guardiola is going to be playing on Thursday nights next season. One draw where we equalled their abilities, two wins where we played them off the park, our park and their park. Out-thought, out-fought, out-classed. These are the moments when we see our abilities. Add consistency to this and we're looking at something. We've won this at a canter, we've put City in their place and we've managed it without the two players that you would consider to be our best.

There's no point in this book where I've felt the need to go with the whole 'here's the team-sheet' approach, but these lads deserve to have their names checked.

Mignolet: faces a shot in the ninety-third minute. Other than that, can't be entirely sure how he kept warm.

Flanagan: let's be honest, Sterling worries him a few times in the first half, I'm ready to call for him to be subbed at half-time but then he appears in the box, in a somewhat 'shopkeeper from Mr Benn' moment to deny Aguero a genuine chance. Sterling has the rest of the night off and Flanno becomes the most comfortable full-back in creation.

Clyne: he's at left back and he's not Moreno. That's a decent thing. He gets forward a lot and he gets back a lot.

Dejan Lovren: looks like the defender that we thought we'd bought, keeps calm, stops things, wins things, steps out.

Kolo: Kolo, Kolo, Kolo. Brilliant, brilliant Kolo. Arrives from nowhere, takes the ball off lads' toes, deals with everything, does everything. He's suddenly twenty-five again.

And then there's the lads in the middle, a four, most of the time, a proper old-fashioned four with wingers, but those wingers are swapping round and making sure that they're everywhere, and we have two proper lads in the middle who are bossing the game and getting into things.

From the middle outwards then:

Emre Can: Emre does all the good Emre stuff and does it better than ever before. And he does absolutely none of the bad Emre stuff, the stuff where he gets caught dawdling in the middle of the park or pings meaningless balls to nobody in particular.

He's rampaging and blocking and tackling and digging and pirouetting his way through a City midfield that doesn't know what's happening. Best game in a red shirt? Quite possibly.

Man of the match? Would be if it wasn't for the lad in the number twenty shirt.

Next to Emre, though, in the middle, doing the rest of the harrying and pushing and probing and carrying it forward and appearing next to Flanno, screaming encouragement and praise at the very moment that Flanno sets the tone for the evening by letting Raheem know that he's not having an easy night:

Jordan Henderson returning to the state of Jordan Henderson-ness which we know he's capable of and doing the captain thing in a very, very big way.

James Milner: clearly upset at the weekend's result, clearly upset that he lost a cup to the team that he left, he's decided to make amends tonight. He's everywhere, he's doing everybody's job. Not because he needs to but because he can, because he's capable of making that burst between Otamendi and Kompany to clip the second goal past Joe Hart, because tonight he's capable of doing anything. He celebrates the goal. Properly celebrates it. This means something.

Adam Lallana: has his name sung. Deserves having his name sung because he's incredible. Because he's just had the best game that he's yet had in a red shirt, because he's made a goal for Firmino and he's back-heeled a pass to set up Milner's and because he's the man who decided that striding from the halfway line and shooting was a good idea. And yes, it's a fairly tame shot and nobody in the crowd knows how it's beaten Hart, but it's beaten Hart and it's in the net and it's magnificent.

Roberto Firmino: Another man who's everywhere, a man who can judge a run to just peel off the last man's shoulder and curl a clip past the still-stranded Hart to make it three and then bamboozle the keeper further by stuffing the ball up the front of his shirt before moving it round the back and watching England's apparent number one try and figure what happened. Which is a metaphor for the night, in case you weren't certain.

Divock Origi: runs the channels, holds the ball up and threatens. Does the number nine role and does it to perfection.

Add goals to this lad and we might have something good here. Best game in a red shirt? Are you seeing a thread here?

And we get Benteke and Benteke holds the ball up and brings people into play and we get Joe Allen and he has this wonderfully unexpected dipping volley that could and should have made it four and we see a little bit of Jordon Ibe and he's positive and that'll do fine, thanks very much.

Three-nil, could have been four, five, six. We wouldn't have been flattered. Big numbers would have been appropriate. We were *that* good. We were genuinely that good. Biggest home win of the season, best home performance of the season. By a very long way. Amazing how quickly football can heal you, isn't it? What a gorgeous, gorgeous game.

Crystal Palace 1 Liverpool 2

6 March 2016

In the 96th minute
(which really annoyed the rest of the world)

OH, THE fume is magnificent, absolutely magnificent. The rest of the world hates us for today, hates us for not really looking as though we can impose ourselves on the game for fifty of the first sixty minutes and then deciding, once we're down to ten men, that it might be time to start playing, threatening, making a difference, hates us for benefitting from a reserve goalkeeper who's making his first start in six months and panics a little bit when he sees Divock Origi closing in on him to the extent that he decides to pass straight to Bobby Firmino. You know that moment in FIFA when you think you're clearing it and suddenly it's at the feet of this attacker that you hadn't seen coming? It's that. It's gorgeous and the world hates us for it. A bit. Just a bit. What the world really hates us for is the penalty. That lovely, lovely penalty.

'It's not a penalty,' screams everybody that isn't us. 'It's a dive, it's the most disgusting dive ever.' It isn't. It isn't even vaguely that. We'll come to what it is in a moment, but the blatant truth of what it is isn't enough to stop the lad who decides to start a petition to have Christian Benteke banned for, well, probably life, and have Liverpool docked every point that we've earned since the start of the Premier League. As sad, insignificant gestures go, it's up there with the Arsenal lad who started the petition to force us to sell them Suarez for forty-million and one pounds.

Last time I looked, the new Palace one had six signatures. Sad and lonely and hilarious.

Context though. Context and background: it was Mothers' Day and we had both of ours round for lunch. I had the choice, J gave me the choice, and let's be honest, I couldn't keep the mums waiting until four, until the game was over, 'It's okay,' I said, 'I'll tape it and watch it later.'

I didn't watch it later. I kind of watched the first half with one eye while at the table, doing my best to be the diligent son and son-in-law and maintain conversation while trying not to get too wound up by the match. I watched the second half from the couch with a nice glass of Prosecco. I do enjoy a very civilised way to watch a game.

That's the background, here's the context: we were supposed to go out on Saturday night, had tickets to see Luke Barnes' play *Who's Afraid Of The Working Class?* at the Unity Theatre. It's a fine, fine play, I urge you to see it. J had been at Goodison in the afternoon, though. I'd travelled back up from London (Islington Assembly Halls on Friday night to see Mr Head play a damn fine set with a full band), had a quick shower and picked her up from near the ground as per usual. Everton had led two-nil against West Ham, had a Lukaku penalty for a third to kill the game off despite being down to ten men. Lukaku took the Coutinho penalty shoot-out option and did the little skip and pass to the keeper routine. Seventy minutes in and they're leading two-nil. By the ninety-fifth, they've thrown the whole thing away and lost three-two. J's not going out, she's in no mood. I get it. I wonder if footballers know that this is what they do to us, to us all?

That's your context then, that's your context for the sheer level of anger that comes from the blue half of the city as well. Two weeks ago, they were ahead of us and looking at kicking on. Today they're six points behind, looking at us sitting six points off fourth and seriously looking like we can push on.

It was one of those games, one of those games where you put down a marker and say: 'We can do *this* as well.'

We show some of the invention and pace that we showed against City. We start with that kind of intensity and then Palace put in their own intensity and start to threaten and then it gets all kind of equal, but it's end to end and it's probably a game that's amazing for the neutral to watch. But I don't believe there are any neutrals. In anything. There's always a stake. Everton fans have a stake in this, a 'Palace beating us as they have the last few times'-shaped stake. So do United fans, City fans, Chelsea fans and possibly Spurs. Not a 'we're really worried about Liverpool catching up' sort of stake, but a 'we can't stand those lads in red, we want them to lose' sort of stake. Which I both get and think is bloody great. I'm having the idea of a siege mentality. I'm having defiance.

I'm having the kind of defiance where we can decide that we're going to be as physical as Palace, that we're not being bullied by these lads this time round, not getting caught by Pardew's standard 'long ball to the fast lads on the wing' counter-attack tactic. We're going to mix it, we're going to do that old thing where you earn the right to play. We're going to show that we can defend. And we do. Until there's this one ball that isn't cleared and it drops to Joe Ledley and he gives Palace the lead.

Which, considering that we're an hour in, we haven't had an actual shot on target yet and it's taken a pretty magnificent save from Mignolet to keep us in the game, is a fairly bad thing. We don't look like scoring. We look like passing the ball around on the edge of the area and being patient, but you can't see where the goal's coming from. Klopp's gone very positive to try and sort the problem out. He's pulled Flanno, thrown Coutinho on and pushed Milner to right-back. We can be more ambitious from here.

That feeling lasts for nearly a minute before Milner sees the red mists descend for the first time in his two-hundred year career, picks up a second yellow and wanders forlornly to the bench. Klopp's calm, rearranging, but you still can't see the goal coming. And then the goalie passes to Firmino and we're back in this and everything's gorgeous again.

Benteke's on. Not Sturridge, Benteke. On for Origi, who's done all the tireless running. And the Belgian that replaces the Belgian is looking good. He's moving well, comes close to scoring a couple of times, the first time with his first shot, but it looks like it's one of those days.

Klopp's third sub is interesting. With the ten men, we've been the better side, we've had the energy, we've had the invention, we've had the intensity, we're the side that now looks most likely to score. So, when Jurgen introduces Kolo in place of Firmino, it seems to smack of 'okay lads, we'll take the point, good enough'.

It's nothing of the kind. Can, who had stepped into the centre-back role with Lovren becoming the world's best temporary right-back in the absence of our vice-captain, is back in midfield and pushing from there. We're taking the game to Palace and it might not be what the manager intended, it might just be that the players want this, that they really, really want this.

The ball from Henderson is beautiful in both weight and speed and Benteke has only one intent, he's getting to the byline and he's looking for a man in the centre. Rewind it, watch it, slow motion it, see what he does.

He glances up, glances to his left. He has no idea that Delaney's behind him, he's looking for the final pass of the game, looking for it to be devastating. Benteke's weight is on his left foot, his left foot is arched, he's on his toes and his heel's in the air. His right foot's off the floor. Delaney's knee hits Benteke's left heel. And the world cries 'dive'. It's not a dive, it's physics, your standing foot gets hit and you're hitting the floor. There's laws and stuff governing this kind of thing, physical-world rules and all that. The fuss is ridiculous, bizarre, unfounded, but Pardew's fuming and the southern media love a southern lad who'll give them good quotes and be all matey, so they're going with this nonsense.

The penalty itself is confident, bordering on beautifully arrogant. There's a hesitation just at the moment that the red part of the universe is yelling 'just smack it', but Chris knows what he's doing and what he's doing is showing that he has something and that he *can* be the man who makes the difference. It could yet be a rebirth. It's assured enough to be a rebirth.

It's a moment. This, coming back from one down with ten men to win, is a moment. It's a moment that we've never managed at any point in our history according to the very hastily assembled stats that appear within moments of the final whistle. It's a moment that says 'We're intelligent enough to change a game when you think we can't, intelligent enough on the pitch and intelligent enough on the touchline, our players won't give up, our players know what it feels like to lose big games, to lose finals, they know how it hurts and they're going to make sure they never feel that hurt again and when Jurgen said that we'd never be beaten by a Palace-like performance again he meant it and, oh yeah, one more thing, we've got bigger balls than you.'

The run-in starts here, the top four is no longer an impossible dream and we have a chance to take a measure of revenge for our two losses to United in what is genuinely one of the biggest European ties that we have ever had.

Why is everyone criticising us? Because they're starting to realise what we can be, that's why. They hate us because they realise that it's time to fear us again.

Liverpool 2 Manchester United 0

10 March 2016
(Europa League, round of 16 first leg or
whatever we're calling it.)

OH, NOW there's a nice segue, last line of the previous chapter into the events of this. I didn't plan it, I didn't change it, I wrote it after the Palace game and I left it there. It's not a deliberate connection, it's just the way the world works.

We've got two things to talk about here and we're going to do them one at a time and then we're going to talk about exactly how the second impacts the first and exactly what the first shows us.

A quick editorial note from the viewpoint of Sunday afternoon and how it relates to what I wrote in this first bit on Friday: the chronology is wrong. You'll quite possibly spot the error immediately, but I didn't. Not until I re-watched the entire game this morning. I could rewrite, I could edit but that's fake, that's false. What immediately follows is what I thought on Friday morning, when I was writing with adrenalin, with the immediate post-game buzz and post-game anger. Changing it isn't in the spirit that I started this book with. I'll see you on the other side of this, when the italics appear again, you'll know it's Sunday afternoon and Arsenal are out of the FA Cup. Hopefully the Mancs will follow Arsene's lads' lead.

'Sign on, sign on …and you'll never get a job' they sang. It's what, the third time I've referenced that song in recent chapters? And it's becoming more and more prevalent. And you think, 'hold on lads, you're from Salford. Well, your *club* is from Salford, *the team you support* is from Salford, you lot could be from anywhere, probably need to drive past Liverpool on your way up to United's home games.' Hope that's the case, to be honest because, otherwise...

'Salford's like Liverpool, Mancunians are like Scousers, we're working class, we love our footy, we love our music, we're two ends of the same sodding road, we're more similar than we are different, we've had the same economic issues and you're pulling this 'sign on' shit? Really?'

Which, as you're well aware, was as good as it got. They went further, much further, too far. Far too far.

I'd started the night kind of split on the two thousand lads in the corner of The Anfield Road. United had provided them all with an away shirt each (twenty-seven years in retail, trust me, I know an overstock when I see one) with the idea that they would create 'a wall of white' to greet their team. There were about twenty of them wearing the shirt. Part of me found this failure to create spectacle quite amusing and the other part of me thought 'Well done lads, you've taken one look at this and gone 'fuck that, we're not Chelsea fans, we're not wearing free shit from the club.' I quite admired them for that stance. Obviously the admiration wore off quickly.

'Oh Manchester is full of shit,' we sang, 'It's full of shit, shit and more shit.'

It's an ancient song, it's there to wind them up. It's an insult and most of us know that it's not actually true. There's some really smart stuff in Manchester, good pubs, good clubs, great bands, good people. Those of us with mates in the city know that there are good people.

These people in our city at this point, though? We complain about a free kick not being given and they wheel out the 'always the victims, it's never your fault' chant. They're upping the ante. It's going to get worse.

'Fergie's right, your fans are shite,' we continued as they gave up on singing 'where's your famous atmosphere?' while looking at our flags and banners and scarves and listening to our almost endless songs, entering utter silence as they realised exactly how outclassed their club were. We'll come back to the outclassed in a minute. Right now we're doing the lack of class bit.

I've honestly no idea what Ferguson said about United's fans. Not a clue. That song just suddenly appeared with its damning indictment that their own manager didn't rate them as a set of supporters. As criticism of the people who come to watch you goes, it's far worse than Roy Keane's 'prawn sandwich brigade' comment. It applies to everyone. It insults everyone.

Their reply? You know their reply, 'The s*n *(I'm not typing the word, not here, not anywhere)* were right, you're murderers.'

It's not a minority. I mean, obviously it's a minority in terms of the number of worldwide United fans, but of those lads here tonight? No, not even close to a minority, it's loud, it's distinct (even more so on TV apparently) and it's vicious.

It's the sound of a couple of thousand lads who are really pissed off at what they're seeing in front of them (humiliation, embarrassment, confirmation that their side are basically over) and responding with as much vitriol as they can muster. They've decided that they're going to repeat the discredited lies of a cheap rag and treat them as truth, as a weapon to use against us. Don't worry about the fact that there's a whole report that tells you that the rag lied, don't worry about the fact that our current (at time of writing) Prime Minister (and you know I won't praise him for much) stood up in Parliament, apologised to us all and told you they were lies. You just carry on singing that song. It's a vile moment.

I can't be selective on this, I can't ignore history. I know that there were lads on the Kop in the 80s who made reference to Munich, I know that there were lads who made airplane gestures. I found it hideous at the time, I find the fact that it ever happened hideous now, I remember my dad telling me how distraught everybody, *everybody,* who loved football felt when the news of the Munich disaster broke, how they felt when it became apparent that people had lost their lives. I know that it basically, sadly, took Heysel and Hillsborough and our own exposure to tragedy to stop some of our fanbase making those comments. I don't recall songs sung at that volume with that much hatred at any point. *(An edit at this point: after I made reference to the flag over the Manchester motorway, a United fan tweeted me footage of our fans singing a song at Old Trafford in 2011 referencing the Munich disaster. Then I remembered. Then I remembered quite vividly. I knew the song, I'd heard it many times, I'd wiped it from my memory. It's deplorable, I hope to God that I never have to hear it again.)* I might be wrong but, even at the worst points in our fanbase's antipathy/utter hatred towards United, I don't recall that level, that depth of hideousness.

(I was wrong. Clearly. My stance on that song, those references, is very clear: watch any interview with Bobby Charlton about the disaster. He's an eighty-year-old man still utterly heartbroken by the loss of his friends when he was a young lad playing football for the love of the game. He's no different to us. For the sake of every person who has lost friends or family to football, it all needs to end.)

It's a moment of disgrace for the United fans, it's evil and it's condemned by their own fans who realise the sheer *wrongness* of the moment. It's condemned online, on social media, by the media in general and, as I write, it's just been condemned by the club themselves. *Their* club is saying this: "It has always been the position of Manchester United that chants of this nature, which refer to historical tragedies, have no place in the game and don't reflect the club's values. We're discussing with fans to seek support in preventing this behaviour in future."

Which is fair comment. We're talking idiots. We all have our idiots, unfortunately. It's just that their idiots have managed a whole new low and the world realises this.

That's the first bit. The second bit helps with the 'why' of it all.

But we'll skip back to the Sunday afternoon review of that bit first, shall we?

I was wrong. I had the order of events wrong. I had the order of events based purely on my own not entirely reliable hearing. It didn't go like that at all.

BT Sport did us a bit of a favour here, in their desire to ensure that the United fans' microphones were higher in the sound mix than the rest of the ground to sound as though two thousand Mancunians had turned up in L4 and drowned out the forty-odd thousand singing 'You'll Never Walk Alone,' they made sure that we could hear the Salford lot as clear as day. They started. They started. Their 'the s*n was right' garbage wasn't a reply to 'Fergie's right...' it was their opening salvo. You know that moment when you think that you had appreciated exactly how low it was for people to go and then they show you that they're capable of sinking further?

Yeah, that.

Us, though?

We're impeccable. On the field and off. The atmosphere's the best that we've seen at Anfield since the 2013/14 wonderment. It's not 'Chelsea in the 2005 Champions League semi-final' level buzz, but then nothing ever will be or could be (*edit from the end of April here: yeah, right, just wait, see how wrong that idea is*). Unless, of course, we were to play United at home in the second leg of a Champions League semi-final with a nil-nil result from the first leg. Then the atmosphere will reach a new high. Pray it never happens, they don't deserve it. And, the way that their club functions at the moment, the chances seem fairly slender.

The pre-match *YNWA* is something different. It doesn't do the 'here's the chorus, here's another chorus, time to clap the lads' thing that it usually does, it *just keeps going*. It just keeps going and going and going and building and we're starting the night as we should and every song is getting an airing. Even that bloody awful 'look lads, he's a metal fan, he likes Can, he really, really isn't going to be impressed with this shite to the tune of Opus' *Live Is Life* disaster' tune manages a half-hearted airing. Jurgen needs a proper song, one we can get behind, one we can *all* get behind. There's more flags than ever, there's more scarves than ever, we're doing this, we're doing the twelfth man.

In fairness, even though the team say that they felt the fans gave an extra edge, even though Klopp says that we were incredible, the lads on the field don't really need us. They're perfect. They know what they need to do and they do it and they keep doing it and keep doing it and keep doing it,. They're ceaseless. They are, and I might have already said this, *immense*.

> Mignolet
> Clyne
> Moreno
> Lovren
> Sakho
> Henderson
> Can
> Lallana
> Coutinho
> Firmino
> Sturridge
> Joe Allen. Joe Allen. Joe Allen.
> Divock Origi

Transcribe their names in stone now. We might be only at half-time but write these men into legend for their deeds tonight. They stand for the ages. We encounter the old, bitter, twisted, horrible upstart enemy in European competition for the first time and these men humiliate them. They teach them, they school them, they embarrass them, show them the limits of their ability, show them what glory and dominance are. They show United that their time is over.

The FA Cup exit has benefitted us. I know how that sounds, but it has. As I'm writing, United are playing West Ham. If we were still in the FA Cup, we'd be the ones at Old Trafford, probably schooling United in the ways of football once again but you can't have everything, can you? United are battling, hopefully in vain, we're having a nice weekend off. Roberto Firmino is, apparently, in Tenerife. Good, he deserves a bit of sun. After the shift he put in on Thursday, he deserves everything that he's given. The moment of utter footballing filth that sees him take out Blind and Rojo with one little shimmy, that sees him leave them looking for him somewhere near the touchline that he'd been heading to while he's actually heading towards the United area? Deserves a fortnight away just for that. Then chesting the ball to Coutinho to set up the shot that stings De Gea's palm as he pushes it over? Give him all of next September. You can come back late, lad. Because you're sodding great.

We're having time between games and you can see it on the field. We're having time to work on shape and understanding and movement and we're translating that into practice in the most beautiful manner possible. I'd thought that the in-game intelligence that we'd seen in the Palace game was the finest that we'd witnessed to date. This supersedes that. This far supersedes that.

We can't talk formation. We can talk formations, plural. We're 4-4-2 but that centre 4 is a box, not a line, not a diamond. Except for when it *is* a line, when it *is* a diamond. We're 4-2-3-1 except for when we push the full-backs right up and Can or Henderson drop between the centre-backs and we become 3-5-2. Unless, of course, we're 4-1-4-1. We're everything at all times and United have no idea what we are, but that's okay because United also have no idea what *they* are. Which is the key to the fans and, obviously, something that we'll return to very shortly.

The scoreline is flattering. You know that. And you know that it's flattering to them, not to us. They do very little to deserve the 'nil' in the equation and they should have more than two against them. Six-nil wouldn't have flattered us. The Coutinho flick that Phil should really do better with but De Gea does brilliantly to get to, the Coutinho long-range shot (from the Firmino chest down) that De Gea tips over, the

Lallana clip that De Gea stops on pure impulse, the De Gea, the De Gea, the De Gea…

United are now David De Gea plus ten. And it doesn't matter who the ten are because their manager doesn't seem to have told them what he wants. No shape, no urgency, no passion. Fellaini elbowing people, that's it. This isn't a United side. It's not even the United side of last season or the season before, they're honestly that bad. David Moyes is beginning to look like the messiah that they claimed him to be. They're woeful.

The Sturridge penalty, the Firmino 'I'll just wait here while Carrick passes it back to Adam so he can nutmeg him and then I'll blam it in,' the two-nil doesn't scratch the surface. We're immense, we're impeccable, we're (oh go on then) indefatigable, insouciant, in-anything else you want to add, we're in control. We're Liverpool. And United aren't United.

There's the key. I wrote a column for a website a couple of years ago, said that United wouldn't finish in the top four, that they'd be lucky to get into Europe, that I didn't care that United had won the league the previous season. They were a spent force. They were over. I predicted a top-four finish for us, though. Didn't care that we'd finished seventh the previous season, we were hitting top four. 'In fact,' I said, 'I'll put my neck on the block, we're finishing third.'

Oh, the abuse that I took. From United fans and our own. My favourite comment on the article was the one that said 'This is the kind of stupidity that gives the rest of us Liverpool fans a bad name. Please shut up, you're making us look like idiots'. It was August 2013. I think you know how the season went. I was one place out, but very, very nearly two.

The United team that won the league the previous season wasn't a good United side. Not by any stretch of the imagination. It was a team that won the league purely, totally, completely, based on the strength of will of its manager and his refusal to allow a repetition of the season before, when City won the league with the final kick of the season. Ferguson couldn't countenance that having happened, refused to let it happen again, Ferguson's determination was worth about twenty points to United in that, his final season.

So they brought Moyes in to buy bad players and play poor football then sacked him and brought Van Gaal in to sell all the decent players remaining at the club and spend £300m on replacing them with inferior copies. Their time is over. It's not a blip, it's not a time of transition while they regroup for a shot at the title. We called this two years ago. Not just me, loads of us. They're us in 1991 and it's over. The guard has changed and, while we had twenty-five years of supremacy built on a belief and a passion and an ethos and an organisation under Bill and Bob and Joe and Kenny, their twenty-five was under one man. United had been nothing for a very long time before Ferguson took over and it looks very much, very beautifully, as though they're heading back that way.

It's only half-time, though. Aren't you jumping the gun? What if we rock up at United next week and they do a number on us? Not happening. Did you not see us in that glorious first leg? We can do anything.

And that, *that*, is what's provoking the United fans to scraping this whole new low. They know that it's finished, they can feel it. Most of them have no experience of the old Manchester United, the one that doesn't really matter in the grand scheme of things, and they have started to realise that they're going to have to start coming to terms with the forgotten old order returning. So, they try and destabilise us with anything that they can, try to derail our support with the lowest chants they can muster. They manage one chant of 'twenty times' but everything else is anti-Liverpool rather than pro-United while we respond with the 'full of shit' and 'Fergie's right' tunes but refuse to descend to their bile and don't address their disaster. It would possibly be an easy retort for those who weren't born at the time of the Munich crash, for those of us who know it only as history, for most of the ground basically, but we don't do it. We won't be goaded into this. We'll let our team do our talking and we'll let them carry on with digging deep into their dark hearts for abuse because we know, as they know, that in a week's time we're very likely to be putting them out of Europe while we move forward, and that league title number nineteen is coming sooner rather than later and then we can start talking about 'fucking perches'. They hate us because they fear us.

Manchester United 1 Liverpool 1

(It's a victory, however you put it, it's a victory)
Europa League Last 16 Second Leg
17 March 2016

YOU EXPECT a reply, obviously you expect a reply, a reaction to the events of the previous week. In every possible manner. A reaction to absolutely everything that happened. We'll do the football in a minute.

There's a sign hanging from a bridge over the M602, the main road into Manchester if you're travelling from Liverpool. 'Murderers'. It's the work of five or six idiots. We know this, they've had their photo taken with it. Should be easy to find out exactly who they are. And when they try to claim that the term refers to Heysel and not Hillsborough, we can all point out that they've added the date of the Hillsborough disaster to their hand-painted banner.

UEFA allowed this. There are no two ways around that fact. When they declined to charge United over the fans' chanting at Anfield last Thursday, clearly extremely audible on TV, because it hadn't been mentioned in the referee's report, they gave tacit consent to the idea that chants referring to tragedies were permissible. Repetition of those chants seemed likely, the banner over the motorway was disgustingly inevitable. The hope was that our away support wouldn't reply with Munich references. The hope seems to have been in vain.

I couldn't hear them on TV, couldn't hear any of the chants from either side, too wound up in the match itself. They were, apparently, there. The reports have it that there were United fans singing about Hillsborough, that there were Liverpool fans singing about Munich. There is never a point where two wrongs make a right and there appears to be no end to this. We're two cities with more in common than most and we allow this hatred to fester. This is forever and it's hideous.

Once again, UEFA haven't helped. Both teams have been charged over the conduct of fans during the second leg, both have been charged over items (seats) being thrown, United have been charged over blocked stairways and crowd disturbances, Liverpool over fireworks, illicit chanting and 'late kick-off'(?)

It's obviously the 'illicit chanting' charge that rankles here. It seems that the 'Munich' chants were from a small section of fans in the lower tier of the home end responding to the scuffles started when some of our fans in the upper tier unfurled a pro-LFC banner which apparently upset the home fans. Hence the 'crowd disturbances' part of United's charge, one would imagine.

'Illicit chanting', though? We're charged with illicit chanting yet United escape without censure for last week's widely televised and condemned (not least by the club itself) incident? Are UEFA doing consistency? They charge City over their fans jeering the official UEFA anthem at a Champions League game, they charge us for 'illicit chanting' at Old Trafford but United are exonerated? There are those on Twitter this morning with theories about why that might be. I'm not repeating them. There are libel laws and I don't fancy a day in court, thank you very much. So, let's talk about the football instead.

United couldn't be any worse than they were at Anfield. And they weren't. They came at us, they looked as though they meant business, they looked threatening. They had all the pace and directness that you would expect from a United side. For about twenty minutes and then we started to show what we were capable of. We'd looked cagey to start, looked as though we were determined to protect what we had, which, if you have a two-nil lead and the possibility of scoring an away goal at any moment that would require United to score four, is a pretty reasonable approach. We didn't look at ease, though. We looked as though we could be broken down. The flanks looked susceptible. An injury to Moreno meant Milner at left-back. Which isn't ideal. On the right, Clyne was having a torrid time.

Co-commentator Trevor Francis was questioning Van Gaal's deployment of Mata on their right to face Milner while Martial was on the United left against Clyne: surely Martial would have more success against a left-back who isn't a left back?

No, as it turns out, he wouldn't, Martial's pace was ripping Clyne to pieces and inhibiting his ability to push forward. Van Gaal got that right. Didn't get much else right, but got that bit spot on.

We looked like we'd ridden out that first spell, looked as though we'd survived. We'd started to move up, started to push and then there was this penalty. Stonewall pen. Clyne takes his man, Martial sends Mignolet the wrong way and United's tails are up. The idea of a second United goal suddenly became horribly possible. The notion that we could depart European competition at their hands after only De Gea had stood between us and a six-nil victory in the first leg was looming in the most hideous manner. What we needed was a goal. What we needed was a genius. A magician. A little Brazilian magician.

Coutinho hadn't started well, looked fairly anonymous, but in the moments before the penalty he'd started to assert himself. He'd started making the runs that you would want him to make, the ones that see him arrive in dangerous areas. This, *this* was the run. *The* run. He peels away from a central position towards the empty flank just as Emre Can rifles a ball, on the half-turn, down the channel. Suddenly Phil is in acres of space and bearing down on a petrified right-back. He's going to do the expected, you can see it. He's going to hit the byline and put it across the goalie for whoever's rushing into the area. You can see it, so can David De Gea.

And the ball's in the net and I have no idea how it's happened, but I'm on my feet and screaming and Phil's gone with the idea of 'if you're unsure, just stick it in the net and we'll discuss the possibilities later' and it's beautiful. Possibly the world's best goalkeeper has decided that Coutinho's going to cross, so he's set himself for that but there's a couple of feet to his right, between him and his near post and Phil has simply flicked the ball through that beautiful, beautiful gap. By the time the replays have finished, so has the first half. We're on level terms, we're three-one up on aggregate and United are heading to the dressing room knowing that they need three more goals in the next forty-five minutes, knowing that they're highly unlikely to get those three goals. The tie is over.

Yeah, they push in the second half but they don't scare us, they don't worry us. Not really. Emre Can runs the midfield, Lovren is solid at the back and Mamadou Sakho is imperious. He heads *everything*, he makes last-ditch tackles in the box and they're impeccable. He executes turns and spins in possession, he nicks the ball off red-shirted toes, it's a defining performance. It's beautiful. We're beautiful, all over the field. Not beautiful in the way that we were seven days ago but calm, assured, considered. It's what a European away tie should look like. It's Liverpool being in charge.

Obviously BT's TV coverage spends the next half-hour discussing exactly what's gone wrong for Manchester United rather than giving us the credit for where we find ourselves. And 'where we find ourselves' is here, pushing in the direction of fourth, in the quarter-finals of the Europa League and looking more and more like a Jurgen Klopp side by the day. Which is handy as, between the start of this chapter and these closing words, we've just drawn Borussia Dortmund in those quarter-finals.

Jurgen's revisiting his old home rather sooner than any of us expected.

Southampton 3 Liverpool 2

20 March 2016

AND THEN the arse falls out, the wheels drop off and we all get a horrible dose of reality thrown down our throats.

The day starts comfortably, hits chaotic, becomes glorious and then descends into incredulity and despair. That is, *my* day, the match is comfortable then glorious then hideous. You know this, you remember this, it's another one of those that's imprinted and isn't going to go away. It's the day that we watched careers end in the most public manner.

It's interesting, the distance that two days can give you, I'm writing this on Tuesday morning. Monday was blocked out and Sunday was preparing for Monday, so there was no way to write up the full horror before now.

And you realise 'the full horror' is way too glib, way too light, way too inaccurate, way too exaggerated a term to apply to losing a game of football. No matter how much it hurt at the time.

I'd mulled it over on Sunday evening, tried to find a way too conflate an opinion on Liverpool's appalling second-half surrender with Iain Duncan Smith's shock Friday-night resignation.

I'd tried to find some way to illustrate how his clearly false claim that he was resigning due to the latest Tory budget, which punished the disabled of the country by removing £30 of their weekly allowance and giving it to the rich in tax breaks, in some way related to Liverpool's first half giving us all hope of a better future before it was torn away as the second half proved that the world was always going to be a harsher place than we thought.

I knocked that idea on the head fairly sharpish. There was no way that I could connect the man who had allowed ATOS to assess terminally ill people as fit for work, overseen the Universal Credit debacle and publicly cheered at benefit cuts before lying about his reasons for resignation in order to side with Boris Johnson for a leadership challenge (trust me, it's happening, probably already happened for you) with any of the eleven lads in red, no matter how awful Martin Skrtel was.

As I write, the news is filled with reports from Brussels, at least twenty-six killed in two separate attacks in the Belgian capital, both suicide bombings by the look of it. A week after the attack in Istanbul, which the media gave far less exposure to, and we have yet another atrocity. The fact that I can write a football book but include accounts of at least two terrorist attacks on major cities within these pages is ridiculous but unavoidable. Our world is coloured by the events we live through and these are the events we're living through. It makes being annoyed/disappointed/infuriated/depressed by a football game seem very small.

Let's do it, though. Let's pull Sunday apart.

It was twenty-five past one, I headed through to the living room, turned the TV on. Newcastle vs Sunderland? Really? Flick up the channels. Nothing. BT Sport? Spanish football, Italian football, German football, not us. No sign of us. Surely we must be on TV, though? I mean, what would be the point of Liverpool going all the way to Southampton and kicking off at 1.30pm, thereby inconveniencing thousands of travelling fans, if we weren't on TV? It'd make it look as though the Premier League didn't care about their paying customers and we all know that can't be the case.

Internet stream? Not working. It's half one, we've kicked off and I have nothing. This is clearly the 'chaos' part of the day. I'm in the car, the penalty shout against Lovren comes when I'm in the car. Whoever's co-commentating is saying it looks soft, doesn't think it's a pen. I'm having that. When I see it later, I'm unconvinced. Looks like a pen to me.

I try our local social club. Three guys sitting round a table watching Rafa's lads play 'Big Sam's' motley crew. The barman is shaking his head. It's desperation stakes now. Which is why I end up drinking in a sports bar in the Square. The square is The Marian Square. The Marian Square isn't actually called The Marian Square. It never has been. It's actually called Magdalene Square but it's on Marian Way so there's not a person in the history of Netherton who's used the word 'Magdalene'. The Square is a lovely place. Honest.

But it's a passable bar and it's got TVs, it's got beer and the last time I was in here I watched Xabi score *that* goal against Luton in the cup. So I'm watching it here.

It starts well, it starts brilliantly, we're in control and it all looks so easy. Southampton are shambolic while we're immaculate. We're breaking at speed and finding holes everywhere. The Saints fans have seemingly decided that their endless barracking of Adam Lallana in the League Cup game had the opposite effect to that intended, so they're leaving him alone today. He's wonderful again, he's everywhere and he's making things happen. Coutinho's goal happens because Lallana breaks up Southampton possession somewhere around the halfway line and slots it to the Brazilian on the left, who advances, advances, sprints and shoots. It's a goal from nowhere and a thing of joy. As is Daniel Sturridge's, a fast break from Origi, a feed across the area, a shimmy, a dummy and it's curled in. This is as dominant as dominant gets. There should be more. Allen should bury it from yet another break through the middle but the shot's unconvincing and Forster sticks a foot out to block. Allen sticks it in the back of the net from a corner to make it three but Sakho's offside and apparently 'jumping over the ball' constitutes 'interfering with play' this week. Sturridge has a fine chance for a second but makes too little of it.

We're forty-five minutes in, look supremely confident, look classy and could/should, definitely *should*, be five-nil up. There's no need to change anything.

· So we change something. The barracking that the Saints fans aren't giving Lallana? They're giving it to Lovren instead. He's on a yellow, has already almost cost us with the penalty issue and, with the knowledge that comes from writing on Tuesday morning, Klopp thinks that Dejan's head has gone. So he swaps Martin Skrtel in for him.

As bad decisions go, it's a 'Napoleon waging a land war in Russia in winter' level of mistake. It's the worst decision Jurgen has made and it's telling. It's very, very telling.

Skrtel's on the pitch for about a minute before his wrestling proclivities get the better of him and he's finally caught in the midst of it. Southampton have a penalty. They've made two substitutions at half-time, introducing both Wanyama and Mane, and it looks as though they're about to be given a toehold in a game that they were never within touching distance of.

Mignolet saves the penalty. Excellently. And we're still in this. Unfortunately, we now have Martin Skrtel on the pitch and it's all going to go horribly wrong.

I don't like to apportion blame for defeat to one man – okay, I probably do and you're probably flicking back through the pages looking for examples as I write – but I'm going to do it now. This game, this surrender, this utter throwing away of three totally wrapped-up points, lies firmly at the feet of Martin Skrtel. This is the kind of performance that signals the end of your career at a club, this is the kind of performance that is very hard to ever come back from. This is the kind of performance that makes you realise how far we've come recently while, at the same time, perfectly illustrating just how precarious that progress is.

We've become used to the idea of Lovren or Toure next to Sakho and acting as a partnership. We've become used to the idea of two centre-backs dominating their line and moving together, each knowing pretty much where the other will be. We've become used to seeing aerial threats dealt with. Lovren suddenly able to do the simple stuff with confidence, heading balls clear, heading balls out, dealing with stuff, we've got used to that. Skrtel doesn't do any of that. Skrtel's everywhere. Not in a 'Lallana's everywhere and it's really good' way but in a 'where the hell do you think you are and why isn't it where a centre-back should be' way. The team loses shape. The team is covering for the fact that the centre-back who's just come on is having some kind of epic meltdown. The team has stopped being a team. And while we're not being a team, Southampton are. Southampton quite definitely *are*. They're better than us all over the park. They want everything more, they're battling harder than we are now, they're faster, sharper, bigger, better, *more* than we are. It's horrible. Our midfield is lost, it's having no impact, our defence doesn't exist any more. Everything that we were in the first half is gone.

When the first goal comes, it's been inevitable for a while. Skrtel's involved. He's involved in all three. I haven't gone back and checked that claim, it's just how I feel from the day. It's the remnants of the fury coming through. He's involved either through presence or absence. He's either where he's supposed to be and doing very badly there or he's gone wandering altogether.

I'm calling this as the worst individual performance I've ever seen. Not just the performance itself, which takes every flaw that we've ever seen in Skrtel's game, combines them all and emphasises them to the Nth degree but for the effect that it has on every single player around him. It is, by some distance, the most negative influence I've ever seen a player's presence have on a team. If Craig Bellamy's performance against City in the 2012 Carling Cup semi-final is the single greatest individual performance over ninety minutes that I've ever seen in a red shirt, which it is, then Skrtel's forty-five minutes here is the furthest point that you could possibly get from that.

At two-one, we have a chance. We have a break, just like the breaks that we had in the first half. Our only problem here is that we have Christian Benteke on the pitch and, with a distance to go to goal and a keeper to beat, Christian is currently the last man on the planet that you would trust to put the ball in the back of the net. He doesn't put the ball in the back of the net. Klopp's on-field bollocking at the end of the game is surprising but thoroughly merited. Chris's Liverpool career is dwindling before his and our eyes, all we need is for Danny Ings to step up from jogging round Melwood and Benteke's not even making the bench any longer.

There's a Pelle pile-driver and a second from Mane, where he manages to outwit Skrtel and then outmuscle Sakho, who has moved across to compensate for his missing partner.

Three goals. We've been blown away by a second-half performance that should have been aimed at nothing more than damage limitation. We needed to capitalise on our first-half dominance. We didn't. We needed to be solid when they replied, we weren't. We have a fortnight off now, the joys of Hodgson being allowed to get the England lads together to underwhelm again filling in for real football.

The next game looks a long way off, the top four looks further. United beat City later in the day. We should be basking in victory and plotting our taking the place of the lads from the Etihad in the Champions League slots. We're not.

Opportunity wasted. In a very big way.

Liverpool 1 Spurs 1

2 April 2016

TWO WEEKS. Two full weeks and not a word to write here. So, what happened between?

The details of the new stand seating turned up. Had a little link to the club website and a time slot which allowed you to choose your new seat, handily broken up by block so that you could be as close to where you are now as possible. I tried to work out how the removal of the paddock would affect the row that I sit in, how the fact that seat numbering which now seems to run from the centre out to the sides would affect my seat, picked an aisle flush with the eighteen-yard box and pressed select.

The guy next to me is now sitting somewhere in the centre of the stand, near Jurgen. The guy in front has moved a couple of rows down and a few seats in, the guy next to him appears to be where he's always been. It seems fairly random. People are moving. There's a couple of voices that I hear in every single game that I'll be more than happy to see accidentally move elsewhere. They see the negative in everything. They're seldom happy.

What else? England. England happened. And they happened well and the world went mad and they happened badly and the world that had gone mad went mad again. Upwards and filled with hope and promise and belief and fate and then downwards and filled with despair. While the rest of us shrugged and said 'It's England, it's a Roy Hodgson-managed England team, did you honestly think that they'd follow up that Germany win? With another performance? You've not had to watch Hodgson put teams out game after game after game, have you? Wait for the face-rubbing and the excuses and the bizarre stares from the bench, oh, look, there they are. Seriously, how does this man manage to fail upwards so convincingly and so often?'

The Germany game, we watched the first half, thought England looked halfway okay-ish and then watched them concede. Same old same old, basically.

We stuck Netflix on, watched a film, always preferable to England games, so didn't realise what had happened until we caught Twitter at the end of the game. Film abandoned, back to the game, watching the highlights.

You can't not give credit to an England team when they do something like that, it'd be ingracious, small -minded. No matter how much we dislike Hodgson, you can't take away from the fact that he managed to put out a side that could concede two goals to a decent, though much-changed, German side and then come back with three of their own. You can't argue with a win like that. Not as good as the Germany 1 – Liverpool 5 game, but there you go.

It's about the strikers, the in-form strikers. It's about Vardy's clip as the ball comes across from Clyne and Harry Kane's pushing the ball away from the area with his back to goal before Cruyff-turning the defender (and there's another thing that happened between, we lost Cruyff, lost one of the greatest players in the history of the game. I showed my twenty-year-old son, total lack of interest in any aspect of the game, the Cruyff turn, the first Cruyff turn. He was blown away but you still can't convey the sheer thrill of seeing that for the first time in a world where *it had never happened before*), nutmegging him and slotting home low into the corner. That Kane lad?

The one we thought had been 'found out' at the beginning of the season? That we thought was about to suffer a severe dose of second season syndrome? Some player, isn't he? Real class, natural goalscorer. By the time he hits Anfield on the

Saturday after the international break, he'll have scored more than our top three league scorers combined.

We'll come back to that in a minute.

There are Liverpool cameos in the international break: Lallana gets to play the same role for England as he plays for Jurgen and suddenly the media are talking him up for the first time since he pulled on a red shirt. Clyne provides, Henderson looks busy and Sturridge pulls off this flick in the Holland game that shows his absolute quality.

All of which is a preamble, the bit where I lead up to what I'm talking about. It's all about strikers, it's all about strikers who are in form and putting the round thing into the thing with the nets on it. It's what separated United from us in their league visit, it's what sees Leicester sitting at the top of the league exactly a year after they were rooted to the bottom, looking relegation squarely in the eye and deciding they didn't fancy it. It's what sees Leicester top by seven points by the Sunday night of this weekend and Spurs as their closest challengers. It's what sees us sitting in ninth, twenty-four points off the leaders and chasing a Europa slot that looks further away by the week at the moment.

That's the Spurs that come to Anfield, that's the Liverpool that face them. Sort of. Kind of.

Emre Can gives an interview during the international break (lots of players give interviews during the international break, all our lads are positive, no transfer requests, no agent-based shenanigans like some players — hello Romelu – it makes a nice change) and he points out that our league position doesn't reflect our performances over the last few weeks.

'The last few weeks' is the important thing. Bar the hideous second forty-five minutes at St Mary's, the last few weeks have seen the team grow, we've seen an increased flexibility, speed of thought, understanding and ability to dig themselves out of tight spots on the pitch. We have a team that look like they understand where Jurgen wants to take them, what they have to do, individually and as a unit, in order to get there. They're learning.

Klopp will acknowledge this much after the Spurs game. He'll say that the game showed what we were capable of but also the mistakes that we are still more than capable of making. He'll point out that the 'showing what we can do' was the hard part, but 'sorting the mistakes' will be much easier.

Let's do it then, let's talk about the game.

We face up a team that are basically in a two-horse race for the title (although we've now helped them fall a little further behind in that chase) and, for the second time this season, we match them. We're as good as Spurs: three years ago that would be the dictionary definition of 'damning with faint praise', but now it's a decent place to be. We've slipped behind, we're catching up. They are, let's not be shy about this, a bloody good football team and well placed for a reason. Mauricio Pochettino (spelt that correctly without checking, you have no idea how happy I am) has them well drilled, solid but creative, has used the four transfer windows he's had at the club to build a big, strong, fast, dynamic team, a team that can shift play from side to side on the pitch with ease and speed, assurance and confidence. He's had two years to do this. Jurgen Klopp has been ensconced in L4 for six months and the team that isn't his is already capable of matching Spurs, Chelsea, City and United.

It might not be capable of consistency yet but it's going to get there. Today isn't about today. Today is about tomorrow and tomorrow and tomorrow.

So, what do we learn today about our tomorrows?

Strikers make the difference. Let's do that first. Strikers make the difference. Glaringly obvious but it needs to be noted. Kane's equaliser is class, utter class. It's provided by Eriksen chasing a lost cause, hooking a ball back from the touch line, but it's completed by Kane turning and putting the ball in the one place that Mignolet isn't going to get it. There are those who complain, immediately and after, that Lovren was turned too easily, should have put himself to Kane's other side, ushered the lad on to his weaker foot but come on, be honest, Kane is going to do exactly what he's just done to pretty much every centre-back in world football. The lad is class, I might have mentioned this.

Sturridge is class as well. We know this, we've seen this a million times. We see it again today, not in the way that we'd like to see it, the scoring way, but we see it. The one golden opportunity, gilt-edged chance, use whichever cliche you wish, that he has today is aimed at Lloris's legs. Major opportunity wasted but the lad's still a long way from fit, still being nursed back to form. That doesn't seem to be the reason for his substitution, though. Klopp says afterwards that we needed more physicality upfront, more pace, more strength, says he could have pulled Lallana and played Origi alongside Sturridge but his opinion, and that's the only one that counts, was that he'd get more from Origi and Lallana.

What we do get from Sturridge is as sublime a piece of hold-up play as we've seen at Anfield all season. What we get is the time that he's willing to take in retaining the ball on the edge of the area so that Coutinho can race in, complete the one-two that he initiated with our number fifteen and, quite calmly, pass the ball into the net. And still Sturridge is pulled apart by sections of the crowd. He's pulled apart for being lazy, for not being fast enough, for not converting his chances, for looking pissed off when he's subbed. He's not had a pre-season, he's had two interrupted campaigns, he's had a succession of pace-altering injuries and he's lost the explosiveness that we would want but he's still got the skill, still got the vision. He's still the best forward we have. And there are those who say that they're willing to take £45m for him. Cash in while we can. Good work, lads. Take £45m for Sturridge, pay at least £60m for anybody close to being as good. Give him a pre-season, get his pace back up, get his confidence up, keep him away from Roy Hodgson and his inevitable summer failings and we still have a striker of the highest calibre on our books. And we can spend the money that you wanted to spend on someone less skilled on a Gotze and a Ter Stegen instead. We can build on what we have.

So how does the rest of 'what we have' look today? Sakho has one of his erratic afternoons but Lovren has a day of immense proportions, covers for everything, wins everything and all anyone talks about is the turn that Kane pulls off on him. Clyne is solid but unspectacular. Moreno does little wrong but I think we're all fairly sure of/happy with the fact that he's keeping Jonas Hector's berth warm for next season. Can regresses a little to his early-season habit of losing the ball in odd/dangerous places. Henderson steps up in the second half and offers an urgency and dynamism which drives the team forward, but I have this sneaking suspicion that he's not a long-term answer, not the man who will give us the quality of thought in midfield that we need to take us to the next level. Milner works hard but offers very little, particularly when it comes to corners. If anybody ever sees a decent James Milner set piece, they should video it and send it to the club's museum to be immortalised for the ages. Lallana continues to impress in terms of possession, though doesn't threaten as often as you'd like. We miss Firmino but Coutinho is as magical as ever.

All of that constitutes a paragraph of criticism in a game where we've played well, taken on the team sitting in second and matched them, where we've seen their keeper keep them in the game. All a bit negative, really. Take that as a statement of the way that we're developing, the ability that we know that these players have and the level that we know our manager is capable of taking us to. Take it as a positive for all our tomorrows, take it as promise.

Obviously the first voice that I hear outside the ground is saying "Dortmund are going to batter us."

Told you, seldom happy.

Borussia Dortmund 1 Liverpool 1

Europa League Quarter-Final First Leg
7 April 2016

THE DAY that Dortmund quite clearly didn't batter us. The day that showed that Jurgen Klopp knows exactly where he's taking us and exactly what he has to do to get us there. The day that shows that our manager, six months into his reign and facing the team that he built over a period of seven seasons, has all the tactical acumen that you would want if you were planning to build a bright future.

Once again we face up to a major team, a major European team at the top of their game and we stand as equals. We create the chances that could seal a victory in a ground where very few are victorious.

I'm not going to lie. I was worried about this one, more worried than I've been for any game for some time (I wasn't worried about the Capital One Cup Final, I was calm as hell about that). This one mattered *so* much. This was the rest of the season in one night. Well, this was the *first half* of the rest of the season in two nights. The top four's looking distant, the domestic cups are in the past, further progression in the Europa League keeps the interest going, stops the season dwindling away to a simple scrap for points and places, sets a tone, shows an intention going forward, creates a momentum for next season.

Progression here, and particularly progression against Dortmund, makes a statement.

The warnings had been there before. You know the warnings had been there before: Marco Reus has scored six thousand goals in his last eight matches, Pierre-Emerick Aubameyang is knocking them in at the rate of a goal a second, Moreno and Clyne are dead men walking. Anyone remember Reus or Aubameyang doing a great deal in the Westfalenstadion? Not to disparage them, they're massive talents, but despite the fact that the combination of those two with Henrikh Mkhitaryan (and the only joy of us not signing that lad when Rodgers wanted him is that I haven't spent all season trying to spell Myk…Mhyk…sod it, I've checked the internet and found three different spellings so far, and *nobody* knows how to spell his name) has scored sixty goals in all competitions this season, we handled them. We handled them brilliantly, perfectly, confidently. Mkhitaryan was Dortmund's main threat and we dealt with him. Whether he was on the right, on the left or down the centre we dealt with him. Lovren, Sakho, Moreno, Clyne, dealt with him, dealt with the lads around him.

You want to know the moment that sums up the extent that we dealt with the lads around him? It comes with about quarter of an hour to go as Aubameyang leaves the field and is replaced by a promising seventeen-year-old. One of the most accomplished players on the planet has just been subbed after making no impression on the game. Job done. Job brilliantly done.

If all this sounds like it smacks of triumphalism, sounds like a running down of Dortmund, like a shout of 'See? They're not all that, are they?' it's not supposed to. Dortmund are a good team. A bloody good team. Probably a better team than us. At the moment. At the moment, we're not as good a footballing side as Dortmund, but we will be, we will be, and soon. And last night, we were. Last night we proved that we are a match for absolutely anybody (okay, maybe not Barca, Real or Bayern yet, but you know what I mean). Last night proved that all we need to add at the moment is consistency. Consistency and confidence. Consistency and confidence and a clinical edge.

We add all that and we're laughing. Sounds like lots, it's not. It's what Klopp acknowledges in his post-match comments. He knows what we did well and he knows where we can improve, he's a realist and he's very honest about the fact.

Last night is Klopp's night. It was always going to be, from the second that the draw was made. The story was Jurgen Klopp going home. The back-story was the love-in between the fans prior to the game, the mutual respect, the promise of the shared, spectacular, *You'll Never Walk Alone* (don't know about you, don't know about the lads who were there but, watching on telly, that *YNWA* was a little underwhelming and God knows what version they play at the ground, but it's definitely not Gerry), the adoration both shared for the bloke in the specs on the touchline. The story itself, though, was what that bloke is capable of.

The night hinges on moments and decisions. Lots of nights do. This one emphasises that fact quite magnificently. The decision is huge. Sturridge on the bench, Origi on the pitch. The proven, if not currently completely convincing, replaced by the powerful potential. The need for the change, the reason for the change, is seen within thirty seconds, a chipped Coutinho pass into space for Origi to run on to. This is the intent. Turn Dortmund around, don't let them play from the back, put the ball into space when needed, let Divock run on to it, prove exactly what a machine he's becoming. On that point, he's interviewed afterwards alongside Dejan Lovren. Origi is bigger than Lovren. Did you realise that? I had no idea. Lad could be about to become an absolute monster.

We're looking at two teams who know how to press, who know how to close down space and we're actually looking the better of the two at it. We're playing little triangles around yellow shirts and we're looking good, confident, comfortable until the final ball, until the final pass. The final pass has a tendency to go astray and Dortmund start to look strong, to threaten. And every single Dortmund chance is created by our carelessness. The second our midfield learns to pass as well as it closes, we'll really have something but for the moment,

Dortmund are taking the upper hand. That beating that so many were predicting? It's looking like it might be a thing after all. And then Divock scores. And it's all about proving why he was put in as the sole striker in the first place. It's a clipped ball from Moreno, a header from Milner and it's in space and Origi's got the strength to hold off his man and place his shot past Weidenfeller. It's slightly, kind of, sort of, against the run of play but it's all we deserve and it's marvellous. We've not been cowed by the occasion, not been cowed by the opposition. We've gone out and we've Liverpool-ed the whole thing. We're putting in a proper European away performance and our manager is celebrating, just as he'd said he would because he's our manager now, not theirs.

The other moments then. The moments that aren't Divock scoring or Aubameyang being subbed. There are blocks, blocks by Lovren, blocks by Sakho. They're powerful and vital and timely and they happen again and again and again. They've decided that nothing's getting past them. They're making sure of it. They're essential.

There's the chance for the second on the stroke of half-time as Origi presses down on Weidenfeller. In space again. In space and powerful. If Weidenfeller wasn't so bloody good, we'd be going in two goals to the good. The equaliser is obvious, it's a corner. It's a corner that Hummels attacks in exactly the way that Lovren doesn't attack ours earlier. It could be three-one, though. It could be three-one away at Dortmund, three-one away at one of the most threatening, most capable, teams in Europe but it's not. It's level.

It's our response to being level that's the most important thing here. It's our response to being level that shows where we are at the moment, that shows *what* we are now. We go for the throat. We don't crumble. We take being level as an affront to what we've managed so far and we attack. We want another, we want more, we intend to have more. You could call it a moment but it goes on for minutes: we push Dortmund back into their box and we go for them. In the space of two minutes, Weidenfeller makes a series of saves of the highest order. It might be the first that's world class, might be the second, the third, might be all of them, but the lad's faced an absolute onslaught and kept his side in it, been the only thing standing between us and one of the most glorious nights of European football in history. Is that an exaggeration? I don't think so. Going there? Going there completely un-fancied? Going there and pulling off a win in style? That would have been immense.

As statements go though, last night is a biggie. It says that we're on our way back, it says that we are *already* at the same level as those that are numbered among the best. It says that our league position lies, that we have improved, that our manager has transformed us already. He's bought nobody yet and he's transformed us. He can see the weaknesses in some of our play and he knows how far he has to go to make us what he knows we can be, knows the changes that he'll need to make, knows the big decisions that he'll need to make and isn't afraid to make them.

Tonight, last night, this night, this is what Jurgen has made us. It's half-time. Time to see if he can push us through that next step on the journey back to being Liverpool.

Liverpool 4 Stoke City 1

10 April 2016

IT'S MONDAY morning, I've watched it back on the few minutes that *Match Of The Day* thinks the game was worth while they happily repeat footage from Saturday rather than concentrate on Sunday's games, and I've decided that he meant it. I've decided that, as Divock Origi curls the ball from the touchline, bypassing an onrushing Daniel Sturridge and ruffling the lower side of the Kop goal netting, it's meant as a shot, not a cross. I've decided that he intended it all along and I'm not going to be talked out of this. So don't try.

But before we get to that, before we get to the wonders of two goals scored from set pieces, of two goals being actual headers from actual crosses, of three goals being the result of crosses (if you count Divock's second, which we've already established that I have no intention of doing), let's talk context. Again.

There's the Dortmund context obviously, the fact that we played on Thursday, that we dug in and did the job, that we were pushed hard, that we play again on Thursday, that it's all square, even if we have 'the vital away goal', that we'll be pushed hard again, that, against all expectations, Dortmund rested eight players for their derby game against Schalke, that they see Thursday as being as vital as we do, that they are prioritising it in exactly the same way.

There's all that context (and all those commas) to take in for a start. It's why we see seven changes today, why we see first ever starts for Ojo and Stewart. It's part of the reason that we see Joe Allen, though Hendo's collateral cruciate ligament (no, I'd never heard of it before last week either) damage and Can's suspension also contribute to that. It's why we have Kolo paired with Martin Skrtel at the back. I'll come back to one of those. You know I'll come back to one of those.

Swapping in Sturridge and Firmino for Origi and Lallana might not seem a drastic thing, might not seem a weakening or a resting as you'd think of the two returnees actually being the first choices here, but they're changes and they're changes that demonstrate the choices that we're starting to see in the squad. They're vital for now, they're vital going forward. In every possible sense of that latter phrase.

Other context then, before we get to the body of this.

Other context, part one: My teeth. Not for the squeamish this bit. Don't say you weren't warned. I'll tell you when you're safe. I'll put up a big sign saying *You're safe now*. My favourite sentence of last week, spoken to me before the first Dortmund game but not mentioned yet as it didn't seem vital, was this, "Well, the tooth's moving a bit now but we're going to have to move the gum and take a bit of bone out to get to it. There'll be a bit of drilling." That's drilling the bone. Drilling the bone away. That was fun. And then it was agony. Living on painkillers and soup for three days. So, didn't really feel like heading to the match on Sunday afternoon. Particularly when you take into account other context part two:

(Oh yeah, should have said, for the squeamish: *You're safe now*.)

I'd bought my ticket, my latest ticket, yet another ticket to see Michael Head way back when Liverpool/Stoke was a Saturday afternoon game. I do go to see other bands, you know. Honest, I do. They just don't seem to get mentions.

Didn't think that going to see him would be an issue. Didn't think that going to see him *in Leeds* would be an issue. So I'm leaving the game at the final whistle and driving to Leeds for a gig that starts at 8pm. Not an issue. At all. Apart from the fact that it took forty minutes to get from the taxi club on Queens Drive to the end of the East Lancs. Suddenly, it's quarter-to-seven and I'm still in a Liverpool postcode and Yorkshire looks a long way away. All because I refuse to leave a game before the final whistle.

I could easily have left with fifteen minutes to go. Everything that was going to happen had happened. We were home, dry, the lot. Four-one up, job well and truly sorted. There's a moment where it looks like it might be about to turn into 'one of those days', the moment where Martin Skrtel brings down Peter Crouch and the resulting free kick sees Skrtel fall over while Kolo plays Bojan onside so that he can head into a gaping net to equalise for Stoke, but that's it. That's the sum total of the Potters' threat despite having Bojan, Affelay, Crouch and the quite wonderful, if weirdly shaped, Shaqiri on the pitch.

We, on the other hand, have everything. We have James Milner drawing a foul near the touchline and possessing the sense and vision to play it short to an unmarked Alberto Moreno. We know that Moreno has that left foot pile-driver in his locker but it's still a glorious, gleeful, surprise when he unleashes it and we're one up within eight minutes. We have Sheyi Ojo, seemingly supplanting Jordon Ibe in the pecking order of young wingers, having an in-and-out forty-five minutes before being replaced by Divock Origi at the start of the second half but crowning that in-and-out forty-five minutes with a sudden dart past a 'stranded-at-right back' Shaqiri and flicking an inviting cross into an area that has Daniel Sturridge's name written all over it. We have a two-one lead and we're not looking back.

We have Kevin Stewart holding in the centre and doing the simple things, concentrating on the idea that the ball is his until he chooses to let go of it, and when he lets go of it he's going to make sure that it goes to another red shirt. He's sensible and calm and I want to see him next to Emre Can to see what happens. We've got Joe Allen chasing everything that moves, darting everywhere, receiving the most deserved of standing ovations when he's subbed and putting in another of those 'his best performance in a red shirt' performances that has you screaming for a new contract for the lad, has you going back on the myth that he was only ever in the team because Brendan liked him and valuing him for what he is and what he does. We have Daniel Sturridge in his best performance since his return. His best performance by quite some distance. He's dropping off, creating, moving across the line and threatening and his touch is impeccable. He wants the ball, wants to make things happen with it. If anybody had been questioning his attitude post being 'dropped' against Dortmund, then he's shown them what he's willing to do, what he's capable of. He's reminded us of his ability and it's something to behold.

And we have Divock Origi and we're all currently a little bit in love with Divock. The header after five minutes of being on the pitch, which makes us unassailable in our lead, would be enough to add to that love, but it's the moment when he takes the Stoke right- back and he twists him and he turns him and he looks up and suddenly he has the ball in the back of the net that confirms it. It's a cross, obviously it's a cross, it must be a cross, it's *not* a cross, is it? He meant that, didn't he? He only bloody meant it. And I'm having the idea that he meant it and I'm having the idea that we have a new hero. And, more than that, I'm in love with the fact that he and Dan can play in tandem, that Divock can do the running and the physical and the pulling and pushing and Dan can do the scheming. All the scheming, tons of bloody scheming.

I'm having the fact that we can make seven changes in order to play a team who have given us so many problems over the years and have started to give us less problems by becoming a halfway decent football team and we can take them apart as though they weren't an issue. Jurgen's happy afterwards, happy in his pointing out that Stoke have now had to change the way that they play three times in order to deal with us and it hasn't worked. Jurgen has the measure of Stoke. He has the measure of so many teams now. Six months in and he knows what this league is about. This is what he's done to date. We might sit in eighth and it might be unflattering but in the world of the Jurgen league, the league that started on the day that he joined, we're sixth and winning our game in hand will put us fourth. It's the right direction, it's all the right direction.

Those changes that Dortmund made? Drew two-all with Schalke, basically cost them their shot at the Bundesliga title. Their season hinges on Thursday. Our season hinges on Thursday. Could be incredible. Game on. Game completely, totally, fully on.

That night

Liverpool 4 Borussia Dortmund 3

Europa League Quarter-Final Second Leg
14 April 2016

JESUS, EVEN typing the score makes me want to cry. I seriously hope you're not expecting this chapter to make any sense. You can't make sense of nights like this, all you can do is live them, breathe them in, embrace them, try to hold on to the feeling, hope you can hold on to how it felt for as long as you live, hope that there will be other nights like this, hope there will be more moments, hope you can always feel this way.

I'm shaking. I'm still shaking. Some of it might be the lager but most of it's the emotion, most of it's the feeling, the miracle, the wonder, the sheer "we're not letting this go" of the whole thing. We didn't let it go. We looked like we'd let it go, looked that way a few times there, but we didn't. We do not let this slip and all that. All that coming magnificently true.

Snapshots. It's all snapshots at the moment. Brian, who sits in front of me, who despite knowing that my name is Ian, decided a couple of games into the season that I was actually called Paul and I didn't have the heart to correct him because it felt rude, so I'm still Paul to him and always will be (if he's reading this, sorry Bri, never had the heart to put you straight, felt wrong). Brian is stood on his seat filming the Kop, filming the aftermath, filming the glory and the celebration after the fourth goes in. He's stood, balanced, filming. He's in his seventies and he's stood on his soon-to-be-changed seat, filming the whole damn thing. He's seen a lot, he's filming this. This needs filming, this needs holding, remembering, treasuring.

I'm walking down from The Kop to County Road. We're meeting in *The Frost*. We've arranged it earlier, when we separated after the magic of the road to Anfield, after the spectacular pyro party outside the *King Harry*. I'm walking down and I'm working it out in my head and I'm going 'Origi, Sakho, Lovren. Origi, Sakho, Lovren, Origi, Sakho, Lovren' and I know for a fact that there was a fourth lad there, a fourth lad who put the ball in the net, and I know he must have been the second one in but I can't remember him, can't remember anything about the goal. And I'm tweeting 'I have no idea what just happened, but it was fucking immense' and I'm tweeting 'There were goals. Lads scored them. Damned if I can remember more than three at a time'. 140 characters isn't beginning to hold the enormity of this. No matter how many times you post and no matter how many times I post, I'm damned if I can remember who that other lad that scored that other goal was. Hell of a goal, that Coutinho goal. Hell of a goal. Wasn't it, though? Kind of goal you never forget, but I forgot. Absolute quality, pure football, no luck, no fortune, just joy. Milner will do so well to set it up but I want Milner pulled after ten minutes. I want Milner and either Lallana or Firmino pulled and I want Sturridge and Allen on. I want changes immediately because we *need* them immediately and it looks like I'm wrong about that. Milner's terrible all night and he should never take another corner ever but he has two assists. He has the vision to see Sturridge peeling away, taking advantage of the free kick that comes in added time when the ref actually notices that the lads in yellow are kicking the lads in red quite a bit. He has the vision to move into the box so that Dan can dissect the Dortmund defence and take three lads out with one ball; and when he really needs to he puts in this cross and it's the best cross you've ever seen. And when he really needs to, Dejan Lovren decides that the time to be poor at attacking headers has come to an end and he hits the target and he hits the target and he hits the target and he's a hero. And Brian's on his chair filming the whole thing.

And there's a photo on my Twitter account. It's a photo of a can of Skol and nobody realised that off-licences sold Skol any longer. 'We've gone the game in 1987' I tweet and we're drinking Skol from an offy because we can't get served in the '*Arry* because everybody who was on the street five minutes earlier is back in the pub now. They'd called for it a couple of days before, the lads from 'Spion Kop 1906' had called for it, others as well, but God knows those Spion Kop lads get the job done and the flags, the flags, the flags, the flags are immense tonight and the Dortmund lot are good, the Dortmund lot are great but we're incredible and the Kop is something to behold. They'd called for it. Maybe meeting the bus before the game like we did *that* season might be an idea. And you think people will turn up but you know how many were there in that season and this is more, this is so much more, and it starts so much further down the road. There are lads on scaffolding and nobody knows where the scaffolding came from but we think they might have put it up just to have a decent view of all this because all this is gorgeous and Alberto Moreno's filming it from the bus and it's all over Twitter later on and he's filming the other lads all filming this and you realise that, behind those blacked-out windows, they're watching us, they're seeing us, they're affected by us. How could they not be affected by this? This is unique and I feel sorry for anyone who supports any other team because they don't get this. They don't get this and they disparage this but they don't have it, they'll never have it, nobody does this like we do, nobody does nights like this like we do. What are we supposed to do after a night like that?

We're in Mathew Street. I'm buying beers in plastic glasses from a pub that I last went into sometime in the eighties and I'm talking to a lad at the bar in a Dortmund shirt and he reckons that we need better pressure on our pumps because they're all too slow over here and the lager comes out too slowly and we're comparing German lager with Carling and I think we all know who wins on that one. There's a lad on an acoustic guitar with a bloody loud backing track playing *Sex On Fire* and, honest to God, there's never any reason to play 'Sex On Fire' and I'm in a good mood but I'm still not letting that one go. I've never done a European away, I need to do a European away, *need* to. Really need to. This is what they're like, isn't it? This is a European away in the middle of our own city. And Mike came into town for the game, up from London, and decided he needed a scarf and bought one from the club shop and had it for five minutes before a Dortmund lad decided he wanted to swap it for his, a black and gold 2011 league-winning scarf, and, afterwards, after it's all over I'm telling Mike 'At three-one, I was calling you and that fucking scarf for everything.' He's framing that scarf. That scarf's legendary.

At three-one, it looked over. At two-nil, it looked over. At two-nil and not even ten minutes gone, it looked over. If we were only chasing one, we'd be okay but two meant we needed three and Dortmund looked magnificent. You looked at the pitch and you knew that they were everything that we want to be. They were everything that we wanted to be and we beat them. Everything that we wanted to be and we decided that we should just be more than them, decided that we didn't like the way our hearts felt broken after ten minutes and after an hour and decided to break theirs instead.

And in *The Frost*, I'm arguing that their first was way offside, that Mkhitaryan was off in the first phase of the play and I'm insistent, as insistent as I was in the ground, as everyone around me in the ground was and I'm wrong and Accy (or Akki or Akky, we didn't discuss spellings of nicknames) is telling me I'm wrong and I'm arguing and we're watching the highlights and I can see that I'm wrong, but I'm still arguing it and I'm wrong. Mkhitaryan wasn't offside and Mignolet saved well and he was just where he needed to be, when he needed to be and that's what we want to be and that's what we'll become, that's what we'll become before the end of the night, where we need to be when we need to be, to be what we need to be. And I'm hugging Fleety in *The Frost* and dancing round singing 'Jurgen

Klopp, na na na-na-na' and the last time we did that was in Wembley in '86 and we were tumbling backwards down the steps going 'we've done the fucking double' and all this goes back a long way.

That wrongly assumed offside nature of the first is a hammer blow, a moment that feels like cheating, feels like injustice and is nothing of the sort, just a bloody good goal. The world-class Aubameyang finish on the second is a knife to the heart. You're looking at it going 'Sakho should cut that ball out, why doesn't he cut that ball out?' And then it's in the net and the lad's somersaulting in celebration on our touchline, right under us and it's horrible. We're looking for the impossible here, we're pushing our luck one step further than we have any right to. It doesn't matter how many dreams we have, doesn't matter how many songs to sing, at some point you have to stop dreaming, stop singing. They're more than us, far more than us and we can't drag ourselves up to their level. Dragging them down to ours, no matter how many claim that *that* is Jurgen's enduring gameplan, his mission statement, his reason for being, isn't happening. We can't drag a team this good down to anywhere and we're not ready for the step up yet, we're too early. Maybe a season too early, maybe years away, maybe we'll never catch up. Dortmund look imperious, we look humbled.

Except we don't. We look like we're going for it and from the point where, ten minutes in, everything seems to be over, we've decided that nothing's over and we're more threatening than Dortmund. We need three, though. We could get three, though. We could do this. We have forty-five minutes and anything could happen in forty-five minutes. We've made anything happen in forty-five minutes before now, we've made legends happen, we've made great European nights happen and we can add, we can add, we can add, we can equal, we can put our names on that list with those lads who were there for Saint Etienne, we can have heroes who will sit alongside Fairclough, we can have last-minute winners, we can take our place in legend.

We need changes, though. We need half-time changes. We don't get half-time changes. We don't get Sturridge, we don't get Allen, we get the same eleven lads. And then big Divock's sliding the ball under the Dortmund keeper. He's the first name that I remember in my repeated litany of three on the way to *The Frost*. I'm still struggling for the fourth as we stand and attempt to decide who played the sumptuous, gorgeous, beautiful, through ball for him. And I can say it now, now that it doesn't matter, it's as perfect as the slide rule pass from Hummels to Reus for Dortmund's third. And we stare at the telly and we ask was it Firmino? Was it Coutinho? It's Phil, isn't it? Only Phil could play that pass and it's this morning before I realise that it's Emre Can.

And I haven't watched the whole match back yet, I need to watch it back, I need to watch it forever, on a permanent loop, on a loop of daze and glory and giddy and I need to keep watching this, feeling this, forever.

And the three-one feels over. Feels over again. We want to know why Mignolet's not off his line and we want to know what Clyne thought he was doing. We don't accept yet that it was all just the Hummels/Reus axis being basically bloody brilliant; bought for nothing and made into something by the man who's making us bigger than we thought we were. The man who's stood at half-time and told the lads in red that Istanbul shows what this club can do and that they should go out and make bloody sure that they have stories to tell their grandchildren. And they have.

They have the story of the Milner turn to feed Coutinho to prove that he can do what those other lads can do and we're back in it and it's what? An hour in? And we still have time, still have all this time and we can push and legend is calling us forward and Dortmund look less, look less, look smaller, look tired, look leggy and we look like we're everything that we need to be and then we have a corner. Was it a corner? I think it was a corner and I need to watch this again and again, to check and to bathe in every single second, and Sakho's bending and he's flicking that header and I don't even remember how wild we went because suddenly we're level and everything seems possible.

And the bloke next to me, the bloke who's been next to me a few times now, is on a stick and he's unsteady and he says, at three-three with no time left, he says: 'I need to get off, I'm not steady enough. it's been a cracking game, though.' And it has, it's been a cracking game though and you're thinking, "Well, if we go out on away goals like this, there's no shame, is there? We gave everything we had and that first goal was offside by a bloody mile, so we were robbed, same as we were robbed in '65" and none of us know for sure how we were robbed in '65 and if we do we've forgotten because all that matters is right now, right this second, this moment, nothing else, but we know we were robbed in '65, we've been told and we accept it. And there's no shame and we weren't robbed. Even if it ended there, we weren't robbed but we've done everything and if we go out then it's just one of them, isn't it? And the bloke next to me's gone. At three-three, he's gone and the night is about to enter glory.

It's the header but it's not the header. It's Daniel Sturridge making the run that nobody else is thinking of making and it's James Milner spotting him and playing him and Sturridge nearly falling over before playing that pass and Milner making that cross and you think the header is coming back across the goal but it's not, it's in the net and Dejan Lovren, the man who wouldn't be king at any point last season, Brendan Rodgers' expensive folly, is a hero. Dejan Lovren is winning this.

And we're in Mathew Street drinking with Germans before and we're in *The Frost* topping up the lager levels after and thinking about kebabs and cabs home and watching the highlights and singing 'Jurgen Klopp, na na na-na-na' and we're still at Wembley and we're in our early twenties and some of us had had a really shitty day and we're drinking Skol on the streets in our fifties and one of us is a grandfather and we're all these things at once, at the same time, and we've never lived through anything like this. Never. None of us. Nobody has ever lived through anything like this. Olympiakos with Rivaldo falling over every few seconds and Mellor and Pongolle and Gerrard bringing us through, fades away. Chelsea with Jose's much complained about 'ghost goal' and the resilience that followed, fades away. Saint Etienne, which none of us were at, is more firmly in the past than ever. And Istanbul, where our Keith convinced Fleety not to head back to town at half-time, at the point that we looked over fades away. Even Istanbul, where Gerrard and Smicer and Xabi did all that because we're never over, fades away. Even Istanbul. Keith and Fleety are saying that even that didn't feel like this. And it might be the night and it might be the lager but they all fade in comparison and we're pretty sure this is as good as anything has ever got. We have no idea what just happened but it was fucking immense and when we talk about the fact that nobody does European nights like we do European nights and nobody does comebacks like we do comebacks, this, this, THIS is what we'll be talking about. This is what we'll be talking breathlessly about and we'll be trying to tell you how it felt and endlessly, endlessly failing because you can't tell people how nights like this felt, you can only feel them, can only hope they felt them too.

Nights like this aren't supposed to make sense. Nights like this are just supposed to be and to let you know that you're alive and that anything, anything, anything is possible and you can do anything and you can change anything and nobody can stop you when you believe and you know that you can be what you need to be when you need to be it. Nights like this are for glory and history and destiny and legend and for watching again and again and again and feeling forever.

Does that make sense?

15 April 2016

THERE'S A moment, just before we start to sing the hymn, where I look at our Keith and he looks back at me. There's quarter of a century in that look. I'm to my mum's right, Keith's on her left, we're high in the Upper Centenary stand, Kevin, Collette and their boys, Dan and Josh, are elsewhere in the ground, I'm not entirely sure where. It has to be either the Centenary or the Kop, though. There are reportedly twenty-thousand of us here and we're filling these two of the four stands.

The hymn we're about to sing is the one that starts with *I Watch The Sunrise*. It's called either that or *You Are Always By My Side* and I'm never entirely sure which. It was sung at my dad's funeral, hence the look. At the end, before the service continues, we both ask mum, quickly, quietly 'Are you all right?' She nods, again, quietly.

The fact that this is the last Hillsborough memorial service to be held at Anfield, that it takes place as we await the inquest jury's verdicts, adds an indefinable extra weight to the emotion that is always present. I can only speak for myself, but I feel more choked than at previous services.

I haven't been to every service. I'm not going to pretend that I have. I tended to be in work on the day of the anniversary. It always seemed the right place for me to be as I was in work on the day itself. Each year, I felt it my responsibility to ensure that the silence was observed properly in whichever store I was working. It always was.

I was at the twentieth, though, and thoughts of the twentieth can't be far away today. Ending the most public aspect of remembrance seems right now. The job that was started with the first, that escalated with the unprecedented size of the twentieth, where the demands for justice became so spontaneous, so overwhelmingly necessary, seems to be done. As I write, the jury is still out. By the time you read this, their verdict might have long since been returned. I might return to the much larger subject of this day twenty-seven years ago before we reach the end of the book but, for now, there's little that should be said here.

I can tell you what I can see, though. From this vantage point in the Upper Centenary stand, where you can gauge so clearly the sheer size of that new stand we're building, I can see three things. I can see three things and none of those things are here. All three belong to the past, all three are with us forever.

I can see my seat. That is, I can see my dad's seat. I can see the seat that he sat in for decades. I can feel him there, can feel him with us, can feel him watching over the day. He didn't miss a single service. You couldn't get him into a church (births, deaths and weddings the only reason my dad would bother with church), but every single memorial service at Anfield without fail. He's here today, not with us where we stand, but *over there* in his seat, standing, watching.

I can see the sea of flowers. I can see the single most desperately beautiful thing that I've ever seen. I'm looking at the lush green of the post-Dortmund pitch and I'm seeing the flowers edge and flow from the Kop goalmouth toward the halfway line and then past. As I'm standing in 2016, I'm seeing 1989.

And I'm seeing our Kevin. I'm seeing him sitting on the steps of the Kop, by the bar where we used to stand. I'm seeing him breaking down. It's only days after, he's a lad of twenty, and he's seen too much. He's seen more than anybody should ever see. He's seen it, Keith's seen it, my dad's seen it, my family and friends have seen it. So many people saw so much that they should never see.

I wasn't there, I was in work, I saw nothing. They saw everything.

And this is the day to remember them, remember them all, the 96 that were so horribly, needlessly lost and the thousands who came home and could never be the same people again.

Bournemouth 1 Liverpool 2

18 April 2016

AND THEN you get some games that aren't about glory and legend, they're just about getting the job done, about being good enough.

They're the sort of games that follow on from European glory, that find you marooned on a coast somewhere with a team that has ten changes, that you don't expect to win, but still win. Still win while leaving no imprint on your soul whatsoever.

They're the kind of games that find you watching on a TV channel that might be Spanish, that has no commentary and manages to make the 'only the atmosphere in the ground' approach sound like the worst idea ever, that make you long, bizarre as it sounds, for Michael Owen's dreary tones and dull opinions. They're the kind of games that see you drinking with a friend, meeting your friends and somehow ending up in a conversation with this lad that you've never met before and that your friend would rather avoid and later apologises for. This lad, clearly Class-A'd up to the eyeballs, is unhappy with, well, everything the world has to offer and he doesn't like your opinions and all you've had is a pint of very weak lager shandy, so you're staying out of this one.

On the telly, in the corner there are lads running around in white shirts against other lads in red and black shirts and, because the team is so changed and because you can't see very well and because somebody who knows the other lad has just come in and told him that he's a 'fucking robbing bastard' and is leaning over the table and quite happy to kill him, you're not entirely sure who anybody is or how they're playing.

It's one of those games.

Somewhere in the game, the angry class-A lad wanders off to argue with others and you get to have a chat with your friend, who's a nice bloke, and his mate, who's seventy and a nice bloke. You're introduced as 'the posh one', which loads of people seem to think despite the fact that you were born in Bootle, grew up in Fazakerley and live in Netherton.

On the telly in the corner, the game looks dull but there's a back-heeled shot from Daniel Sturridge which Boruc palms in front of Firmino and the ball's in the net and there's a cross from someone and Dan's nodding the cross home and two-nil looks comfortable. Two-nil looks like a case of 'we've sent the ressies down to the south coast because those lads who played all of Thursday worked their arses off and they could do with a bit of a sit-down and we've started with Ward, Randall, Smith, Kolo, Lucas, Stewart, Allen, Ibe, Ojo, Firmino, Sturridge and these lads haven't played together before, but they're more than good enough to do the job. Wasn't expecting Ibe, though. After his whole, 'I'll wipe all reference of Liverpool FC from my social media accounts' mini-strop, I never expected to see him in red, or white, again. It looked very much as though Ojo had moved ahead of Ibe in Jurgen's thoughts and Ojo looked more threatening on that TV up in the corner while we drank lager and debated the morals of the junior doctors' strike but, when watched back later, the fact that Ibe is integral in the first and takes the free kick for the second are pretty good arguments against the idea of Ojo being better on the day. The joy of being closer to a decent telly.

It looks as though there are about a million handballs from Kolo and Lucas and Smith and possibly some other lads in white shirts on a screen in the corner. It looks as though the Bournemouth lot have reason to be aggrieved but seriously? It's not a biggie, is it? Not for us. There's probably a handball in the Bournemouth consolation as well, but seriously? It's not a biggie, is it? Not for us.

There's a Sturridge chip from a gorgeous Allen pass that hits the post and, honest to God, is of the quality that deserves to settle games on its own. There's a Sturridge turn and shot that's class and deserves a goal that it doesn't get. There's a lot of Daniel Sturridge and he looks sharper by the second. Rest of the lads? Not a clue. Need to watch *Match Of The Day* later. In English, with a commentator. Get a grasp of the situation.

Sometimes you need that distance, that re-watching, to appreciate what happened. That chapter about the Dortmund game? I fell gloriously in love wth Emre Can's final ball to Divock for the first. Until this morning, I had no idea that he'd just one-two'd his way the length of the pitch before playing it. I woke to a gif of the whole move and refused to rise and greet the day until my viewing count was in treble figures. A thing of marvel and wonder.

Three days after glory and madness, then, we head south and we don't do the whole 'Lord Mayor's Parade' thing (never understood that term, to be completely honest with you), we just do what we need to do. And that's fine, sometimes. On afternoons when you really have no true grasp of whether the lads you were watching were good, bad or indifferent, good enough is good enough.

Liverpool 4 Everton 0

20 April 2016

BY THE end we're in full on training session mode, pinging the ball round with a sense of humour to the sound of thirty-five consecutive *olés,* one for each pass completed to a red shirt. The only sane response from the stands is applause and laughter. We're so in control, it's ridiculous. The only complaint, apart from the woman behind me screaming 'get a grip, Liverpool' in the second minute of the second half after seeing us wrap up the game as a contest before half-time, is that we don't score eight. Or ten.

It wasn't supposed to be like this. This was supposed to be the pointless derby, the least relevant of modern times, a team whose only focus was the FA Cup semi-final visiting a team whose only focus was the Europa League semi-final. Everton were, we all agreed, going to play the kids. Rumours of Tony Hibbert starting circulated and were met with hilarity.

Martinez pulled a flanker. Rested everybody on Saturday for a dismal draw against, *somebody*? I want to say Swansea but, honestly, who's arsed checking? They drew, the fans called for his head. He staked everything on tonight and the semi-final. Part one of that gamble didn't go well, did it?

Thirty-seven shots to three. Alberto Moreno had more shots than Everton and at least two of his were on target. Which is two more than the blue lads managed. There's about ten minutes where they looked like they might be up for playing a bit of football, might be considering threatening and then they realised that Sakho and Lovren, one absolutely *towering*, pitch-length header for each, had the measure of Lukaku and you could see everything slip away. You could see Barkley vanish into the midfield, see big Romelu thinking about his agent's number, and we took over.

We could be three-nil up before we score the first. Lallana, excellent throughout but a far from clinical finisher, could/should have a hat-trick. And then James Milner decides it's time for a couple of crosses again.

Corners might not work for our current captain, but stick him a few feet further in and he's going to deliver. Origi's header is a carbon copy of Lovren's against Dortmund, Sakho's is just another joyful Sakho moment. His charge to the bench to celebrate with Kolo is a moment of massive beauty.

The second hits the back of the net, the celebrations happen, everyone heads to the centre circle, the whistle blows and the game's over. Forty-five minutes in and the game's over. Whatever threat Everton had is long gone.

And then it gets worse. For them. For us, it becomes marvellous. Funes-Mori walks for that shocking, appalling, probably season-ending stamp on Origi's ankle, he's a flurry of protests and badge embracing, clearly under the impression that he's done something heroic rather than possibly cost his team any chance of a comeback, any chance of an FA Cup win.

The £50m John Stones, the man who destroyed Chelsea's season and then lost his place in blue affection, passes a stray ball into an area that Lucas Leiva fancies the idea of, watches it zip past him for Sturridge to hit his fiftieth goal in eighty-seven games and then leaves the field, substituted after a little sit-down.

That thing where teams with ten men are harder to play against? Everton have missed that one. Martinez has no defenders on the bench, that's *no defenders,* and suddenly his team has given up on shape, spirit and fight. I don't think I've ever seen a capitulation quite like it. They have nothing and we're embarrassing them. Our lads are playing round them and deciding to go for the kill by setting their mates up for goals. The lads on the pitch clearly want Moreno to score, Lucas to score, Clyne, Joe Allen, they want the lads who don't normally get on the scoresheet to get on it and this is as good a chance as they'll ever get.

In the end, Sturridge tries to claim another Coutinho wonder strike as it wafts past his shorts on the way in and we play out the remainder at a canter.

It's almost too easy and there's a sense of regret that we don't really destroy them. An utter destruction of Everton would be a hell of a thing. Let's settle for the idea of twelve goals in the last three games at Anfield and unbeaten since Southampton.

That horrible south coast second half seems a distant dream at the moment. That was the old us. We're something new now.

Liverpool 2 Newcastle 2

23 April 2016

THEN EVERYTHING got a little bit darker. Victoria Wood first, on the Wednesday night, before the derby, suddenly, we lost Victoria Wood at the ridiculously early age of sixty-two. A wordsmith of rare talent, a writer who could find brilliant comedy in the utterly mundane, a talent we all aspire to when we sit at a screen. It was shocking, unexpected and difficult to process, another loss in a shocking year.

Then Prince died. First Bowie, now Prince. Fifty-seven years old, only five years older than me, a towering genius, one of the most naturally talented musicians ever to walk the planet, one of the greatest live acts you could imagine, gone.

There had been a warning a week earlier, a 'medical emergency' forcing his plane into an unplanned landing. A friend had posted the news on Facebook, I'd replied with 'if we wake up in the morning and there's no Prince, there's going to be fucking murder'. When J looked up from Twitter and said 'They're saying there's news coming out of Minneapolis,' it could only mean one thing. There's no Prince. We've lost another great. The year's unreal. Needs rebooting and starting again.

Which makes the Mamadou Sakho news pretty minor in comparison. Fat burners? Really? Never struck me as a lad who needed to burn fat. If you'd told me that Kolo was on fat burners I'd have understood, but Mamadou? We've done the right thing by taking him out of the picture while the charge hangs over him. No actual suspension yet but if the lad's accused of using illegal substances, then unilaterally deciding not to play him makes sense.

It's another hit to the spine, though. The last fortnight has rocked the centre of the team, Henderson, Can and Origi all sidelined for the rest of the season and now Mamadou out for the foreseeable with a potential ban hanging over him. Six months? A year? Two? Seriously? Potential two-year ban? Everything changes depending on which 'expert' you're speaking to, but things are looking just that little bit lumpy.

So we pick today to go all Southampton again. First half of brilliance, the kind of procession that seemed to be a natural successor to Wednesday night's joy, two goals of pure ease. Sturridge chesting, turning, curling after an entire minute and eight seconds. You're looking at the eleven lads running round in red and you're thinking 'double figures'. Lallana with one of those goals that's all football and talent and placed just under the bar. Half an hour in and you're thinking 'record score here'. Two-nil up and you're talking 'this lot are relegated now' and 'if they'd sacked McClaren in January, like they should have, they'd be safe now, it's a shame' but you're not really that arsed because, Rafa or no Rafa, it's only Newcastle.

And then half-time happens. And then Simon Mignolet happens. Again. From my position in the main stand, level with the Kop end eighteen-yard line, I clearly hear him shout 'keeper' *before* the Newcastle lad has even put the cross in. He's shouted, the defence know he's shouted and then he watches the cross loop as he flaps backwards in its general direction. He's just turned what should be goalkeeping practice into catastrophe. Again.

The damage is incalculable. Suddenly, from a position of relegation, Newcastle have their heads up and the equaliser's more than inevitable. We dig and we try but we've surrendered the game again.

The options aren't there. There isn't a goalscoring threat on the bench.

There's an Ibe and an Ojo and Ojo gets on and tries, but he's not a saviour of lost causes. Origi might have made a difference, Can *would* have made a difference. Stewart does little wrong, but Can's a class above him.

Klopp comes out later and says that, without a single second of better football, we could be seven points better off: Sunderland, Southampton and now Newcastle. In fairness, Mignolet's only responsible for four of those seven points, today and Sunderland, but those four alone would see us in fifth position with a shot at the top four. Stupid, unforced, careless mistakes, need to end them, simple as that.

26 April 2016

I RANG Tom on Saturday while J and Matty were on their way to Wembley for the semi-final.

'Are you doing anything on Tuesday?'

'No, why?'

"Me and mum are going to come down and see you for your birthday."

Our Tom, born on his granddad's birthday and named for him. J's dad would have been 72 today, we lost him at 64, he'd have been proud of the young man that he only knew as a boy.

So, Tuesday is for driving down to Bangor University's halls of residence, that's why we're in the car when the news starts to come through. We'd known from the Monday afternoon, when the announcement was made that the jury had agreed its determinations, that this is how we would hear the results. We thought that we were ready for it. We weren't. I wasn't.

We didn't expect all the answers to come through so quickly, I don't think anybody did. Eleven days ago, I was of the opinion that the jury members could possibly take months to return their decisions. When we realised yesterday that those decisions were made, I still thought, with no understanding of how inquests work, that it would take hours to cover every answer that was about to be given.

The emotions were already there, bubbling. Obviously we knew from yesterday's announcement that the jury had answered thirteen of the fourteen questions unanimously and sought guidance on the fourteenth, or, more accurately and far more vitally, the sixth. Obviously we had no idea what nature their unanimity took, but we believed, we hoped, that they had been able to see what we'd always known, always maintained, always fought for. Question six was the one, question six was the big call, the moment where they would decide if one man was responsible for ninety-six deaths. Question six was the question we worried might not go as it should.

The first 'yes' was fine, the formality of agreeing the tragedy. We were listening to Radio City Talk on a poor medium wave signal on a coast road, J was following the answers coming in on Twitter. Coming in quicker than we expected, quicker than commentary could cope with.

The second 'yes', police planning, error and omission. The first sob came there, huge, unexpected and overwhelming. Another sob on the third 'yes'. Driving in tears. 'We need to pull in, this isn't safe,' says J. Questions four and five have passed with the same reaction each time before we reach a turn off. Question six is answered before we get chance to pull in. I'm simultaneously punching the air and questioning *exactly* what it means.

'Does this mean they've said he's guilty then? Are they saying it's his fault?'

That, apparently, is exactly what they've said, exactly what they're saying. The radio is explaining this as the seventh answer arrives: there is no blame attached to the fans.

We're sitting on the sea front at Colwyn Bay. The sea's grey, the waves are wild, it's blowing a gale, the sky is threatening, it's almost unbearably beautiful. There are a couple of old women walking a dog as we leave the car. I've no idea what they made of the tearful couple standing on the sea wall. Something's happening that doesn't seem to be part of their immediate world. We have all fourteen questions answered and all fourteen say everything that we always knew they should. All fourteen place the blame firmly where the blame always belonged.

We stand on the front at Colwyn Bay holding each other, exactly as we held each other on the night itself, when I arrived home to find J already there with my mum and the news that the lads had rung home and that "they're all right, they're all alright," exactly as we held each other on the touchline at Anfield as we saw the flowers grow to fill the pitch.

There are twenty-seven years in that hug, there were twenty-seven years in the sobs that burst in the car. The reaction is physical. Deeply physical. And we were the lucky ones. We were the ones whose family came home. It's still impossible to comprehend the pain of the families of the 96 and always will be.

Does this feel like justice? Does it feel like we thought it would? I don't know. It feels like another step. It feels like all of the truth, it feels like some of the justice, it feels like vindication. It needs accountability. The one word that came through so firmly in the news reports. Justice is nothing without accountability.

We know the names. We know the institutions. The criminal investigations continue. This isn't the end but hopefully it means that the souls and spirits of the 96 who we can finally say without contradiction were unlawfully killed at Hillsborough can rest a little easier now. Hopefully it means that their families are nearer the moment where they are able to grieve without the need to defend their loved ones against lies and insults.

RIP the 96.

Villarreal 1 Liverpool 0

Europa League Semi-Final First Leg
28 April 2016

I HOPE the weather was nice for the travelling lads. Hope they were able to have an afternoon in Spain's late spring sun before the game because, God knows, it was bloody weird at home.

The game kicks off on the TV to the accompaniment of thunder, lightning and hail. All at the same time. We're three days away from the start of May and the weather's decided to reset itself to November. It probably is the tribute to Prince that everyone had expected, *Sometimes It Snows In April* and all that.

It was a gamble, wasn't it? It was a gamble and it didn't quite work. It almost worked, it was *almost*, but not quite, satisfactory. The idea of playing for a draw doesn't really sit well with me. It certainly didn't sit well with the Twitter crew. That Benteke had suddenly, unexpectedly, returned from his knee injury and was on the plane seemed to make up, slightly, for the missing Origi. It seemed to indicate that we would play with a striker and have an option on the bench. When we discovered that the bench contained both Benteke *and* Sturridge, we were convinced that it meant that we intended to tire the Villarreal back line and then introduce Dan on, let's say seventy, shall we?

It looked as though we intended to 'Man City' them, all false nines, the six lads who weren't technically defenders moving round in a manner that the Yellow Submarines were

318

unable to follow. We had speed and dynamism and creativity, we just didn't have a final ball into the box that made any real impact. BT Sport had Owen Hargreaves commentating. He spent the first forty-five minutes complaining that Firmino wasn't in the box often enough, which I took to mean that Owen had spent so much of his career on various treatment tables that the concept of tactics is foreign to him and he has no understanding of Firmino's role in the team.

It was nearly one of those nights where you don't need somebody in the box, you just need possession and a chance. If Joe Allen shoots either side of the goalie instead of straight at him, if there's any lift on the ball, then we're one up. If Firmino's shot hits the inside of the post, we're two up. Fine margins.

BT has Messrs McManaman and Owen on the touchline for half-time. They're surprised by how weak Villarreal are, how easily we're controlling them, how easily we're dealing with the supposed threats of Bakambu, Soldado and the improbably named Denis Suarez (it might be spelt exotically, but you say it 'Dennis' and it sounds like the name of a minor seventies sitcom character). They think that the game is screaming out for a change and a threat. Half-time is surely the time for Sturridge.

We get Jordon Ibe. And the shape doesn't change and we plough on as before. We take Daniel Sturridge and Christian Benteke to Spain and we leave them both on the bench until big Chris emerges on the ninetieth minute. Two minutes later, we're one down. A long ball into the area that Moreno should be defending; Moreno has mysteriously chosen to push up and attack. It's an interesting choice.

We've gambled. Gambled on the idea of nil-nil being a decent base to work from and the prospect of snatching a goal a bonus. If they don't punt forward in the last seconds, we're all relatively pleased. But they do and we aren't.

Klopp pointing out afterwards that this is only half-time and Villarreal's celebrations are just the tiniest bit premature is probably for our benefit as much as theirs. If the game had remained a stalemate, we would have had to come back to Anfield and win. What do we have to do now? We have to come back to Anfield and win. Same difference, we've done it before.

Time to break out the pyros, the welcome parties in Anfield Road and the atmosphere we pride ourselves on. We're one-nil down at half time. Time to turn this around.

Swansea 3 Liverpool 1

1 May 2016

I KEEP trying to tell myself that it doesn't matter. That there's no consequence, that it's just an interruption between legs of the Europa League semi-final, that it's just something that we need to get out of the way so we can concentrate on business. That a noon kick-off on a Sunday when the team only landed back in England at four on Friday morning is some kind of TV-based practical joke and it doesn't matter.

It doesn't matter because all that matters is the weekend response to Tuesday's determinations. All that matters is the way that Everton's planned minute's applause lasted at least three and that their response to the presence of some of the families was as magnificent as it has been ever since the day itself. All that matters is the way that Newcastle's tribute became a spontaneous rendition of *You'll Never Walk Alone* and that alone means that, against everything I might have ever said about the club and the owner, I want those fans to see their team avoid relegation. All that matters is the dignity that Swansea afforded us prior to kick-off with their applause and the presentation of a wreath to Barry Devonside. I don't know what other tributes were paid. I'm pretty sure Stoke did something, don't know if Southampton did anything, don't know if Spurs will tonight, no idea if United held anything before Leicester moved one point closer to the title at Old Trafford, but it doesn't matter.

And if that doesn't matter, then the performance of a Liverpool team with the lowest average starting age of the

Premier League era shouldn't matter. A midfield two of Stewart and Chirivella being pulled out of position at Swansea's whim shouldn't matter. Chirivella appearing completely out of his depth against a side that has struggled with relegation all season shouldn't matter. Kevin Stewart's least convincing game to date shouldn't matter.

The five minutes which see Benteke's header bring us back into the game at two-one down before our combined defensive forces of Skrtel, Lucas, Clyne, Smith and Lovren combine to allow Swansea to regain their two-goal lead shouldn't matter.

Jordon Ibe continuing his less-than-inspirational form on either wing should be unimportant. Sturridge seemingly refusing to shake hands with opponents or applaud the travelling fans who'd been up since the night before in order to arrive in Wales for noon should be a minor irritant.

It's not. They're not. There's not a single second of this that doesn't matter. It's hideous. The whole lunchtime fiasco matters. The lack of fight, lack of shape, lack of creativity, lack of comeback. All of it matters. We're Liverpool, of course it bloody matters. Swansea away, worst first forty-five minutes of Jurgen Klopp's reign. There are players who, if they weren't already aware, saw themselves become part of the rebuilding process in South Wales.

Because it always matters.

Thursday then. Flares and flags and fans in the street. Start again.

Liverpool 3 Villarreal 0

Europa League Semi-Final Second Leg
5 May 2016

AND THERE were. Flares and flags and fans in the street. Despite the lunchtime warnings from the emergency services that any flares brought into the ground or the surrounding streets could see the game cancelled and lifetime bans issued. Intimidating stuff. Good luck with policing that one, lads, there's about a million of us and we're filling the streets with the reddest smoke you've ever seen.

The scaffolding's grown since the Dortmund game, the scaffolding's packed, banners, flags, men who are clearly old enough to know better. There's no such thing as old enough to know better. Knowing better suggests you've stopped enjoying the madness. You should never stop enjoying the madness. The madness is everything.

Devastating. I thought long and hard on that one, looking for the right word to capture everything that we were last night. Imperious? That's Emre Can. Tireless? Adam Lallana. Intelligent? James Milner. Creative? Coutinho. Staggeringly brilliant? That's the Firmino turn that sees the endlessly irritating, whining, diving, petulant Soldado trying to figure out what the hell happened to that lad that was there a second ago. Resilient? Kolo. Disciplined? Alberto Moreno, bizarrely enough. Endlessly available? Nathaniel Clyne. Deadly? Dan. Dan in a starting line-up, Dan showing his necessity, showing just how much he bloody cares about this. Imposing? Dejan cleaning up everything with such bloody authority that we should all queue outside his house to beg forgiveness for ever doubting him, every day until we all have to go to that Switzerland place. Secure? Big Si. Who saw that one coming? Safe, secure.

Devastating, though, we're doing devastating. And, yes, there's one very, very major name I've missed here. You know that. I'll come back to him.

It's not Dortmund. Nothing could be Dortmund. Dortmund wasn't devastating, Dortmund was dramatic, Dortmund existed on the twists and turns, on the fact that we were out, that we were over and then that we weren't and then that we were again and then that we were in the game, but out on away goals, and then on the last-second revival and the drama and relief and outpourings of elated, astonished emotion.

Villarreal isn't that. Villarreal is the awareness that we start already behind in the tie. Villarreal is the awareness that one goal from them could make the night very difficult, the awareness that we're facing a team who are more than capable of countering. It's about knowing that any risk could be dangerous. But risk *should* be dangerous shouldn't it? Risk is where the fun is.

I leave the game thinking that there's every possibility that Daniel Sturridge has scored a hat-trick. I think that the third might be Lallana but I don't know. It was at the Anfield Road end and I couldn't tell and there was no way of hearing George announce the scorer of the winning goal in *all that*. And *all that* wasn't the outpouring of relief that we saw with Dortmund, it was the celebration of the confirmation that we were through. Not that we doubted.

At one-nil up (and I know now that it wasn't Sturridge, it was an own goal but, good God, Sturridge's sheer presence is everything here), we don't doubt. We know that an unanswered Villarreal goal would see them two-one up on aggregate and put us out, but we don't doubt those fabulous lads in red who are giving everything you could want them to give.

At two-nil (and I realise now that Dan didn't just slip it under the goalie as I thought at the match, he clips it off the goalie on to the first post, on to the second post and into the net, a scruffy goal, a fine move but a scruffy finish, our second fine move but scruffy finish after the 'not really Sturridge, actually an own goal' first), we don't doubt. We know that an unanswered Villarreal goal would be the crucial, equalising, away goal and put us out. We know that a two-one win here would still be a loss, we know that a third is essential but we don't doubt those fabulous lads in red who are giving more and growing stronger by the second.

We know a third is essential so we do the essential. We score when we need to score. We score each goal when we need to score each goal. We're clinical, we're incisive, we're devastating.

The third? The third's the devastation incarnate. The third's the moment that breaks Villarreal, that leaves them with nothing left. I think it's Sturridge's hat-trick but it's not. It's Lallana. It's a gorgeous little flick and, watching the highlights in the pub, we're convinced it's offside. The more we watch it, the more offside it gets. It's the lad on the floor, isn't it? His body's off the field but his arm's in the box, the ref's pointing at him. He must be playing Lallana onside. Is that how it works now? Does anybody care? The Spanish lads aren't appealing. The Spanish lads are finished. There's nothing left.

This was the team that we weren't going to break down. This was the team that we weren't going to prevent from scoring. This was the team whose first-leg late sucker punch goal had ended our dream. This was the team who had seen Jurgen Klopp's first major misstep, had exposed his first leg caution as folly. No. No on all fronts.

This might be as complete a European performance as you will ever see. This was almost undoubtedly the finest performance of Klopp's reign to date. This might have been perfect. This felt perfect.

This is the answer that our manager gives to anybody who doubted him last week. The team that he designed to absorb

Villarreal's pressure seven days ago tweaked ever so slightly to become the most attacking side that he could field and sent out with the brief to attack. So they attack. Wave after glorious wave of attack. Intelligent football, emotional football, decisive football, coming at the Villarreal back four from every possible angle. It looked like a 4-1-3-2 to me but who really knows? We're so flexible now that it could be anything changing to anything else as these wondrous lads in red and our incredible manager see fit. Six months of Jurgen Klopp and we have flexibility. We have intensity, we have belief, determination, courage, creativity. He said that he would convert doubters to believers and he's done that, done it with us, done it with the players.

You can see it in us, see it in the ground with the noise levels rising with every vital game, with the main stand singing, with the centenary stand singing, with the fervour that comes with big nights and those big nights becoming bigger and bigger. You can see it in the way that we never doubted.

You can see it in the players, see it in the way that Dejan Lovren has become a colossus, become the man that you know, absolutely *know* will be first to every single ball, the way that Bakambu and Soldado and the still improbably named Denis Suarez are nothing to him. You can see it in Kolo but then Kolo's job has always been to believe, it's his essential Koloness. You can see it in the way that Moreno measures his runs tonight, is where he needs to be when he needs to be. See it in the way that Nathaniel Clyne is an endless threatening presence, in the way that Adam Lallana, that player that some still regard as lazy, indulgent, inclined to take too many touches, is all pressure and closing and moving and creating. He's the perfect player for the European stage for us. He keeps the ball, he steadies everything, he keeps you as a permanent threat high on the pitch.

You can see it in the sheer, experienced, masterful game intelligence of James Milner. I was as disparaging of Milner as any (flick back, re-read if you don't remember), thought he added little to the team. He adds guile, adds thought, adds awareness. Bizarrely, when watching the highlights, it appears that Milner had little involvement. On the pitch, he was nothing but involvement.

See it in Daniel Sturridge. Those who say that he's aloof? Those who say he doesn't care, that he's not got Liverpool in his heart? See him whirl away, screaming. See the joy on his face. No casual, prearranged, arms waving, just sheer honest delight in an evening when he never stops moving, never stops probing, never stops threatening.

And see it in Emre Can. See it in the form of a lad who was supposedly sidelined for six weeks, comes back after three and does *all that*. Can is imperious, Can makes everything happen. Can puts in the ideal central midfield performance. The words Rolls and Royce are often mentioned when Emre is spoken about. Tonight they're used again and again and again. Call it hyperbole if you wish but watching Emre Can dictate Villarreal's fate held glimpses of Souness in his pomp. Say what you like, that's what *I'm* saying.

And see all of it in Jurgen Klopp. Furious at all times, two-nil up and screaming at his players to get it right. It doesn't matter how right they're already getting it, he wants more of it, he wants more of the right. He *gets* more of the right. He's improving these lads day by day, week by week. All those lads that we listed, all those virtues we ascribed, they've all come from Jurgen. Six months in and he's made Liverpool into this juggernaut of pressing, of speed, of determination. He's made us devastating and we recognise that in the endless singing of his name as the final whistle and Switzerland beckon. As glory beckons.

And this is what we were tonight. This is why we don't have the drama of Dortmund, simply the grace and power and knowledge that we know how good we are. We're ruthless and calm and determined and aggressive and powerful and icy and clinical. We're everything we want to be and we're in another European final. We're looking at UEFA Cup number four. Champions League Group Stages as a reward? Fine, all good, but the cup's the thing. Liverpool Football Club exists to win things. We're beginning to look very much like that Liverpool Football Club again.

This wasn't supposed to happen. Two finals in his first season? Without adding to the team? Not supposed to happen. This is how good Jurgen Klopp is, this is how good Jurgen Klopp has made us, this is what we are: devastating.

The Inevitable Comedown

HOW COULD you possibly take the shine off an evening like that? Easy, stick the ticket details up on the club website straight after the game.

We're in *The Frost* again. It might not have the passion, madness, buzz of *The Sandon* or *The King Harry,* but you can get served at the bar and find a nice table to sit at.

We're discussing transport and routes. Fleety is talking about this coach that gets to Basel about four hours before kick-off and leaves four hours after the game and we're not taking this as a good idea,

"All it takes is an accident on the M25 and you're buggered for kick-off."

Paris is discussed. Paris for lunchtime, nice day out, three hours on the train to Basel. Our Keith points out that Switzerland is pretty much central to everything in Europe, so we could go anywhere. Tommy is favouring Hannover and the train from there. There's flights that won't go through the roof because the routes aren't expected to be used and train prices in Europe are train prices in Europe. Their ability to stitch us up is limited.

We're already wary about ticket prospects. We've heard that it's going to be nine thousand tickets for a thirty-eight thousand-seat stadium. That's nine for us, nine for Sevilla and …oh, that leaves twenty-thousand, doesn't it? For the UEFA family and their mates. None of which will hit the black market for stupidly inflated prices, honest.

'Twas ever thus. Every final ever played. No chance of half the stadium to each set of fans and the atmosphere and spectacle that would go with that, no attention to the simple beauty of the game connecting with the people, not when there's a non-specific family to cater for.

Nine thousand tickets. Anyone really think there'll only be nine thousand Liverpool fans in that stadium? Anyone think that a lot of them won't have been fleeced by a lad in a pub who got his tickets from a bloke who knows a bloke who knows a bloke?

And then the extra details hit. Forty-seven per cent of those tickets will go to general supporters. That's us, we're the 'general' supporters. From UEFA's pitiful allocation to Liverpool, the lads who were greeting the coach in the streets and singing and setting off those evil flares and adding all the atmosphere outside and inside the ground, the ones who the players have said pushed them over the line and into the final, the club's twelfth man, are getting 4,800 tickets.

The lads who've got eight European games on their cards this season are guaranteed a ticket. That's the lads who've done at least one European game. That's cool, that's how it should be. The rest of us, the ones who've only done every home game, are in a ballot. If you weren't in the 'auto cup' scheme, you don't even get a place in the lottery.

The UEFA family, the football family, doesn't include the fans. Why should the fans get to go to the party? The game will survive so well without us, won't it? Fairly sure we've made a stand on that principle already. Time for all fans to organise another stand on the subject, something that will get the world bodies to pay attention.

Don't look at me, I haven't got the answers. I'm just asking the questions.

So we drift away and we know Fleety's sorted because he's done the aways, but Keith's not because he's not auto-cup. He's done Augsburg but that wasn't on his card and Tommy's said that he's not going to contemplate the old 'do anything to get in' approach, the 'holding up a ciggy packet to get in' that was used in Athens in yet another unorganised stadium that should never have seen a major final grace its unsuitable surroundings.

A nice barbecue, a few mates round, watch it on the telly with some beers. But if we hear of anyone…

The next thirteen days consist of a lot of lads who love their team using the phrase 'but if you hear of anyone'.

It's wrong. It shouldn't be this way. Look at what we make this game and treat us as we deserve.

Liverpool 2 Watford 0

8 May 2016

THE SUN'S shining. Lauren Laverne's playing Curtis Mayfield's *Move On Up* on 6 Music. She was, a second ago, she's now playing The Beastie Boy's *Sabotage*. Small moments, all good.

Yesterday's small moments. Me and J went for a bike ride. First time in years that we've done that. First thing in the morning, pleasant, warm. Down Dunnings Bridge Road and back. Twenty minutes at most. My knees are wrecked, I feel my age.

Played footy in the garden with Matty. First time in a couple of years. You realise these things as you're doing them, realise how quickly everything moves. I was never any good, he's always been. Cruyff turns, rabona flicks, nutmegging me. Endlessly. My knees are wrecked. I'm checking my life insurance halfway through. This all seemed so much easier before he was the same height as me. I feel my age. It's bloody great. The idea of going the game seemed like an interruption to a nice day. I think the other 42,000 in the stadium felt the same way.

Credit to the lads who came up from Watford. Paraded a banner along the front of their section as we sang *YNWA*. 'Justice at last for the 96. YNWA. From Watford FC Supporters.' It's a beautiful touch. Classy support, glad they're okay, nothing to worry about football-wise. Decent team, play well, pose us a few problems, force a good save from big Si in a game that nobody's really arsed about.

Oh, the Kop tries to get a few songs going but it's too sunny, too nice, too warm, too unimportant, too close to Thursday. Could have done with a few more days to bask, to breathe out, relax. Watching the Villarreal game again on Saturday night probably didn't help my appreciation of a routine 'end of season/nothing at stake' game. Just didn't measure up.

Eight changes. But only because Brad Smith was suspended and Danny Ward injured. No way it wouldn't have been at least ten otherwise. And the lads do fine this time. All half speed, all relatively safe. Score when you need to. Benteke makes one for Joe Allen, Ojo blocks a tackle and Firmino capitalises. Big Chris does okay and probably deserves a goal. Would have been in double figures for what's been a poor season. Martin Skrtel's sound, Lucas is fine. No-one does anything wrong and we win two-nil. In the sun. Nothing wrong, no mistakes, no drama, just a pleasant day out. Sometimes it's enough.

Tuesday 10 May

'THE BALLOT results are due at one. You'll find them on this link. And we'll e-mail you.' That's what they said.

Our Keith gives me the advice. I'd said that I'd wait until I'd found out if I was lucky before I sorted travel and accommodation. 'Don't do that,' he says, 'Have everything ready for when you know or you'll get nothing.' He knows this stuff, he's done the hard miles, I take his advice.

So, I've got multiple screens open. Flights from Liverpool? Not happening. From Manchester? No. Leeds? Birmingham? He's already given me the suggestion that I end up going with and I've everything ready for that. Ready for one.

One comes, one goes. There's no e-mail. And the website has fallen over. Facebook and Twitter fill with questions about servers and load capacity. I throw the old 'dial-up' tone and image up on Facebook to amuse myself as I'm getting nothing else done. When I finally give up and decide to do some real work, that's when the e-mail pings its way in. I get as far as the word 'congratulations' and bounce off the walls. Leaping, screaming, swearing. I'm fifty-two years old. Apparently. Bollocks to that, age ain't nothing but a number, baby.

Stick my head into the living room, J adopts mock sincerity,"Unsuccessful, darling?"

Lime Street. Euston. The Tube. Victoria. Gatwick. Milan. A car. A hotel. A drive from Italy to Switzerland. The match. Repeat in reverse. With no sleep. Tuesday morning to Thursday night. One-in-seventeen chance? Never doubted. Not for a second. Basel beckons.

Liverpool 1 Chelsea 1

11 May 2016

'THIS IS a public service announcement for all supporters in the main stand. Unauthorised removal of club property is theft and you may be arrested.'

As announcements go, it doesn't have the snap of the opening lines of The Clash's *Know Your Rights*. 'This is a public service announcement...*with guitars!*' It's not cool, it's not classy, it's not credible. It is, however, very likely to get you in shit with that steward right there who's decided his job is to stare out everybody who looks like they might be considering the idea of taking a souvenir from the old main stand on its last day.

You can hear the snapping noises as we wait for the 'lap of appreciation' which tons of people have decided that they're going to swerve in favour of the bus home. See those lads there? They've got us to our first European final in years, give them a clap, they kind of deserve it. The snapping noises are coming from back and to the left. They're the sound of chairs being liberated. Hence the polite announcement from the guy who generally only gets to say 'Commence Operation Anfield Exercise.' Prefer his other gig if we're honest.

But I want a seat. Change that, I don't want *a* seat, I want *this* seat. This is my dad's seat, this is the seat that his back leant on to watch the glory. Those grooves in the top of the backrest? They're his leaning, they're the feet of the lads behind him over the decades, this is his. If I take it, am I really stealing? Particularly when, by the time I write this, it'll be in a large skip and the club, despite all the rumours, haven't mobilised well enough to say: 'Fancy buying your seat, lads? Cost you thirty quid?' 'Cool, where do I sign?' Nothing. Profit margins there you know, easy money. I'll come and do the CEO job for you. I've got vision.

So I'm leaning back on it. I'm not kicking this, I'm not breaking this, breaking this isn't the point. I'm stepping over into the row behind, flexing my knees against the back, seeing if there's any give. There isn't.

I'm not getting this. So I get the photo instead. I get the seat, I get the view from the seat. I get the memories. I keep the memories. The memories are everything, you know this. Would have been nice to have the back of that seat mounted on the wall over my desk, though.

The game? Yeah, pretty entertaining on the whole. We start off as though we've decided that fifteen would be a nice number to score. We're everywhere, we're terrorising Chelsea, we're fast, inventive, and we appear to be playing a 4-2-4, which is a pleasantly attacking notion. Sturridge is playing the wings. Both the wings. He's looking for other wings to add to the two he gets to play on, but dropping deep to attack from the middle will do.

Firmino is being Lallana, who's being Coutinho, and they all seem to fancy the idea of being Daniel Sturridge and James Milner at the same time. We're swamping and we're beautiful to watch. For fifteen minutes. And then we slow down and Chelsea look at us and think 'these lads don't fancy tackling, don't want to chase us round too much, might as well have a crack at this'. So they do and they reinvent themselves as the best version of Chelsea that they've been all season, built on the idea that Eden Hazard feels like being the best version of Eden Hazard that he's been all season.

They're good. And for long stretches, they're better than we are.

And you can see that everyone's kind of got one eye on the final and I'm fine with that. I was at the league game in '88 when Spackman and Gillespie contested the same header and ended up playing the FA Cup final against Wimbledon's collection of yard-dogs in decorative headgear.

We're late out for the second half and it seems that it's down to Jurgen suggesting to the lads that running around a bit more might be a good idea. Because they do. And the running round and closing down's pretty cool, but it looks like nothing's going to happen and we're going to close off the old main stand with a one-nil loss to this least offensive of all versions of Chelsea until we combine Ojo with a Begovic disaster and a Benteke header and we're back to being unbeaten in thirteen games.

So we end the home section of the season with another chapter of the Benteke conundrum. He's in double figures, which isn't bad, really. I can think of at least seven points that he's solely responsible for off the top of my head. Two late one-nil wins and, now, this one-all draw. I have a sneaking suspicion that he's responsible for ten points but can't prove this without research and really? Does it matter? For a terrible footballer who's had a terrible season (cleaned up version of Twitter fume), he's not done badly, has he?

Now that's a conundrum.

Goodbye to the main stand then, thanks for everything, it was great, saw some good stuff there, this year and other years. Me and my dad. Separately, mostly, but there were a few occasions we were both in there and close to each other.

Won't miss pillar number three, though. Neither of us ever saw a single thing that happened by the Anfield Road End corner flag.

Wish I'd got my seat.

West Brom 1 Liverpool 1

15 May 2016

IT'S ABOUT fifteen minutes since the match ended. I'm writing this without having re-watched, reviewed, revisited. I'm watching it without consideration or contemplation. Let's be honest, I'm getting it out of the way. Seems apt, after all, you're not really arsed about reading this chapter are you? With a bit of luck, all you're thinking about is getting to the next bit. So let's keep this short.

I hate watching matches in pubs. Hate it. Might be okay if you're with your mates, but on your own? No. The pub that I used the last couple of times? I get there and they're messing with the telly. It's dead on three and they're messing with the telly. 'Do you want serving?' 'Are you showing the match?' 'Just sorting it.'

I get a bottle of Becks and wait. Once we've hit the ten-minute mark and nobody's made any further attempt to sort out the jarg stream, I abandon the bottle and head for a pub that I've studiously avoided drinking in for two decades.

Their TVs are showing both Liverpool and Everton's games. I order and immediately realise that the coked-up lad from last time out is stood next to me. He's demonstrating something that seems to be MMA-based to a bloke who's twenty years older than him. And he's moving a lot in order to do it. I'm waiting for the 'did you spill my pint?' moment. It's coming. Another guy's quizzing him 'Are you on Charlie? Show us your eyes.' Really, mate? You really need to check his eyes? 'I'm not on anything.' Fooling no-one mate.

That's my problem with matches in pubs on my own, other people. Can't be doing with them. The atmosphere you want is gone, replaced by other lads' conversations. 'Well fuck off back to the army then.'

The telly's too far away, there's little blokes in red shirts running round quite close to little lads in stripes and you can't tell if any of it is achieving anything.

Obviously West Brom score the very second I get to the bar. Looks like an issue with our grasp on the concept of defending combined with the idea that Adam Bogdan isn't very good. I have a feeling that the only reason he's playing is because the rest of us missed the phone call from Jurgen.

We respond nicely, we run round and try things. And then Jordon Ibe does this little turn just before the halfway line, runs the length of the pitch and slots home and we all remember, for a brief moment, why we loved him. And it's a draw.

Eleven changes and we get to see Ibe and Ojo and Brannagan and Stewart and Smith and Flanno. And Danny Ings gets to come on in the second half and I genuinely have no idea if he did anything. Ditto Hendo. Nice to have them back. And we get to see Sergi Canos in the first team. Again, no idea what he did. By the time he's on, I'm trying to figure out whether Benteke's still on the pitch or not, and if he is, when we last saw him. And I'm trying to find out whether this is the first time a team has fielded the shirt numbers 14 (Hendo), 24 (Joe and his Pirlo beard), 34 (the world's gingerest keeper), 44 (Brad Smith), 54 (Ojo) and 64 (the just arrived back from loan Canos). Shame Kolo wasn't there, would have had a full house.

And, as the heavily pregnant singer for somebody's 60th birthday 'do' lugs speakers across the room, I think, 'can I go home yet?' Because none of this really matters. With the results above us going the way that those above us wanted them to go, we finish eighth. Which is unimpressive but, sod it, Leicester only just avoided relegation last season and they've done okay, haven't they? We'll be fine. All that matters now is Wednesday.

Liverpool 1 Sevilla 3

Europa League Final
18 May 2016
A Hard Rain

SO, THIS is how it ends, not with a bang but with a whimper.

I've just looked up the origin of that quote, one of the many things that I've been doing today to avoid writing this part, it's T.S. Eliot apparently, comes from the poem *The Hollow Men,* a piece which concerns itself, in part, with the difficulty of hope. Seems somewhat accidentally apt, that. *The difficulty of hope.*

The rain, which seemed mildly amusing as we marched towards St Jakob Park with flares in our hands and songs on our lips, an invading army intent on nothing but glory and pleasure, all 'sorry love, you can have your city back tomorrow' and laughter, as me, Keith, Fleety and Mike abused Mongoose for his desire to shelter and keep dry, was bitter now, bitter and heavy and unrelenting. I had entered the day, the country, the ground, filled with hope and expectation and certainty and belief. I left feeling nothing but old and cold and wet and tired, very, very tired and unable to see anything positive, any reason to keep moving forward other than to get out of the bloody rain.

And it had all started so well.

I'd thought it would be just me. Well, just me and a few thousand others, obviously. Apart from those few thousand others, the season that had started with me picking up my first season ticket in my own name was ending with me going to my first ever European away game. At the age of fifty-two, I was going to my first ever European away. Might as well be a final, mightn't it? Do things the right way. Alone but right.

I knew I'd meet Fleety there, knew Fleety was sorted. Long coach trip but sorted. Then our Keith rang me. Thursday night, I think it was. Late, I'd been out, no idea where. 'Could you do us a favour?' 'Yeah, what?' 'Could I get a lift off you from Milan to Basel?'

So, Keith's in. Within a day, Mongoose has a ticket and there are three of us heading for Switzerland. There's a message from Mike, he of the swapped Dortmund scarf that brought the luck and the drama, he's coming. So's the scarf. There are four of us, we'll need to upgrade the car. Now this, *this* is right, this is how it should be.

'But you won't need a full tank,' says the girl in the car rental place near Milan Malpensa airport once me and Mike (met up in Gatwick after I'd raced across town having corrected my original, almost disastrous 'Victoria Line in wrong direction' mistake) have negotiated the 'having to locate the shuttle bus when their English is only marginally more existent than our Italian' issue. 'Yeah, love, that's what you reckon, we're driving to Switzerland in the morning.' Didn't say it, obviously. Not out loud, not to her.

Mongoose is on the later flight from Gatwick. He's Whatsapping us on his progress from the city centre to the hotel that's just found out that I'm no longer on my own and, upon being asked if they could move us to a twin room or maybe a double, offers us a room with a double bed. "But it's okay, the bed is big enough for a couple."

Yeah, mate, we're *really* not a couple.

We don't bother telling Mongoose that the second he arrives we're going to drag him back into town because it's funnier that way. We quite fancy seeing Milan. We've never been there. He has, he's our guide.

We see the Duomo, all intricate and carved and beautiful and we see a bar which proudly displays the name Martini and menus which contain myriad Martini-based drinks. So we're drinking Martinis. Well, me and Mike are drinking Martinis. Mongoose is having none of that behaviour. And we're talking to Danny, a cheerful, bearded fellow Scouser who's been working in Canada and has now ended up here as a stopping-off point on his way to the same destination as us.

And that's where we meet Keith. Martinis in hand, overlooking the Duomo Square, pointing at those below, going 'there's our kid' and marvelling at how easy it is to meet up in nice places in theses 'far foreign lands'. Sitting, drinking, talking about the possibilities ahead. Which are endless.

We meant to eat. I'm sure we meant to eat.

That was supposed to be the first line of this chapter, 'We meant to eat.'

'But you won't need a full tank.' That was supposed to be the first line as well. You write this in your head as it's happening, as you're taking everything in. You change it as you go along. Events take over.

The radio is playing as we leave Italy. The Italian version of Capital that we had discovered the previous evening with its constant, obvious, fast-paced Italian and its terrible euro-pop is leading its breakfast show with Joy Division's *Disorder*. On the 36th anniversary of Ian Curtis's death, an Italian breakfast show is playing the opening track of Joy Division's first album. I'll guarantee that Capital in Liverpool isn't doing this. They follow up with The Who. It's a marvellous soundtrack to the start of an awfully big adventure.

Want a spectacular backdrop for your drive to the match? I fully recommend Milan to Basel. Snow-covered mountains, lush green forests, perfectly blue lakes, sun kissed scenery, motorways that seem to exist on stilts with vertigo-inducing drops to either side. Eighteen-kilometre long tunnels through mountain sides, slowly trickling streams wending their way down the hills, traditional Swiss housing that seems to be made from a mixture of chocolate, gingerbread and Lego. Magical, enchanting, wondrous, until Thursday morning when you're doing the whole thing in reverse with a hangover that's equal parts shop-bought Swiss lager and heartbreak.

"Look at it," I said to Fleety. We were two rows and six seats apart after managing to persuade the lad sitting next to him that moving forward and swapping with me was a good idea. 'How are they supposed to cope with all this?'

The 'all this' was all us. Thirty-thousand of us, must have been thirty-thousand of us. Thirty-thousand of us in the ground and God knows how many more outside. We were that marching army, that singing army. We were the people who popped into a pub on the way down to the ground to use the toilet (the bushes? I'm not using the bushes when there's a bog over there) and found ourselves in a chorus of 'The ball, the ball, they never touched the ball, we played the shite on a Wednesday night and they never touched the ball, the ball, the ball...' that went round and round and had an older bloke, younger than me but still older, asking: 'Why are you singing about them?' 'Well, we're only singing it in a pub bogs, we're not going to sing it at the ground, are we?'

And we weren't, because at the ground we were singing *Poor Scouser Tommy* and *The Fields of Anfield Road* and *Three Little Birds* and the next day I was looking at a photo of Bob Marley and going 'I don't know if he's a lying get or not'. For one glorious two-minute spell at half-time, while we were still happy, still having a party, we sang, we *all* sang *There She Goes* and it was bloody special and anything was possible. It would only take seventeen seconds to prove us wrong and forty-five minutes to show just *how* wrong.

'All this? How can they cope with all this?' And the 'they' was Sevilla and the answer was 'pretty bloody well, in all honesty.'

There are ten minutes at the start where it's all a bit scrappy and then we calm down and we get into it. And we look like we can score. There's a Sturridge header that's cleared just before the line and there's a Sturridge shot that's saved and it's clear that this match means something to Dan. He's up for this. And when he scores his goal, it's right and appropriate and deserved. Deserved by him, by the team, by us. It's world class. Honest to God world class, outside of the foot, curling all the

343

way and we're going wild. We're everything that Sevilla aren't and I genuinely think that we'll win by three or four or five because I'm stupid and optimistic and naive and hopeful and drunk. And Liverpool are honestly that convincing. You know this, you watched this, it's part of the disappointment. How good we were to how good we weren't, the difficulty of hope.

There's the square with the TV that's a lot bigger than the one we'd all seen on Twitter the day before and we're standing drinking our shop-bought lager and talking and laughing and having the best time you could ever have and it hasn't started to rain yet, but it will. And there's the neutral zone and we think that'll be worth a look, see how the neutral fans are partying. But there aren't any neutrals. There's a five-a-side pitch but it's for the kids and there's no chance of us getting a game no matter how much we want to. And it's me suggesting it, us against a few Swiss lads or Spanish lads. Because I'm drunk and I've forgotten I'm fifty-two and shit at football. Mike isn't. Mike's taking on the bloke who's running the skills competition and he's not happy because the rules are getting changed so the bloke wins and we're back to our zone because neutrality's dull. God knows why the Swiss think so highly of it.

And I know that Basel's the wrong place to have the game and I know the stadium's too small, but right now? Right now? Right now I'm kind of thinking, 'I'll give UEFA this, they've made an absolute pils of the whole thing here but it's a cracking day out, isn't it?' And it is.

And it's winding down and we're moving and we're going the ground and we're trying to figure out how many of us there are and the figure's getting higher by the second. And the rain's coming. But how can they cope with all this? Look at us, look how magnificent we are. Nobody does this like we do this. We're beautiful and powerful and destiny's coming.

Moreno heads it clear but 'clear' is the space between Coutinho and the Sevilla lad and the Sevilla lad's racing at Moreno and he's probably shouting 'megs' as he goes through him, and Lovren and Kolo are nowhere near Gameiro and it's a tap-in. Seventeen seconds. All that work, wasted. In seventeen seconds. And you can see it in the lads' body language. And our heads go. On the pitch, in the stands, our heads go.

I'm saying, 'it's okay, it was one-all in Rome' but I'm not sure if it was or not. I believe it, though. I believe we can come back. Fleety's not sure, Fleety's convinced the team's mentality is all wrong, is too soft, too weak. Thinks they thought they had it wrapped up at half-time, same as we did, got a bit cocky, same as we probably did but come on, we were having so much fun and I think he's probably got a point here.

Then it's two. Lovren's the one who's megged this time but we're still all blaming Moreno and I'm sure we had a reason, sure he was involved. Those who were watching the replays, watching the coverage, they're convinced, they must have had reason. And I've watched the goals back and I'm not sure but there's a line here and it's a line that Alberto can't possibly come back from.

And then it's three. And we know it's offside. We *know* it. We see the flag go up and we're screaming and we know. But we're wrong because Coke wasn't offside when his lad played the ball. The fact it bounced off three of ours on its random way to him means he was very much onside.

And we can't come back. I'm invoking Istanbul and Dortmund and I'm trying to believe it can happen. It can't. Sevilla are pulling us apart. We have no shape, no apparent ability to pull ourselves back into this game, our midfield has disappeared, our defence is struggling, our attack is at the point where 'living off scraps' is an ambition rather than a complaint. And we're quiet. We're shellshocked. The endless, joyful singing has gone. There are pockets, attempts, nothing that quite takes off. Origi and Allen and Benteke are on the pitch but it makes no difference, it's too late and there's the possibility that Jurgen got this call very wrong. There's the argument that he should have bolstered the middle of the park earlier, possibly at the point that Sevilla started to make it their own. There's the argument that we've got all the creativity and movement, but we needed grit. The grit isn't there, there's no coming back from this. Not tonight.

Can is struggling, Milner's trying but he's in all the wrong places, Firmino's disappeared and then subbed, Lallana's pressing's ineffective and then leaves the field with him. Coutinho manages to remain, to continue the anonymity that he had, unusually, brought to the first half. It has to be hope, it has to be the hope that Phil can pull something magical out of his locker to change this. If it's not that, there's no reason for him to be there now, not like this.

It's horrible. The whole thing, all of it. Hideous. Embarrassing. Pathetic. It's probably the worst thing I've ever seen happen to a team. It's a total capitulation, a humiliation. We've been given a lesson in football and courage and resolve. We've been made to look like a very, very young team (which we are) totally out of our depth. Which we are.

It wasn't supposed to end like this. But it has. All that's left is the walk back in the cold, bitter rain and the wait for the others. But Mongoose has jumped the first train out and is on the station in Olten, where we have a lovely loft to sleep three which is unofficially sleeping four and has a pool table and table football, neither of which will ever be used by us. Keith and Mike are in a McDonalds somewhere and my phone's dead so I'm standing there, wet and cold and old and heartbroken and all I want is a cup of tea and my own bed, but they're far away.

The drive back to Milan happens in torrential rain and hangovers and there are only so many recriminations and investigations you can manage before you're on the plane and in separate seats and drinking wine and then on English soil and in a pub near Euston with nothing to do but eat your first actual meal since Monday night and start drinking again.

That's a miserable way to end a story though, isn't it? With despair and cold and rain and your expectations dashed, the difficulty of hope and all that.

How about if we sign off with this? We went to Switzerland. At the end of a rollercoaster season which saw some incredible nights and incredible victories and incredible comebacks. At the end of a season that allowed us to dream, we went to

Switzerland for a European final. No other English team did that, I've checked. At the end of this season of incredible nights, we ended up coming just short of that one last incredible moment.

We still went, though. We went and we had an adventure, me on my first European final, my brother and my mates adding another to their collection. We went and we had good company and we had Martinis in Milan and beers in Basel and we had *one hell of a time*. That's what's important, isn't it? Good company, good times, the memories that live on. For the doubters who took pleasure in the loss, the admittedly horrible loss, there is only this:

We've seen things they'll never see.

It just wasn't supposed to end this way.

Postscript

Everything that comes after

AND IT doesn't, of course. Seasons end, stories don't. Seasons are just chapters in much, much longer stories.

I said this on the 21 August. Words that have gone unaltered since the day I started all this:

The key to any story is knowing which part to relate. Knowing where your story starts and where it ends, telling the most important part of your character's life. Not the whole life, simply the crucial part, the life-changing part.

Perhaps this was the life-changing part. Perhaps I've been telling the life-changing part.

Look at what changed during the telling: I was convinced by Benteke, then I wasn't. I defended him and then I gave up on him. I thought the team couldn't survive setbacks, then that they could and then watched as they finished the story by not being able to when they needed to most. I thought we might have seen the end of Daniel Sturridge, but he ends his season with *that* goal. And then England break him again.

I knew that Kolo was over and then he was as Kolo as he's ever been when he most needed to be. He was the experience that we needed when we needed it. It just wasn't enough. I thought Bogdan 'looked secure.' No need for that level of stupidity, is there? And I said, 'Top four, trust me on this.' Soz lads, feel like I've let you down.

The story goes on, though. Brendan's got a new job at Celtic, Rossiter's signed for Rangers. So's Joey Barton. Jerome Sinclair's gone to Watford and we want four million for him. Fair enough, if you don't ask…

Karius has signed in a move that means Emre is no longer the most handsome man in the team and Gotze is signing. Or he isn't (he signed for Borussia Dortmund). The story goes on.

We'd been talking on the terrace just before that final night as we looked at the stadium filling and we'd talked about the importance of the game, not just to the season but to the club. This was massive. This was the first European final in nine years, this was to show where we were going. Finishing eighth in the league was unimportant if we won this. Winning this would be everything. Winning this would put us back in the Champions League. I wasn't bothered about that last one, that was a nice bonus, the silverware was everything. The glory was everything.

Fleety was more concerned that this was vital in giving us a platform to build from, winning this was what would make us Liverpool again. The real Liverpool, the Liverpool we grew up with. There was so much riding on this game, all of *that* was riding on this one game. And I had to agree with him on that.

But what if it wasn't? What if we've already started building our way back to the real Liverpool? What if greeting the coach before Dortmund and Villarreal was the real Liverpool? What if it was the lads in the square in Switzerland? What if it was the new manager that we'd appointed? What if the real Liverpool has already started to come back? What if this really *was* the life-changing part?

Jurgen Klopp has taken us to two finals in seven months after we had only reached two in the previous seven years. He's taken us to these with a team that he inherited, that he improved, that he has yet to add to. You doubt that Brendan would have done that. Brendan proved against Aston Villa at Wembley that he was unlikely to do that. That's got to give you hope for the future.

The names are out there, the names that he wants to add to this squad. And if this squad's mentality wasn't enough to take us to that last incredible moment, perhaps that of the lads that come in will be. Certainly Karius, Wijnaldum, possibly Chilwell, Hector. Who's going to say that these lads, alongside Matip and Gurjic and Ings and Gomez (and those last two will seem like new signings) aren't the upgrades necessary?

The lack of European football next season? Disappointing but look what happened last time we had no midweek distractions. And yes, you can argue Suarez and Gerrard, but what if Coutinho is our Suarez? What if Wijnaldum and Can are our Gerrard? We've seen what some of these lads are capable of: a finally, hopefully, Hodgson-permitting, fit Sturridge, a confident Coutinho, a growing Can, a rejuvenated Lovren, a fully settled Firmino, all these can improve further under the guidance of the right manager. *Our* manager. What if our manager is the single best man that we could have for the job that needs doing? Because he is. You know he is, you knew it when he came in and *look what he's already done.* He's the man that we all wanted because we believed he could do exactly the job that he's doing. Think of what he can do next.

You know what I think? We're going to win the league. Say it, think it, feel it, feel how the winning feels, throw it out to the universe and believe in it.

We're going to win the league.

This, this is how it starts.